HARKING

OTHER BOOKS
BY GEORGE MERCER

Dyed In The Green

Wood Buffalo

Jasper Wild

Fat Cats

HARKING

A NOVEL

BY
GEORGE MERCER

Mercer, George, 1957-, author
 Harking/ George Mercer.

Issued in print and electronic formats.

ISBN 978-0-9879754-8-5 (pbk.)
ISBN 978-0-9879754-9-2 (pdf)

Cover art and design: Dan Stiles
Editing: Kate Scallion
Manuscript Review and Final Edits: Jody Carrow
Typeset in *Fournier Petit* at SpicaBookDesign

MIX
Paper from responsible sources
FSC® C016245
www.fsc.org

Printed and bound in Canada

For our family,
Jan, Joey, Emily and Claire

This story never happened. It is a work of fiction.

Although place names are real, all of the characters in this book are fictitious, and any resemblance to actual persons living or dead is purely coincidental.

■ ■ ■

PROLOGUE

The dream.

As the howling whiteout raged around her, Harking struggled to stay on her feet, the biting cold piercing every part of her body.

There's no way we'll make it, she thought as she stood there, shivering.

Barely able to see the tips of her skis as the heavy snow encrusted her eyelids, she swiped a gloved hand across her face then tightened the scarf over her mouth and nose.

Grabbing the front of her toque she pulled it down across her forehead then fumbled with the drawstrings of her hood, cinching it tight so only her eyes were showing.

Turning her head, she peered behind to see if the others were still with her. Just able to make out a series of shapes distorted by the squalls, she returned her attention to the ski track she'd been following.

Peering into the whiteout, she called out to her father, but there was no reply.

"Dan," she repeated, yelling his name again.

Hearing nothing but the wind, she leaned into the tempest.

Every step forward was a confused struggle for balance, trying to decipher up from down as the intense cold confused the senses, any notion of depth perception nearly impossible as firm ground morphed seamlessly with the air above it.

Without warning, something or someone pushed past and she stumbled.

Ramming a ski pole into a drift, she saved herself from falling face first into the snow then cursed out loud.

Regaining her footing she carried on, confused by what was happening out there in the whiteness.

Mustering every ounce of strength she fought to catch up, gaining ground.

"Stay back," she could hear her father yell.

"Dan," she called out, ignoring his warnings and forging ahead, trying to catch sight of him.

"Stay back, Har..." he yelled again, her name lost to the wind.

Still she edged closer.

As she powered through the deep snow, thigh muscles burning, she could just pick out his ghostlike shape.

She had almost caught up when a loud *Crack!* reverberated across the slopes. "Get back..." her father yelled again, his voice vanishing in the confusion just as the *whumph!* of the snowpack's collapse shuddered through her body.

For an instant, time stood still.

And then it hit her, the torrent of air knocking her off her feet.

Tumbling downslope, struggling to breathe, her mouth choked with snow, she clawed at the emptiness, instinctively swimming for the surface, straining to reach out, to pull through the waves of white dragging her into the depths, fighting for her life.

When the madness stopped, she was buried up to her waist.

Panicked, her eyes swept across the mounds of snow searching for any sign of her father.

Nothing.

Then she saw an arm and head protruding above the surface.

"Dad" she screamed.

Shifting her body, she tried to pull herself free but the weight of snow held her captive.

Realizing her predicament, Harking frantically clawed at the hardening snowpack encasing her body, extracting one leg at a time.

2

Free at last, she leaned back and rolled away from the hole.

Struggling to her feet she scrambled through the debris field and fell to her knees next to him, digging for all she was worth.

"Dad," she screamed as she cleared the snow away from his head and shoulders. But there was no response.

Carefully she eased his head to the side to clear his airway, but his face was suddenly lost in a blur of swirling snow.

CHAPTER 1

The rumble of the train slipping into the railyard sent tremors through the old house. The subtle shaking worked its way along the stone foundation, moving into the floor joists and walls, finally making its way into the beams and roof trusses, rattling the light fixture above the bed.

Her heart pounding, sweat beading across her brow, Harking opened her eyes and looked at the ceiling, her mind sifting through the details, trying to distinguish dream from reality.

Her father had been reluctant to lead her class on the back-country trip, claiming he had other more pressing things to do, but she'd finally convinced him to help chaperone. He was an excellent skier after all, a trained guide, well versed in backcountry travel. He also knew the park like the back of his hand.

Although the trail to the hut was relatively straightforward, climbing out of the forest of lodgepole pine and winding its way through Englemann spruce and subalpine fir, avoiding most of the avalanche paths in the area, the storm had changed everything, slowing down and separating the group, increasing the risk as the daylight hours faded.

When Harking realized how quickly the day was slipping by, she urged her father to push a track through the deep snow, a last-ditch effort to make it easier for the others. She knew he'd try *for her*. He'd get to the hut then backtrack to help the stragglers.

They were now so close; there was no turning back.

They'd come this far; they were committed.

Turning back would have been *suicide*.

Slowly, almost imperceptibly, like the tremors from the morning trains, an uncontrollable shaking racked Harking's body as the memories of that day came flooding back.

Her father was dead.

And she was to blame.

No one said it to her face, but she could see it on theirs.

Behind her father, in the lead group and desperate to get out of the storm, she knew she was pressuring him to take risks, crossing avalanche paths he'd normally avoid.

And she knew he'd do whatever he could to be a success in her eyes.

Even though he always had been.

Whatever his reasoning, he went for it.

And whatever the reason, it was a moot point now.

When the snow gave way, Dan was in the lead.

And she was tight on his heels.

Following *too* closely?

Perhaps.

That's what she remembered.

The rest was a blur.

In the end, she and two others classmates were also caught in the slide, but only her father had been killed. The others, like Harking, had been partially buried, self-rescuing or helped by students and teachers who'd been following behind.

Harking had collapsed by the time they got to her and remained in hospital for two days after their rescue. She remembered almost nothing else about that day. Even as the details were revealed to her, most of what happened remained clouded in guilt, convinced she'd triggered the avalanche.

Efforts to console her had largely failed, the almost unbearable weight of grief and sense of responsibility at having caused her father's death, pulling her down.

It was more than a year later but she had finally managed to come out on the other side.

■ ■ ■

Lying there as the sounds of the train faded, Harking struggled to refocus, consciously trying to slow down her breathing and the whirlwind of thoughts racing through her head.

Drying her eyes she was determined to move on.

Tossing off the heavy quilt, she slid her almost six-foot frame out of bed and walked to the open window, parting the curtains as the first rays of sunlight made their way into the valley.

She loved this time of the day, when sunrise eased its way down the mountain slopes, bathing the valley in its warmth, the stillness of the night subtly giving way to a morning chorus of songbirds.

Standing in her pyjamas, absorbed in the moment, she sucked in the cool mountain air and stretched, massaging the back of her neck, oblivious to the trio of boys gawking up at her from the back alley.

The first catcall startled her.

"Hey, Harking," one of the boys yelled, repeating the shrill whistle as Harking shoved a middle finger into the air.

There was a chorus of laughter and the boys raced off on their bikes.

"Assholes," she muttered as they disappeared around a corner.

Harking quickly changed into her bike shorts and grabbed a jersey from the hummock of dirty clothes on the floor. Hauling the shirt over her head as she rushed downstairs, she hesitated at the landing.

Not wanting to wake Marion, she nudged the bedroom door and peeked inside. Seeing no sign of movement, Harking eased the door shut and slipped into the bathroom.

She was out again in a few minutes, her long auburn hair tied back and hanging down the centre of her back. Once again, she checked the main floor bedroom, this time standing silently against the door and listening for any signs of movement.

Hearing nothing, Harking tiptoed into the kitchen. She quickly made a peanut butter and jam sandwich, slid it into a plastic bag, then added it to her pack along with an apple from the bowl of fruit on the table. Standing at the sink, she ran the tap and filled the dented water bottle, took a sip, and then topped it up.

"In a hurry?" said the voice behind her.

Harking's shoulders slumped as she screwed the lid on the bottle and turned around. "Sorry, Marion. I didn't mean to wake you."

"Not to worry." Marion pulled the housecoat tightly around her lean frame as she walked to the stove and picked up the kettle. "I can't stay in bed on a beautiful day like this," she added, making her way to the sink. "Tea?"

"No thanks," said Harking. "Gotta run."

"Those boys are going to drive you crazy, young lady."

Harking hesitated. "You heard them?"

"Hmph," Marion muttered. "The whole town probably heard them." She pulled out a chair and sat at the small wooden table. "Sound carries pretty far at this time of day."

"Oh well," said Harking. "Nothing we can do about that. Boys will be boys."

Marion smiled and ran a hand through her shoulder length grey hair. "Isn't that the truth?"

Harking finished loading her pack and stood at the doorway. "Do you mind if I take off?"

"Not at all," Marion sighed, as if she knew trying to quell Harking's energy would have been pointless. "But where are you taking off to, exactly? In case I have to send out a search party."

Harking laughed. "I thought I'd check out the area up back of the lake."

"Still looking for that bird?"

"Yeah. I know it's out there, but I have to actually see it to add it to my life list. That's the birder's rule."

"Well, you'll have more time to look for it now that school is almost over for the summer."

"You mean for good."

"Goodness, that's true. I can't believe you're almost finished." Marion paused. "With this stage anyway."

"Couldn't happen soon enough. I'm done with school."

Marion smiled. "Don't be in a rush. Once you start working, you'll be working for the rest of your life."

Harking waited impatiently by the door. "I kind of do want to get going, though. The birds are more active in the morning. I thought I'd put out Dad's recorder and his remote camera to see if I could pick up anything interesting."

"Killing two birds with one stone, so to speak," said Marion. "Okay, get out of here. But please be careful. The bears are out now and it would be easy to surprise one charging through the forest on your bike."

"Don't worry," Harking countered. "I'll leave my bike by the main trail. It's easy enough to hike in."

"Smart girl," said Marion. "Hopefully those boys are as smart."

"I doubt it," Harking said with a shrug. "Anyway, they're off doing their own thing. I never see them."

"Just as well," said Marion. "They seem like trouble. I've heard they're cutting their own trails all over the valley."

"It wouldn't surprise me," said Harking. "They think they can go wherever they want in the park."

Marion shook her head. "Some people's kids."

"They're okay," said Harking. "A little misguided perhaps. Tyson is the only one I really need to keep an eye on." Harking's voice faltered.

"Hmph." Marion seemed about to launch into a sermon but Harking quickly cut her off.

"Please let it go, Marion. I don't want to get into that now." Harking's body slumped noticeably. "Anyway, when Match is around, Tyson and the others are pussycats."

"Hmph," Marion repeated. "Match. What a name."

"Yeah," said Harking, pulling herself up, glad to change the topic. "I'm not even sure what it's short for."

"No doubt something cryptic," Marion scoffed. "Probably makes no more sense than his father does sometimes. But don't get me started. Ever since he came here as park superintendent, he's been hard to pin down."

Harking raised her eyebrows, but didn't respond.

"Go on and get out of here," Marion shooed her; not having to repeat the offer as Harking vanished through the doorway.

CHAPTER 2

Keen to get on with her next quest, Harking raced through town, smoothly shifting gears as she climbed the winding road leading to the benchlands. She didn't think the boys had discovered the area she was interested in, but didn't want to take a chance. At the trailhead, she veered off the pavement and followed a narrow path to the far side of the lake. Carefully, she hid her mountain bike behind a large Douglas fir toppled during last winter's biggest storm.

As she made her way through the forest, Harking left the main trail and followed any wildlife trail she thought might lead toward her goal, a small hill above the lake where the lodgepole pine forest gradually gave way to aspen. She knew from helping her father that higher ground had the added advantage of capturing sounds from a larger area. If there were Lewis's woodpeckers in this patch of forest, the recorder would pick up their distinctive *churs*. If not, she'd move it around to sample different areas in the valley, using the information to fine-tune her search for the elusive woodpecker. She had to see the bird to add it to her life list and while there were few other birds its appearance could be confused with, its atypical flight, slow and deliberate instead of the quick, undulating wing beats of a woodpecker, could easily be mistaken for a crow or jay.

Climbing the hill, Harking paid attention to the early morning chorus of songbirds resonating through the trees, the sounds of warblers, wrens and thrushes interspersed among the calls of crows and ravens. She was getting better at deciphering most of them, but she still needed help with what her parents used to refer to as "LBBs" or little brown birds. This last thought brought a smile to her face as Harking finally crested the hill and plopped down on the ground, sliding the heavy backpack around to her side.

Sitting with her legs draped over the edge of the knoll, Harking removed the recorder from her pack and placed it in her lap. She used the screwdriver on her father's Swiss Army knife to open the face of the unit and quickly programmed the schedule, then replaced the cover and inserted the two small external microphones.

Surveying the surrounding clump of aspen, Harking selected a tree then strapped the recorder to its trunk, cinching the strap tight to ensure it stayed in position. Using her father's GPS, she recorded a waypoint, just in case she had trouble finding this spot again, and assigned it a name: Woodpecker Hill. She would be back in a few days and hopefully get lucky with her first series of recordings. In the meantime, there was one more place she wanted to check out.

■ ■ ■

Retracing her steps to the base of the hill, Harking located a well-used wildlife trail she'd found on an earlier outing, the trail from which she'd spotted the slight rise of land that now hosted the recorder. Farther beyond the small knoll, the land rose sharply toward the base of the mountain, but here the ground was flatter and easier to navigate. She assumed it would be easier for wildlife as well and wondered what animals might be using it. Determined to find out, she headed down the trail to look for a good spot to set up her father's remote camera.

As she hiked along, Harking was alert to the signs left behind by wildlife: the tracks in the dirt and mud, dried piles of scat here and there, and tufts of hair snagged and left behind on the small branches of trees laying across the trail. At a creek crossing, she noted the tracks of deer and elk, and what looked like either a dog or coyote. Seeing no human footprints, she assumed it was the latter. Jumping from rock to rock, Harking crossed the narrow stretch of moving water and continued on her way.

Rounding a turn in the trail, her attention was drawn to a massive pine tree. The tree's full crown suggested the pine had started its life with little competition from neighbouring trees, probably in an opening created when one of the older Douglas fir fell decades or maybe even centuries before.

But there was something else that made the tree stand out.

As she got closer, a series of depressions in the moss led off the trail toward the pine. It was obvious they were bear tracks, worn into the moss from years of use.

Following the tracks to the tree, Harking could see the outer bark had been worn off in many places while clumps of hair stuck in the pitch oozing from the tree's scaly trunk. She pulled a strand of hair out of the pitch. The subtle curls and tinges of brown suggested it belonged to a grizzly bear. Investigating further, the silver tips of some of the other hairs confirmed her first suspicion.

Definitely grizzly.

Years of bears rubbing against the tree had given portions of the trunk a polished sheen, leaving a record of their passage. Harking ran her hands along the lowest branches, just above her head. Even though they were at least six feet off the ground, the hairs stuck to these branches suggested bears were standing taller than her and getting a good back and head rub from the stately pine. The image brought a smile to Harking's lips.

As she continued to check out the tree, Harking thought she heard something moving in the bush not far away. She stopped for a moment and looked around, listening carefully.

Maybe the boys are using these trails.

Unable to tease apart any sound other than the babbling of the creek, she wrote off her initial suspicion and returned to investigating the tree.

But there's that noise again.

This time she was certain something was moving toward her along the trail.

Looking away from the tree, Harking's heart skipped a beat as a silver-tipped grizzly made its way around a bend in the trail, followed closely by three small, multi-coloured cubs, the mix of light and dark brown fur coats giving the siblings a distinctive appearance.

Harking froze, her mind racing as she focussed on the mother grizzly and tried to figure out what to do. Her dad had always told her to stand her ground when encountered by any wild animal—to assess the situation and quietly let the animal know she was there by speaking in a low, confident voice. Bears in particular had notoriously bad eyesight, he'd said, and often they stood on their hind legs to catch a scent. It was usually mis-interpreted as an aggressive response, but her father stressed not to take it as such. Being overly dramatic won't help the situation, he advised.

"Hey, bear." Harking whispered the words but the grizzly kept coming.

"Hey, bear," she repeated, a little louder this time.

The mother grizzly stopped suddenly and gave a short, sharp huff that brought the three cubs to a halt. Slowly, the sow regarded Harking, remaining stationary but rolling her head and shoulders sideways as she made her assessment. Seeming unsure, she gave two more quick puffs, sending the cubs scrambling past her and into the underbrush across the trail from Harking.

Harking could feel the hair rise on the back of her neck. Her heartbeat felt like it was echoing around the forest as the grizzly watched her with cold dark eyes.

Giving Harking no quarter, the sow slowly continued along the trail, taking forever to place each step. Finally she took one more sideways glance at Harking, then turned and followed the cubs into the forest.

As the grizzly disappeared into the trees, Harking let out a huge sigh and leaned against the old pine. It was only then she noticed her whole body shaking.

Suddenly thirsty, Harking pulled the water bottle from her pack. She steadied it and took a long drink, then splashed a handful across her face. Harking wiped off the water with her sleeve and returned the bottle to her pack. Noticing the sandwich, she wondered how far the smell of food might travel and worried about the potential for other bears to be in the area. Without a second thought, she pulled the sandwich from the plastic bag and devoured it.

Harking gave the bears ample time to create distance between them and her. Then she crossed the trail and found a good location to place the remote camera. Taking it out of her pack, she aimed the infrared beam across the trail toward the old pine and strapped the camera into position at the base of a smaller tree just like her father had shown her. Next, she placed broken branches and other pieces of wood around the setup to camouflage the camera so no one would find it, including Parks staff. She then made her way back to the trail to see if it was visible to anyone or anything going by.

Satisfied, Harking tested the setup, triggering the camera by walking through the beam, then checking the photo to make sure everything was working properly. Although she figured the tree would be hard to miss when she came back, she also recorded the location with the GPS. Satisfied she'd done everything she needed to, Harking closed her pack and threw it over her shoulders, then beelined back to her bike, hoping not to run into the bears again.

CHAPTER 3

Marion was setting the table as Harking walked into the kitchen, towelling off her hair.

"So how was it today?" Marion asked, barely looking up as she carefully placed each dish, obviously conscious of the subtle tremors in her hands.

"Fine," said Harking. She reached across the table and stuffed a piece of lettuce into her mouth, narrowly avoiding Marion's slap.

"Now, young lady," said Marion. "Mind your manners."

Harking smiled and pulled a chair out from the table and sat down.

"I put out Dad's recorder and camera. I'll check them next weekend."

"The apple doesn't fall far from the tree," said Marion. "Your father lived for the outdoors."

Harking liked to be reminded she was her father's daughter, but she liked it less when Marion suggested she also had lots in common with her mother.

"*Now* you can help yourself," Marion said as she placed the pasta dish on the table.

Harking loaded her plate then topped it with salad. "Looks awesome, Marion. Thanks."

"I've told you a hundred times, you don't have to thank me." Marion took a small helping of pasta and salad. "I enjoy your company and I'm glad you decided to move in with me after Susan moved away with the kids."

Harking smiled and dug into the food.

"Besides, it's nice having a younger person around. I think

it keeps an old lady like me healthy, mentally and physically. And it's the least I could do for your parents. Dan and Paige were always both so good to me, especially after we lost Malcolm."

Harking closed her eyes, the memory of her parent's separation still raw and simmering beneath the surface. It had been close to three years and she blamed her mother for it all.

She never gave Dad a break, always on him about something.

When her parents split, Harking decided to stay in town with her father, rather than move away with her mother and younger brother. But then the avalanche changed everything.

Marion's offer to come live with her couldn't have been better timed.

"Sorry," said Marion. "I shouldn't have brought it up." She hesitated, wanting to steer the conversation away from any further discussion of Harking's parents.

"Did you see anything interesting ... out there?"

Harking wiped a hand across her eyes and stared away. "Yeah. I actually saw a mother grizzly with three cubs." She looked up to see Marion's reaction and quickly added, "Nothing happened. They were fine."

"Harking Abigail Thompson." Marion's brow furrowed. "I worry about you."

"It was fine," said Harking. Her green eyes shone. "Marion, she was beautiful. And the cubs, oh my God. They were just small bundles of fur ... all shades of brown. Adorable."

"That's a dangerous combination," said Marion, sounding *very* serious. "A sow and cubs. You have to be so careful. My goodness." She let out a heavy sigh and regarded Harking with concern.

"Marion, it was fine." Harking was emphatic. "I spoke to her and she sent the cubs off. It was textbook. Just like Dad said." Harking stumbled on the words as she recalled one of the last hikes with her father when they'd run into a mother black bear with two cubs on one of the park trails. Reminding Harking to stay calm and not make any sudden movements, Dan Thompson had spoken quietly to the adult bear, watching as she slowly guided her cubs past them into the forest.

Others in town may have thought he was *different*, but Harking was impressed with how her father seemed at one with nature, his calm and cool demeanour always seeing them through any challenge.

"Where were you exactly?" said Marion, interrupting the memory.

"Huh?"

"Today," said Marion. "Where were you today, exactly?"

"Like I told you. Up back of the lake."

"And like I told *you*, that's an important area for wildlife, one of the few areas available for them to move safely around the valley, without coming into conflict with people. According to what your father used to say, it should be permanently closed."

"But it isn't," Harking insisted.

"Well, that's another story." Marion sighed. "Either way, it's an area you probably shouldn't be going into."

"But I wasn't up there for very long. I put out the recorder then checked out a new wildlife trail I found. There was an old pine tree with lots of bear rubbings and that was when she came down the trail toward me. But neither one of us overreacted."

"It could have been a different story if you surprised her, especially on bike."

"But I wasn't on my bike."

"Well, you do ride everywhere," said Marion matter-of-factly. "And you could run into a bear as well as the next person."

"Maybe."

"Maybe?" Marion paused. "*Maybe* you need a bell on your bike."

"Right." Harking scoffed before she could catch herself. "Sorry," she said sheepishly. "The boys would think I was a dork if I used a bell. I take enough crap from them for wearing a helmet."

"Oh, who cares about the boys? Better safe than sorry."

"Yeah, well." Harking shrugged.

"Boys," Marion muttered, shaking her head.

"Anyway," Harking continued, "I'm pretty sure they haven't found this trail," Although she was worried they might.

"Not yet, perhaps, but they will."

"I'll keep them out of there. They'll listen to me."

Marion raised her eyebrows. "I'm not sure Tyson Griffin listens to anyone."

"I guess we'll see." Harking stopped and thought for a moment. "Either way, I don't want anything to happen to them."

"The boys or the bears?" Marion raised her eyebrows.

"Both I guess. But I'm more concerned about the bears." Harking motioned to the grizzly bear talisman hanging from a rawhide lace around Marion's neck. "They're a keystone species, aren't they?

"Absolutely," said Marion. "Protect them and you protect a lot more." She stroked the talisman. "Some call them an umbrella species ... but they're more than that. They epitomize everything that's wild about these parks. Lose grizzlies and we lose the very reason this area was set aside as a park."

"But that doesn't sound fair," said Harking, finishing her food.

"Fair?" Marion laughed to herself. "No, it's not fair at all. And if the bears can't make a go of it inside a national park, then they're probably doomed everywhere aren't they?"

Harking got up from the table and collected the dishes.

"Then, what can we do about it?" she asked as she carried everything to the sink and turned on the tap.

"We?" Marion walked over and nudged Harking aside. "Don't waste water." Turning off the tap she slid the talisman inside her top then began to wash the dishes, handing them to Harking to dry. "Malcolm and I were fighting this battle ever since we got here. Now that he's gone, I'm not sure I have the energy to keep going."

19

Harking laughed. "You have more energy than people half your age. And besides, you're a warrior." She looked at Marion with raised eyebrows. "That's what my parents always said."

Marion chuckled and turned on the old radio sitting on a shelf above the sink. The melody for "Four Strong Winds" resonated from the speaker.

"One of your favourites," said Harking.

Standing elbow to elbow, they began to hum the tune together.

Marion smiled and nodded then looked at Harking with a mischievous grin.

"So they said I was a warrior, did they?"

CHAPTER 4

After dinner, Harking lay in bed, thumbing through a stack of her father's field notebooks as the last rays of sunlight faded from the valley. The small red hardcover books were about the size of a paperback, but thinner. Crammed with writing that ranged from detailed notes describing some species of wildflower to seemingly spontaneous musings about a hike that went sideways, the notebooks, as much personal journals as anything, were the main reminder Harking had left of what made her father tick.

Turning on the bedside lamp, she pulled the quilt around her and picked a notebook out of the pile. As with all of them, there was something intriguing about the writing. It was efficient and to the point, similar to the journals their parents read to her and her brother Col, written by some of Canada's earliest explorers.

David Thompson was one of their favourites, possibly because their father claimed he was a distant relation, although he was never able to prove it.

As Harking thumbed through the pages, a square of paper fell to the side, fragile from repeated opening and refolding. Gently picking it up, she carefully separated the folds and scanned its contents again.

It was a letter to Harking that her father had written after he and Paige had divorced. In it, he apologized for screwing things up with her mother and brother, complicating all their lives, but the letter really focused on what he saw in Harking:

I'm still in awe of the young woman you've become and wonder sometimes where did you come from, for surely you are more than the sum of our parts. To be fair, you have your mother's hair. But that's where it seems to stop. Hers would never find itself tucked beneath a Crankworx ballcap, the ponytail poking through the back.

And your eyes!

Green may be the eyes of jealousy but in truth, we are the ones who are jealous. Transfixed by them, we seem to overlook the tall, strong, lean and limber biker, and birder, with a soft spot for bears and the backcountry, who wears her heart on her sleeve (and a soaring peregrine tattoo on her arm!).

How did you ever convince us to let you do that?

Nose ring and tattoo aside, you remind me of your grandfather, a powerfully built man whose genes seem to have skipped a generation and landed in yours. I'm laughing to myself because you are so much like him, your presence filling the room, even when your voice hasn't.

And there are traces of your grandmother as well, the quiet confidence firming up the hard resolve hidden behind the smile.

I'm proud of you Harking Abigail Thompson.

You will move mountains.

Harking usually stopped there. The rest of the letter was more than she could handle most days.

And on those days or nights when she could make it to the end without losing sight of her father's handwriting through a veil of tears, she would bite her lip to keep it together, thinking about him and their last day together.

Putting the letter aside, Harking lay back on her pillow and returned to the notebook, digging into the detail. Like David

Thompson, her father had been a meticulous note-keeper, not to mention a bit of a data nerd.

But where Thompson's journals listed detail after detail including intricate maps and survey coordinates, her father's notes were interspersed with short anecdotes that drew the reader along, uncovering hints and clues that led, finally, to a sighting of something spectacular or intriguing:

> Climbed The Notch this morning. Steep. Slow going. Found an old wildlife trail leading to a ravine littered with bighorn sheep bones including three huge racks ... all trophies, full curl plus some. Won't share this for fear someone will poach them and sell to a collector. Left in situ ... on their way back to the earth.'

He often ended the detail of a find with the notation "mls."

It took Harking some digging on her own to realize it was short-form for "my little secret." The books had been his alone for the longest time, but then became a record of a shared existence, entries with an implied second person, "hiked the Skyline this weekend," later modified by "we" when he and Harking's mother first started dating.

After her parents became an item, the tag changed to "ols" and the note-keeping became slightly less prolific.

It seemed he had other things on his mind.

Similar to Thompson, Harking's father also filled his notes with cryptic symbols. And although she understood David Thompson's to be related to his surveys, directional arrows and other mapping symbols used at the time, she had no clue what her father's notations meant.

Dan Thompson also had a penchant for sketching animals in the margins of the pages, especially birds. She locked in on his sketch of a woodpecker, its silhouette, clinging to the margin of the notebook as if it were clinging to a tree trunk, searching for carpenter ants and other insects.

Closing her eyes, she pictured the Lewis's woodpecker swooping through the mixed forest of poplar and pine. It might be difficult to tell it apart from crows and ravens but they tended to have a straighter flight path. The salmon-coloured underside also separated it from those local corvids, but it was the dark red face that distinguished the Lewis's woodpecker from all other possibilities. Fixing the picture in her mind she decided that would be her search image then returned to the detail of the notebooks.

Each book was dated and each observation seemed to be numbered and cross-referenced, but the more she tried to figure it out, the more the numbers seemed to be a random scattering. She had no clue what they stood for. If it was a system, it was one she didn't understand.

Still, each time Harking opened one of the books, she discovered something new hidden in the details.

Of particular interest to her were the pages referencing the births of her brother Col and herself, found in separate notebooks, the corners of the pages preceding their birthdays dog-eared, suggesting her father had returned to them often.

Her father had said her name was a reference to J.B. Harkin, the first commissioner for the Dominion Parks Branch, a precursor of the present-day national parks service. But the more Harking researched the man, who suggested parks were as much a commodity to be marketed as they were special places to protect nature, the more Harking preferred her mother's insistence that her name was a reference to the expression "harking back," hearing voices that once touched us and now guide us.

Col's name, on the other hand, was a direct reference to the low point between two mountain peaks, a pass of sorts, a way through. In some ways it spoke to the notion that her baby brother had been an attempt by her parents to get through some of the challenges in their "partnership," as her mother called it.

Harking had never liked the term and didn't like her mother using it. It seemed cold, devoid of the love and caring a marriage should be based on. And in some ways, Col bore the brunt of its disintegration, rebelling at times when what his parents probably needed was an easing of the stresses they were inflicting on each other, not more stress added on top.

After she and Col came along, Harking wondered if her parents regretted lost adventures, even if her father's notes painted a different picture.

The flair of the handwriting around their birthdays seemed to suggest a new take on life, with a propensity for exclamation and question marks, and the occasional ellipsis suggesting uncertainty about what might be coming their way.

Harking started to drift in and out of sleep even as she tried desperately to cling to images of her father, recalling how, after her parents separated and she went to live with him, he would try to spend as much time with her as possible, especially helping with school outings.

Until that last day and the avalanche.

Fighting off tears Harking tried to think about other things, still struggling with the notion she was at least partially responsible for what happened to her dad. Even though Simi and others insisted it was an accident and no one was to blame, Harking couldn't push herself to accept that truth.

Following the advice of the grief counsellor, to help get to sleep, she tried to focus on positive thoughts and those things that brought her joy; a breathtaking view after a challenging hike, sighting a rare bird, or spotting a black or grizzly bear going about its business, kicking over an old log to feed on ants.

She smiled at the thought of a grizzly standing against the old pine tree, its antics resembling a dance as it scratched its back.

Bears, especially grizzly bears, had always intrigued her.

She wondered how they coped, especially outside the park where the landscape was sliced and diced by forestry cutblocks, oil and gas wells and coalmines. And where poachers still took a significant number of bears.

Even inside the national park she wondered how they dealt with so many people on the landscape during summer, when the bears were focussed on feeding, putting on enough fat to make it through the following winter.

And what other challenges did they face?

Perhaps her father's camera would open up a window into their lives

CHAPTER 5

The young male grizzly was new to the valley, having spent the first several weeks after emerging from its den on the lower slopes of the mountains, slowly making its way north. Despite being large for its age, the young bear had been pushed along by even larger grizzlies, fighting to defend their own territories from the newcomer.

Moving across the landscape, unhindered by any physical obstacles, the bear followed a series of streams springing from their source in the icefields, tracing their route as they combined forces, merging to become swiftly flowing torrents of milky, silt-laden meltwater.

Traversing gravel flats, crossing back and forth as necessary where the growing river carved its way through narrower notches of rock, the bear worked its way northward, stopping at times to feed on the rich bounty of emerging plants at the base of avalanche chutes before continuing along, following the river's rich riparian habitat.

Once in the main valley, the young bear was drawn toward the abundance of deer, moose and elk that called the valley home, making its way up and over ridges as it sought prey and staked its own claim, feeding as it went.

Gradually working its way toward a series of lakes, the bear turned over large stones with its front paws to uncover grubs, tearing apart decaying tree stumps to feed on the bounty of ants scurrying for cover. Routinely stopping to sniff the air, the scent of carrion pulled the bear to the top of a slight rise. Standing on the knoll, the smell was now overpowering. Taking its time, the bear descended into an alder thicket, sending a trio of ravens into the surrounding stand of lodgepole pine. Perched on the lowest branches, the birds shot quick glances back and forth between the bear and the carcass of a partially eaten moose, rotting in the bottom of the gully.

Carefully inspecting its find, the bear pushed its nose into the carcass and tore off pieces of flesh, sitting back and grinding the meat between its jaws as the ravens squawked their displeasure from above. Winter had come late and ended early. Still, the need to satisfy the pangs of hunger that accompanied emergence from the den was a powerful force that had to be satisfied.

Eating his fill, the grizzly slowly picked its way out of the gully and continued toward the lakeshore, leaving the remains of the moose to the ravens and the newly arrived competition, a lone bald eagle now eyeing the prize as its own.

At the small creek, the bear turned eastward, ambling along a wildlife trail leading to a large pine draped with the scent of a female bear. Approaching the tree, the bear made its way around the base, sniffing the trunk and raising up on its hind legs to run its snout along the lower branches. Reaching above its head, the bear raked its long claws down the trunk, ripping a series of parallel marks into the bark.

Leaning its shoulder against the tree, the bear rose up once again, turning and rubbing against the bark, standing tall as it scratched itself, leaving large clumps of fine hair stuck to the tree's resin.

Dropping to the ground, the grizzly circled the tree one last time. Picking up the scent of a female bear, it began to follow it into the forest. But an unfamiliar smell drew it off the path.

Walking across the trail to a small pine, the bear stood back and raised its nose into the air, trying to tease this new scent from the resinous aroma of poplar buds and pine pitch. Reaching out with one paw, it pushed aside the small pile of branches surrounding the base of the tree and sniffed again.

Suddenly, a flash of light and a whirring sound sent the young grizzly bolting from the tree. Stopping some distance away, it turned around, raising and lowering its head and rolling its shoulders. Rising up on its hind legs the male grizzly sniffed the air one last time before finally dropping to all fours and turning away. Picking up the scent of the female again, it ambled off down the trail.

CHAPTER 6

Sitting in class later that week, Harking was chomping at the bit, waiting for the school day to be over. Desperate to get back to the recorder and remote camera, she was anxious to know what they'd captured.

The area behind the lake was new territory, the tree like nothing she'd ever seen before.

And the trail was her little secret.

She smiled to herself as she looked around the room at Match and his pals. She knew they'd kill to know about it. Especially Match.

He can be such an ass sometimes, she thought, recalling how he taunted her before class, his two buddies parroting his antics as they described seeing her in the window.

Still, there were times he seemed so nice, almost as if he had a split personality. Like the time he helped her with a flat when she'd left her tools and spare tube at home. She'd been on her own, as usual, on one of the back trails far from town, and he'd appeared out of nowhere and asked if she needed a hand.

Despite her protests that she could take care of it herself, Match quickly pulled the rear wheel off her bike and handed Harking his spare tube. She replaced the tube and they had the wheel back on in a matter of seconds, silently working together as if they'd routinely practised the repair. When they were done, Harking was about to offer him some of her lunch, but Match just smiled and jumped on his bike, disappearing down the trail without a word.

As Harking watched him ride away, she felt like a small hole had opened and closed in her stomach, a tightening in the pit of her belly that left her wondering what kind of effect he'd had on her. There seemed to be a mutual interest, however brief, yet there were other times when they crossed paths that he seemed indifferent. But the other boys were with him then and Harking figured it was all about looking cool.

Not that he needed help with that.

He wasn't hard to look at.

Momentarily distracted, Harking shook her head, bringing her back to the present, and her eyes into contact with Match.

Great. Now he thinks I've been staring at him, she thought as her face flushed.

Snapping her head back to face the front of the class, she was met by the pointed stare of Ms. Peacock.

The science teacher pouted her lips and shook her head slightly.

"Focus, class," she said, speaking through Harking to the other students. "I know we're almost at the end of school, but there are still final exams. Don't come this far only to lose focus at the end of the match."

The British accent drove Harking bonkers, not to mention the fact that since Harking's mother took a position in another school district and moved away with Col, Ms. Peacock had gone overboard "looking out for Harking's best interests," she claimed. It was worse than having her mother hanging over her shoulder, which she would never have done anyway. At least Paige treated her as an equal. Ms. Peacock on the other hand ...

Phhh! Harking thought. *She's going to drive me crazy.*

"Focus, claws," Simi's voice, coming from the seat behind her was almost too much, the Nigerian lilt and British intonation forcing Harking to choke back a hysterical laugh.

"Stop," Harking whispered, her head tucked into her elbow as she tried to nix her best friend's antics.

Not taking any of it, Simi poked her pen into Harking's back. "Nowww, claws."

Harking shot her a quick glance and turned back around.

Thankfully, Ms. Peacock was too engrossed in drawing a diagram on the board to notice and when the bell finally rang Harking was out the door, waiting for Simi.

"Now, girl," Simi said when she finally emerged, this time employing a bastardized Southern US accent. "What you got your feathers all in a tizzy 'bout?" She laughed out loud as Harking pulled her in against the wall, away from the line of students exiting the classroom.

Taller than most of her peers and definitely more striking, Harking figured Simisola Odili could pass for a teen supermodel, her unique looks accentuated by the tribal facial markings she'd acquired as a young girl growing up in Nigeria.

So very cool, Harking thought, even if it also sparked a hint of jealousy on Harking's part. But not enough to stop her from loving Simi like a sister, especially since their family situations had been somewhat similar.

Being the only daughter of Richard Odili, one the local RCMP officers, Simi had left Africa with her father because of her parents' disagreement about how they would raise their child.

Not wanting to subject Simi to the threat of child marriage and other traditional practices, Richard separated from his wife and took Simi to Britain where he went on to study criminal justice. One thing led to another and eventually they ended up in Canada where Richard applied for a position with the RCMP as a forensic specialist.

Forced to take basic training before the Mounties would consider placing him in a more senior role, Richard realized he liked the day-to-day challenges of policing, opted for a posting anywhere in the country and ended up assigned to Jasper's fifteen-person detachment. There, he realized he and Simi also shared a passion for nature and the outdoors.

Simi and Harking had hit it off immediately, two outcasts with a shared interest for anything with two wheels. They were often the brunt of the others' jokes and taunts. *Ginger* and *Ebony* they were called when within earshot, although both girls knew what was said behind their backs was worse.

"Stop doing that in Peacock's class," Harking scolded, looking around to make sure no one was paying attention to them, then lightly pushing Simi away and turning toward the exit. "I already have enough to deal with from her."

"What's your rush?" said Simi, walking along beside her as Harking headed outside to the bike stand. "Gotta place you need to be?"

"Yeah, kind of," said Harking, unlocking her mountain bike and straddling the seat

"Mind if I tag along?"

"On that?" Harking looked at Simi's cruiser.

"I can go home and get my hardtail."

"Not right now," Harking said over her shoulder as she rode away. "I'll text you later."

In a flash she was out of town, headed toward the lake.

As she made her way back down the main trail, Harking was curious to see what the past several days would reveal. She hid her bike and picked her way through the forest toward the small hill.

As she crossed the wildlife trail, she decided to leave the camera for later and headed upslope. Gaining the top of the hill, she was happy to see the recorder setup was just how she had left it. She loosened the straps holding the recorder to the tree and undid the clips, then sat with the recorder in her lap. Opening the front cover, she pulled out the memory card and carefully replaced it with a blank card. She placed the first card in a small plastic case and slid it into her pack. She would wait to listen to the recordings at home.

Excited to get back to the camera, Harking pulled on her pack and started downhill. Picking up speed, she jumped over a fallen log and stumbled, impaling herself on a branch stub that nearly brought her to tears. Grimacing, she shook it off and pushed through the bushes, limping back to the wildlife trail at the base of the hill while keeping an eye out for bear tracks and other signs of wildlife.

As she approached the creek crossing, Harking stopped short, surprised to see tire tracks emerging from the mud.

Mountain bikes! What the ...?

Harking knelt down to get a better look. The tread marks were on top of a set of bear tracks, suggesting that whoever was riding the trail had come through after the bear.

But how long after?

She ran her fingers along the dried mud, tracing the outline of the bear track like her father had shown her, noting the claw prints well out in front of the toe prints, a sure sign it was a grizzly and not a black bear.

Feels firm.

And not that much older than these tire tracks, she thought as she traced her fingers down their length.

They probably only missed each other by a few hours ... at most.

Not a good sign.

CHAPTER 7

Harking had been surprised to see the camera knocked slightly out of whack, but happy to discover it was still working as she limped through the set-up, testing the camera before retrieving its storehouse of images. She assumed the mountain bikers had found the camera but decided to leave it alone, probably thinking park staff had put it there.

Now sitting at the small desk in her bedroom, Harking was curious to check out the pictures she'd downloaded to her laptop and also curious to know what the songbird recorder had captured. Pulling on her headphones she plugged in the memory card from the recorder and listened as an early morning chorus of songbirds brought a smile to her face. The sound recording was superb and surprisingly rich with a diversity of calls and songs, most of which she recognized immediately ... *Robins, white-throated sparrow, northern flicker, ravens, of course,* ... and some she didn't ... *warblers for the most part.*

With the recording playing in the background, Harking slowly scanned the images from the remote camera, laughing at the slightly out of focus pictures of a large raven sitting in the lower branch of a Douglas fir. It must have been sitting just on the edge of the camera's infrared beam, triggering several shots of the bird's antics.

As Harking flipped back and forth between the series of pictures, the contorted head of the raven suggested it was listening intently to the whirring of the camera as it automatically focused and refocused in an attempt to capture its fidgeting subject.

Crazy bird.

Just then, a raven's call echoed through Harking's headphones.

Checking the time and date of the raven pictures she noticed they didn't line up with the time stamp on the audio file. Most likely, the raven cackling in her ears was not the bird in the photo, just a happy coincidence. But as she continued to look and listen Harking realized how powerful the combination of recordings and images actually was.

Moving past the images of the raven, Harking quickly skimmed through the next pictures: a deer and her fawn, a coyote and a stellar image of a bull elk.

But it was the next series of images that glued Harking to the laptop screen.

One by one, she watched as a mother grizzly and her cubs, no doubt *her* grizzlies, visited the tree, rubbing and scratching before moving out of camera range and disappearing from view, the last shot showing the hind end of one of the cubs scampering after the other bears. Scrolling back and forth she carefully examined each image, spellbound by the cubs in particular, especially the variation in the colours of their fur; combinations of lighter and darker shades of brown with one cub sporting a dark brown face mask that contrasted sharply with its lighter-coloured body.

Not one for naming wild animals, Harking was tempted to call this last cub *Mask* or something similar, if only to distinguish it from its lighter-faced siblings, but she resisted, even though deep down she was already enamoured by this little bundle of fur.

Finally moving past the pictures of the bears, Harking was disappointed to discover several blurred images of mountain bikers, with the last shot in the series showing only the rear wheel of one of the bikes. Although they were out of focus, Harking immediately recognized the bikes by their distinctive colours and realized the boys had found her trail.

From the date and time stamps, Harking knew exactly when they'd been on the trail and decided to fast-forward to the recording from that day to see if it had also picked them up.

Sure enough, as she lined up the recording with the time captured by the camera, she could hear the boys' hoots and yells. Harking imagined them racing down the trail, "poaching single track," as they liked to call it, drawn by the cachet of getting off the park's official trails and finding wildlife trails they wouldn't have to share with others, cutting them out in places to clear deadfall and other debris that had accumulated over time.

Seeing the full suite of photos, Harking worried the boys would have been oblivious to the other wildlife using the trail. Even more concerning, when she compared dates and times of the photos, she was shocked to realize the boys had only missed the bears by a matter of minutes.

So not good, she thought.

Curiously, after the boys appeared on the camera, no wildlife was recorded for the next two days, with the exception of the *crazy* raven, or one of its brethren. Likely intrigued by something about the camera, it (or they) seemed intent on having their pictures taken on both days.

After the sequence of raven photos, the next images showed a cow moose followed by a shot of a lone wolf. Having never been that close to a wolf before and intrigued by its expression, Harking scrutinized that photo for several minutes.

What is that look?

Like it somehow knows the camera is there but doesn't give a shit about it.

Mesmerized by the size of the wolf and the rich black sheen of its coat, Harking lingered for a few more seconds, then scrolled to the next image.

Once again she was drawn to the edge of her seat

Another grizzly.

Obviously a different bear than the sow she'd met on the trail, this bear had the large square head of a male and a massive shoulder hump. It was also darker, chocolate with none of the silver-tipping of the female.

37

In the first image, it seemed to be investigating the old pine, but the next photos showed it making its way across the trail before it went out of view of the camera.

A few minutes later something large and quite dark seemed to knock the camera out of position. Harking assumed from the time stamp it was the same bear, checking out the camera and quite possibly scared off by the *whirring* of the autofocus or the bright flash.

The last picture the camera captured was a slightly off kilter self-portrait of Harking as she walked through the set-up to test it. She shook her head as she leaned into the image on the computer screen, scrutinizing the dishevelled hair and sweat-stained top.

God, clean it up, girl.

Noting the streaks of dirt and dried blood on her left leg she unconsciously slid her fingers along the scrape.

Finished with the first pass through the photos, Harking listened to the other audio files, noting a few other birdcalls she didn't recognize. She then reviewed the photos and began recording their times and dates as well as the subject matter; deer, coyote, elk raven, grizzlies, boys ...

Boys.

She wondered how to best deal with them and wasn't sure if she should tell Marion.

She'll be mad as hell and won't want me to go back there.

And she'll probably confront the boys' parents or go to the park and tell the wardens.

Or both.

Probably both.

Sitting there, rubbing her bruised leg, she was still thinking about the possibilities when a door opened downstairs.

CHAPTER 8

Hearing footsteps padding up the stairs, Harking bolted from her desk to the bed, quickly sliding under the heavy quilt as Marion nudged the bedroom door open.

"Harking, are you in there?"

"Huh, yeah, I was just laying down for a bit."

"Busy day?" Marion inquired, walking into the bedroom.

"Yeah. I'm kinda tired." Harking feigned a yawn, hoping to head off any possible interrogation.

Marion walked to the edge of the bed and sat down, scrutinizing Harking. "Did you find what you were looking for?"

"Not entirely."

"But something of interest? You were certainly gone long enough."

Harking tried to avoid Marion's stare as she squirmed out from under the quilt and slid to the edge of the bed. "Yeah, I'll show you," she said with a sigh. Turning her back to Marion she eased her legs into a pair of sweat pants and pulled them up over her shorts.

"The boundless enthusiasm of youth," said Marion as Harking made her way gingerly to the desk.

Ignoring the comment, Harking settled into her chair and started the recording from the beginning. "I never heard the woodpecker, but the soundtrack is kind of cool."

As Marion leaned over her shoulder, Harking turned up the volume.

"God, I'm not deaf," Marion straightened up and took a step back.

39

Harking smiled and turned down the volume. Carefully monitoring the time of the recording scrolling across the bottom of the computer screen, she opened the first of the photos.

"So this is the trail on back of the lake?" said Marion. "The trail people call Battle Axe."

"Not quite," said Harking, somewhat sheepishly. "But it's near there. This is actually a new wildlife trail I found that comes off of it."

Harking looked over her shoulder, curious to see if Marion bought her story. "Battle Axe is kind of a cool name, though, eh?" she added. "I think it's named after those medieval shows everyone's hooked on, although I also heard it got the name because it was so tough a trail to cut out they needed a big axe to clear it."

"Nice try," said Marion, tapping Harking on the head. "But I wasn't born yesterday. I know it's named after me. But if names are the price to pay for raising hell about human use in the park, so be it," she sighed. "And I guess the name could be worse." Marion pinched Harking's shoulder. "Just let me see those photos."

Wincing, Harking zoomed in on the first picture of the raven, as a medley of songbirds filled her room. After adjusting the volume of the recording, she flipped back and forth between the photos of the raven as it stared into the camera.

"Crazy old bird," said Marion. "I guess they could have also called the trail Old Crow."

"Yeah, I guess." Harking laughed. "But it's a raven."

Marion pinched her again and motioned for the next photo.

"Mule deer," Marion stated.

"Look at those ears," said Harking. "Not hard to tell how this species was named."

Marion was silent as Harking slid past the photos of the coyote and elk but leaned in closer as the first image of the mother grizzly filled the screen.

"My Lord, she's beautiful."

"Wait until you see the cubs," said Harking, scrolling slowly through the series of grizzly bear photos and stopping at the masked cub as a raven gurgled and croaked in the background.

"Incredible," said Marion, her head brushing up against Harking's. "They're all stunning."

"Yeah, but this one's gorgeous," said Harking, unable to take her eyes off the screen as an undercurrent of hoots rippled through the silence. Quickly she reached to turn down the volume but Marion's hand pulled her away from the controls.

"What is that?"

"Huh, nothing." Harking quickly scrolled past the next several photos.

"Oh no you don't." Marion pushed Harking's hand off the computer mouse and fumbled with the mouse, scrolling back through the blurred images of the boys on their mountain bikes. "Damn."

"They only show up one time," said Harking, sensing the impending storm.

"Once is too many," said Marion, flipping back and forth between the photos. "And look at the times. They could have run into those bears."

"I know. I'll talk to them."

Marion scowled. "As if they'll listen." She scrolled to the next photo of the moose and hesitated before moving on to the picture of the wolf.

"See. They only show up that one time." Harking slid her hand toward the mouse but Marion pushed her away and zoomed in on the wolf.

"Beautiful," Marion said, crowding Harking. "Looks like the alpha male in the town pack."

"Do you know *every* animal around here?"

"Well it's not like there are lots of them," said Marion. "And this one is pretty distinctive. The black coat sets him apart. And he's figured out how to live in the valley and keep his pack out of trouble. I like that."

41

"But there's something about him," said Harking. "Like he knows we're watching."

"Hmphh. He knows more than you think. You don't get older without getting a little smarter." Marion slid the mouse back to Harking. "Are there more?"

When Harking hesitated Marion took over control of the mouse one last time, scrolling to the final images showing the large male grizzly bear.

"Harking Abigail Thompson," Marion's voice rose with each word. "Enough. I'm going to the Parks office." She turned to leave.

"Marion, don't. Let me talk to the boys first. Besides, I don't want the wardens to know the camera is out there. They'll make me take it down."

"You *should* take it down. It's not safe going in there. For you or the bears."

"But I'm careful. And I'll get the boys to listen to me. Let me try at least."

Marion paused at the bedroom door. "You know if something happens, we'll both regret it."

"Nothing will happen. Please," Harking pleaded.

Marion stood motionless. "You're going to drive me crazy, young lady. Or worse. I *will* become the old crow." She paused. "Dinner will be ready soon," she added as she walked out of the bedroom. "Get cleaned up."

Harking hobbled as fast as she could to the door and gently closed it as Marion's voice trailed off down the stairs, " ... and put something on that scrape before it gets infected. It looks terrible."

CHAPTER 9

After dinner Harking was back in her room, lying in bed with her laptop, thinking about the day's events.

Despite Marion's silence at dinner, Harking knew she wouldn't let the issue die and would likely go to the Parks office and report the boys.

Accepting the inevitable, Harking finished recording the data from her camera and sound recordings. When it came to tagging the files with a location, she preferred to give them names that were meaningful to her, but not to anyone stumbling across her records. No point telling people exactly where she'd been. She had her own secrets.

She smiled to herself as she went through the list, adding "Woodpecker Hill" for the site she'd chosen to collect sound recordings. She wrestled with the idea of an appropriate name for the trail camera site and laughed out loud as her fingers typed "Pecker Head."

If Match doesn't listen to me about staying out of there, I just might have to revise the name to Dickhead!

As she copied and pasted the new site name for each of the photos into her spreadsheet, she couldn't help but be amused by the range of possibilities for site names. Most trails already had an unofficial handle. Psycho, Corkscrew, Destruction, and Battle Axe were just a few of them.

Reaching for the GPS, she quickly found the waypoints she'd collected, her thumbs a blur as she entered the new names. Following her father's protocol for recording sites, she also added the names to her own journal. Although she was more comfortable working within a digital world, the value of a paper copy wasn't lost on her.

Her Dad had also tried to teach her the practical values of map and compass and usually recorded bearings and distances in his own records. "You really should try to understand this," her father had said as he pored over a topographic map spread across the kitchen table amid Harking's protests. "Hey, if it worked for David Thompson," he'd pointed out, "it should be good enough for you."

But she was lost when he tried to explain the intricacies of the compass and opted for the ease of the GPS instead.

"It's so old school," she'd countered. "And David Thompson never had this," she added, holding up the GPS. "God Dad, my phone even has GPS."

"But what if the GPS doesn't work? What if you can't get a signal? What if the batteries die? You still need to keep your head about you and know where you are. A compass will help you get home. A compass doesn't lie."

"Oh yeah," she'd said. "What about the time in the Maligne Valley? You and Mom thought you knew where you were going and ended up having to pack Col and I out on your backs because we were too bagged to go any farther? We were lost for hours."

"Not lost. Just momentarily confused." Dan Thompson was notorious for defending his slip-ups and never admitting to having made a mistake. "And we were using that old compass. I'm pretty sure the declination was wrong."

Yeah right, a compass doesn't lie. Harking shook her head as she recalled his explanation about declination, something to do with deriving true bearings from magnetic bearings, east is least and west is best, and so on. It all seemed like voodoo.

When she'd asked Ms. Peacock about it in science class, the teacher made it even worse, confusing Harking further and making it clear that her science teacher wasn't the navigational expert she purported to be.

But her father's notes were riddled with compass bearings and the first page of each of his journals bore a reminder to readers, carefully printed in large letters: "ALL BEARINGS ARE TRUE."

Harking understood it was a way of saying that the compass bearings recorded in his notes were true bearings as opposed to magnetic, making them easier for users to follow as long as the compass declination was properly set to compensate for the difference.

But she knew anyone picking up the notebooks, without some prior knowledge of her father's quirks, might take it to simply mean that his bearings were correct.

Any way you read it, she figured it was confusing, and so much easier just to simply go with the GPS and the waypoints it provided. As for the compass bearings in her father's notes, she'd use those only if she had no other way of figuring out where he was referring. Even then, she'd argued they gave the user no idea when or where to stop as they merrily followed his bearings through the bush.

"Oh, you'll know," he'd said, pointing to the other notes next to the bearing. A typical entry read something like "follow the chain of small lakes on a bearing of S45E until you come to the large pine with the eagle's nest on the NE side of the last lake."

The detail was too much for Harking and she preferred just to scroll to the "Eagle Nest" waypoint she'd entered in the GPS and punch the GO TO button.

And as for the other numbers lining the margins of her father's journals, seemingly added later, she would ignore those much as she ignored her mother's musings that the rules that applied to the navigational compass applied equally to her moral compass.

"Stick to the values we've taught you, Harking. Stick to what you believe in. Don't let people steer you down the wrong path."

Increasingly Paige had tried to piggyback life lessons onto Dan's more practical teachings, and increasingly that became a source of tension between her parents.

"But she doesn't listen to me otherwise," she'd overheard Paige telling Dan. "The only way she'll listen is if I speak through you."

"She doesn't need a lecture," Dan had replied. "Show, not tell, and she'll figure it out. She's a smart girl."

Although she agreed in principle, Paige couldn't seem to let go of the need to reinforce the message time and time again, ultimately leading to more and more blow-ups between mother and daughter.

As Harking finished entering her data, she placed the laptop on the bedside table and lay back on her pillow, thumbing through the pages of her father's last journal one more time, unable to ignore the numbers embedded in the margins as she struggled to keep her eyes open.

What do they mean? Why did he add them? It just doesn't make any sense.

She was slipping in and out of sleep when the idea came to her.

I guess I'll follow one of his compass bearings ... just for once to see where it takes me ... maybe then the numbers will make more sense.

CHAPTER 10

The following day, Marion headed straight to the Parks office, just as Harking suspected.

"I'd like to speak with John," she said, looking down at the superintendent's assistant who had been forewarned she was making her way upstairs.

"He's not in," said the young man, nervously eyeing the door behind him.

"He's never in." Marion stormed past the desk, almost knocking him over. Turning the knob, she threw the door open, the frosted glass pane rattling as it slammed against the wall, sending a hairline crack across its surface and briefly stalling Marion's momentum.

Surprised by the intrusion, the superintendent bolted upright in his chair as his assistant rushed in behind Marion, trying to explain the outburst.

"I told her you weren't in," he stammered. "She just pushed past me."

The superintendent collected himself and waved the young man off, motioning him out of the office. "I'll deal with it," he said, inspecting the glass in the door before closing it and turning to face his elderly intruder. "What is it this time, Marion?"

Marion resented the insinuation.

"*This time!*" She pursed her lips but a small gob of spittle threatened to dampen the effect before she could pull it back in. "This time," she repeated, extracting a tissue from a pocket and wiping it across her mouth, "is the same as the last time. And the time before that."

She caught her breath and was about to launch into her main offensive when John Walleski held up a hand and walked around his desk.

47

"Marion. Calm down and have a seat."

She looked around then grudgingly lowered herself into a chair as John settled in next to her. "Now tell me exactly what's bothering you?"

"People," said Marion. "More specifically how you manage people. Or *don't* manage people, I should say. You can't continue to let everyone do everything they want to, everywhere in the park. It's a dog's breakfast."

"I'm still not sure what you're talking about, Marion?"

"You need to deal with those young mountain bikers," Marion said, sounding exasperated. "They're taking over the wildlife trails, using the few areas left in this valley that bears and wolves and cougars need to get around the town. Before you know it, there'll be no places left for wildlife to go."

"Where exactly is this happening?"

"Everywhere," Marion exclaimed. "For God's sake, John, get out of the office and go in the park. It's happening *everywhere*."

"But where *specifically*?"

"Up back of the lakes, in one of the best wildlife corridors left in the valley. One of the only places the animals can travel without having to deal with the railway, the highway and everything else Parks has allowed in this valley."

"But that's an area we've asked people to stay away from," said John. "Technically, it is a closed area."

Marion scoffed and threw back her head. "John, how naïve are you? You've put in place a *voluntary* closure. It means nothing."

"I disagree," John said, sounding defensive. "It's still a closure. Give it time for people to comply."

"No John." Marion shook her head. "You and I both know that no amount of time will stop some people from going where they want to go. You need something with teeth, a *permanent* legal closure that is enforceable. And enforced."

Adamant, Marion bristled at John's seemingly cavalier attitude and lack of a sense of urgency.

"Good God, John, your park wardens are chomping at the bit to do their jobs and deal with these types of situations, but you have to give them the means to do it. If you don't get serious, you're just setting things up for an accident to happen. One of those boys will get hurt."

"*Those boys?* You know who's using the trails?"

"Well not exactly, but I have a pretty good idea."

"And how exactly do you know this?"

Marion hesitated.

"It's Harking, isn't it?"

Marion hesitated and shuffled in the large chair, but before she could say anything else John launched into her.

"Damn it, Marion, Harking is picking up where her father left off. Dan Thompson was never happy with the way we ran the park. He always had advice for us."

"Maybe you should have listened to some of it."

John raised his eyebrows, but let the comment slide. "Harking needs to leave the management of the park to my staff."

"But she has no confidence they'll do the job," said Marion. "And quite frankly, neither do I."

"Still, you're telling me she's out there as well. In areas you say are critical for wildlife. If so, she's as much part of the problem as the others."

"She's just out exploring, John, on foot, looking for birds. She happened on this quite accidentally."

"On *this?* What is *this* exactly?" John ignored Marion's defense of Harking. "You still haven't told me what's got you so upset."

"Harking had her father's remote camera out," Marion admitted reluctantly. "Some of the photos she got show some boys biking on the wildlife trails. There were also several bears using the trail, a sow with cubs and a large boar. Harking's concerned they'll run into one of them and someone will get hurt."

"So she's jumping to conclusions."

"No. She's putting two and two together." Marion's tone became even more serious. "John, I've seen the pictures."

John got up from his seat and walked to the window before turning around to face Marion. "So who are the boys, Marion? I'll have one of the wardens speak to them."

"I don't know who they are," Marion confessed

The superintendent stared Marion down. "Don't know or won't say?"

"I don't know." Marion was emphatic. "It's impossible to tell from the pictures."

John walked to his desk and sat down, seemingly distracted by the mound of paperwork on his desk. After a moment's silence he looked up.

"So what do you want me to do Marion? Close every trail that we see a bear on? You know we can't do that."

"That's not what I'm suggesting and you know it. Just close those areas your own staff have told you are critical for these animals to move around the valley. And then enforce the closures. It's as simple as that."

John laughed. "Simple? Marion, nothing is ever simple."

"That's because you make it hard for people to take the park seriously," she said. "You have authority. Use it."

"And what about Harking? Are you going to tell her those areas are off limits to her as well?"

"She already knows. She'll stay out of there." Marion got up and made her way to the door.

"And the boys?" said John.

"Harking will talk to them. She thinks she knows who they are and seems confident they'll listen. I'm not as confident, but I need to give her a chance to try."

The superintendent stood to see Marion out. "I have a feeling you know more than you're saying. If you know who the boys are, I need to know."

"I honestly don't know," said Marion. "I wish I did."

CHAPTER 11

Match Walleski stared at his plate as his father shot a look at him across the table.

"Well?" said John. "Have you and your pals been riding up back of the lake, or not?"

"Yeah," Match conceded, finally getting up the nerve to meet his father's stare. "We've done the park trails so many times, riding them is just boring to us now. We wanted to try something different." He hesitated. "But we've only been up back of the lake once. Honest."

"Once is too much, Match. If you run into bears back there, you know what could happen?"

"But we didn't see any bears."

"Of course not," John scoffed, "because you were riding hell-bent for leather down the trail. That's exactly when you'd run into a bear and the bear wouldn't give a second thought to reacting. That's what they do. It's instinctive."

"I guess."

"You guess?" John leaned across the table and pointed his butter knife at Match. "You *know*."

Match hung his head as his father looked at Mary Walleski and shook his head before turning back to their son. "Remember that story we heard about the bear in the Tonquin Valley?"

Match nodded.

"The folks who ran into that male grizzly after it had just killed a moose, weren't so lucky. The bear was only defending its food but, in the end, one person was mauled to death and the other was lucky to come out of it alive. In the end, the superintendent had to order the wardens to destroy the grizzly. And Parks is still tied up trying to settle the lawsuit the families filed against us. We'll probably be fighting that for years."

"But that's just stupid," Match offered. "How can they sue you guys for something like that?"

"That's what I'm saying, Match. It was stupid, but they did it. And in the end, no matter how stupid it was or not, two families' lives were changed forever. And not to make light of that, but there's also one less grizzly out there." John swept an arm toward the window.

Match looked at his mother, who nodded in agreement.

"People's safety is critical," said Mary. "But here in the park, so is protecting the bears. Your father's got to try and balance all sides. It's not easy."

"Especially with people like Marion Seawell holding your feet to the fire," John acknowledged with a wry smile.

"Old Battle Axe," Match muttered.

"Match," Mary started, but her husband cut her off.

"*Old Battle Axe?*"

"Yes, Battle Axe," Match repeated, looking at his father incredulously. "Who do you think I learned that from? You're always moaning about her marching into your office, making demands."

"Match," Mary tried to interject, but John cut her off again and glared at Match.

"I may have used that term *once*. But I shouldn't have. Marion is a huge supporter of the park. Even I can see that. She wears her heart on her sleeve, and if she was your age, I expect she'd kick your ass for being on those wildlife trails. Harking Thompson is probably a lot like her and I expect she *could* kick your ass."

Match looked up at the mention of Harking.

"What's she got to do with this?"

"Probably nothing." John's tone softened.

"Probably?" Match glared at his father.

"Leave Harking out of this," said John, pointing a finger at his son. "After the avalanche and everything else that's happened, she's got enough on her plate."

52

CHAPTER 12

After Marion told Harking about her visit with the park superintendent, Harking knew she had to talk to Match right away. Once school was out, everyone would be going their separate ways and even though Parks had closed the trail on a voluntary basis Harking doubted that would be enough to stop the boys. Once summer holidays began, they'd be out riding every day. And if anything happened, it would prove Marion right.

Thankfully, at least Col wasn't in the picture any more.

When their parents were still together and they all lived in town, Col, who was forever consumed by video games, rarely got outside, except when dragged along on hikes by their parents. But when he hit high school, he started riding with Match and his pals, bagging all of the park's official trails multiple times before tiring of them and starting to create their own, determined to take over wildlife trails.

The peer pressure exerted by the older boys seemed to be leading Col away from everything his mother and father had drilled into them as kids. Simple acts of rebellion like his refusal to wear a bike helmet drove his parents crazy.

And his newfound disregard for the park and its wildlife drove Harking crazy, to the point where she was ready to disown him if he didn't smarten up.

She knew getting Col out of town after their father died was probably the best thing Paige could have done, even if it did widen the rift between Harking and her mother and Col. Without his father's oversight, hanging out with Match and Tyson would have been disastrous and there was no telling how far off the rails he'd have fallen.

Not having him around should make dealing with the other boys a bit easier, Harking thought as she waited for Match to come out of the classroom. When he did, he immediately made eye contact and scowled, then quickly turned away. As he tried to walk past her Harking stepped in his way, nudging Match up against the lockers.

"Hey, take it easy," he blurted as Harking stood shoulder to shoulder with him.

"We need to talk," she replied as a stream of other students paraded by.

"Sounds like you already have," Match sneered.

"What do you mean?"

"I mean giving us up to my old man." Match blew a lock of hair out of his eyes and collected himself, folding his arms across his chest.

"About?" Harking played dumb.

"You know damn well what about. Riding the trails behind the lake."

"I've never even spoken to your father," Harking insisted.

"No?"

"No." Harking leaned in. "But you and your buddies should listen to him and stay off the wildlife trails near Battle Axe." Knowing the name referred to Marion, Harking felt guilty repeating it, but she knew it was what Match and his buddies called the trail. He would know exactly where she was referring.

"Says who?" Match replied, standing as tall as he could.

"Says me," said Harking, matching him inch for inch.

"You don't own the trails."

"No, I don't. But there's a mother grizzly and cubs back there and another mean looking grizzly that I wouldn't want anyone to run into."

"How do you know that?" Match tossed his head back.

"I just know." Harking met his stare.

"So you've been hanging back there too?"

54

"That doesn't matter. Besides, the trails in that area aren't official trails and the park wardens won't be happy if they find out you've been in there. Especially since they're closed."

"Right," Match rolled his eyes. "It's a voluntary closure."

"Still, your dad wouldn't be too impressed if he found out you were still going in there."

"Who would tell?"

Harking avoided his look.

"Old Battle Axe, right?"

Harking pushed in closer, pressing Match into the locker door.

"You should watch what you say. 'Old Battle Axe' has bigger balls than you ever will." Focused on Match, Harking didn't notice his buddies Tyson Griffin and Grayson Moberly circling in behind her.

"Balls! Wow, what would you know about balls, ... *girl?*" Tyson chided.

Caught off guard, Harking half turned to face Match's best friend.

One on one, with no one else around, Tyson was fine, a 'pussycat' Simi would often say, reminding Harking that Tyson wasn't so bad, he just had a shitty home life.

And most of the time he was just as into biking and skiing as Harking, Match or Simi. And just as competitive, always wanting to be with the lead group.

He'd also been there on the day of the avalanche, along with her father and Match. Even though Harking thought it was only her father and herself at the front of the pack, it turned out that all four were caught in the avalanche.

Unfortunately, Dan Thompson was the only one unable to self-rescue.

That's how Match and Tyson remembered it.

As for Harking, she recalled nothing.

Apart from what others told her and the blurred details of her dreams, she wasn't able to piece together those final minutes after the avalanche before the rest of the class caught up and helped with the recovery.

And despite Match and the others' insistence that it was an accident and no one was to blame, Tyson always seemed to leave things hanging.

Although he never outwardly accused her of causing the avalanche, it's what he didn't say that led Harking to doubt what others told her about that day.

And it hurt.

Now, here in the school hallway, standing with his peers, Harking could only see the side of Tyson she despised: all mouth, acne and attitude.

And the way he said "girl" just made her want to punch him.

As she took a step back, Tyson and Grayson moved in next to Match.

Grayson was obviously a follower, like Col had been before he left town, but other than his choice of friends, Harking had no issue with him.

Tyson, though, was another matter. A bit of an enigma, he could be tolerable at times, even kind, but at other times a total pain.

She couldn't figure out what hold he'd had on Col in the past, but she resented his influence on her brother. And she could see traces of the Tyson she didn't like surfacing whenever she had taken Col to task about hanging out with him.

Fighting the urge to launch into Tyson, Harking sneered. "Why don't you screw off," she threatened, "before *this girl* kicks your skinny ass?"

"And I kick it a second time," said Simi appearing out of nowhere. As she slid in behind Tyson, he did a doubletake and shuffled sideways.

"Oh right, the cop's daughter," Tyson muttered, appearing to not want to lose face. He stepped closer but Match inserted himself between Harking and Simi as a small group of onlookers, including Harking's least favourite female Brianna Smith, gathered around.

When Brianna moved in closer to the action Harking and Simi scowled simultaneously, causing Brianna to step back.

"Take off, guys. I'll deal with this," said Match. He motioned for the other students to move along. "You too, Brianna."

As the others began to leave, Tyson feinted as if to go around Match and confront both girls, but Match leaned his shoulder into him and whispered, "I'd hate for them to drop you in front of everyone, so back off."

Scoffing, Tyson made a second push.

"Later," said Match, pushing his chest into Tyson's.

Tyson bit his lip. "You got that right," he said, glaring at Harking and Simi. "Later, *bitches*." He took a step back, gave the girls the middle finger and walked away with Grayson and Brianna on his heels.

Match turned back to Harking as Simi stood silently behind her. "Don't worry about him. He's all lip."

"Do I look worried?" Harking dropped her arms to her sides. "He's a moron."

"Why do you even hang out with him?" Simi interjected, scowling toward Tyson as he and the others walked out of sight.

"That's not your concern." Match waved off the comment and turned back to Harking. "So, what's the big deal with those trails anyway?"

"The big deal is it's one of the only safe corridors for wildlife trying to move around the valley. I had my Dad's camera set up in there and got a ton of pictures of bears."

"So?"

"So, I don't want to see anyone run into them. You know how it goes around here."

"Whadya mean?"

"I mean, if someone does go back there and gets hurt, the bears will be destroyed."

Match mulled over Harking's points. "But you're going back there."

"I won't anymore. I just need to go back and get my gear. I'll set up somewhere else."

"What are you up to anyway, Harking? Snooping?"

"Snooping?" Harking laughed. "No, like I said, I was using my Dad's equipment to record birds and capture pictures of wild-life. Just playing around. I recognized your bikes in one of the photos. That's the only reason I knew you guys were back there." She paused. "Look, I don't really care what you do or where else you go. But you should stay out of that area."

"Show me the photos, and then I'll decide," Match insisted. "Or I can bike in there with you and help haul the gear out."

Harking wasn't quite sure how to interpret Match's apparent offer. She squirmed when Simi jabbed a finger into her back.

"You shouldn't even have it there, if the area's closed," Match pointed out.

"I don't bike in there," Harking defended herself as she glanced at Simi before collecting herself and turning back to Match. "I ditch the bike and hoof it. And I'd prefer to pull the gear out on my own. I don't want to draw any more attention to the trail than it already has."

"Whatever. Just sayin'." Match turned to leave.

Harking bit her lip as Simi poked her a second time. "But thanks for the offer anyway. Maybe we could ride another trail?"

"Maybe."

"But you'll stay out of there?"

"I'll think about it," said Match as he turned to leave.

Harking watched as he walked down the hall. When he went around the corner, she turned to face Simi.

"Really?" Harking said, shrugging and raising her palms in the air.

CHAPTER 13

The mother grizzly led her three cubs around the lakeshore as the first hints of morning dissolved the shadows under the thick canopy of fir and pine. At a small creek, she turned upslope, ignoring the antics of her offspring as they cavorted in the shallows, rolling around in the water and playing tag. The largest cub routinely caught up to his siblings, pushing them under his body as he haphazardly leapfrogged ahead, only to have the two smaller females gang up on him as they attacked from opposite sides.

As the mother bear picked her way through the buffaloberry, she methodically plucked the last of the overwintered fruit from the hanging branches. Emerging from the thicket, she followed the narrow trail to the old pine tree and waited for the cubs to catch up. The sow had been raised in this valley and the tree was familiar to her, a routine stopping point as she traversed the berry-laden slopes around the base of the mountain.

From time to time, she would pick up an unfamiliar scent, a transient bear taking advantage of the slope's bounty of wild fruit before making its way past the lake to parts unknown, or the scent of humans and their food, carried across the lake by the prevailing westerly winds from the rows of cabins lining the opposite shore.

With the cubs finally at her side, she continued along the trail toward the large wetland at the end of the lake. Veering off the trail, the quartet feasted on the fresh shoots of grasses, sedge and horsetail, spring's first offerings after a winter spent in the den high above the valley. Finally full, she led the cubs into the thick stand of alder bordering the wetland and bedded down for the day.

CHAPTER 14

Even though Harking had taken it upon herself to talk to Match, there was no doubt in her mind she would also get a house call after Marion's visit to see the park superintendent. When it did come and she opened the front door, she was glad to see Shane Ross, a park warden and family friend, who often visited the Thompsons when he wasn't working in Jasper's backcountry, one of the few park wardens still using horses to conduct patrols, 'riding for the brand' as he liked to call it.

Harking still felt bad about the fact that Shane was the person who delivered the devastating news to Paige about the avalanche, but in many ways, she was glad it was him and not some stranger.

Shane was a no bullshit type of guy with a big heart for anyone who shared his passion for the park. Originally from Saskatchewan, he'd fallen in love with the mountains on his first trip out of the flat lands, but he was still a prairie boy through and through.

Like many of the older park wardens, Shane tried to portray the image of an old-school cowboy, a tough guy who chewed toothpicks and spoke out of the side of his mouth.

But he sucked at it—or so Harking thought.

"Howdy, little lady," Shane started with his trademark drawl.

"Really, Shane?" Harking folded her arms and stared.

"Okay, Harking, cut me some slack," said Shane, looking slightly deflated. "The chief sent me here 'cause he knew I was a friend of the family. I'm just tryin' to help out."

Harking held the door open and gestured for Shane to come in.

"You want a coffee?" Harking headed to the kitchen.

"Nah, this won't take long," said Shane. He kicked off his cowboy boots and followed Harking.

Harking cut a bagel and put it in the toaster then turned to face him. "What's up?"

Shane collected himself and took a deep breath. "Well you probably know Marion tore a strip off the superintendent about kids on those back trails."

"Yeah." Harking raised her eyebrows. "I kind of figured she would."

"And she kind of let slip that you were in there as well," Shane continued. He held up his hands before Harking could protest. "Now I know you're just exploring and I suspect you're smart enough not to be biking through there, but the bears can't tell one person from another. If we're gonna have a closed area to help bears, then it's closed to everyone."

"But it isn't really closed. It's a voluntary closure," Harking scoffed, using her fingers to make air quotes.

"Well it's gonna be a full-on closure. After Marion made such a fuss, the superintendent figures if we leave it open and anything happens to someone, the shit'll hit the fan," Shane frowned. "Pardon my English, but you know what I mean, Harking. We'd be sued big time."

Harking returned the frown then buttered her bagel and sat at the table. Motioning for Shane to take a seat she spread home-made jam on the bagel and bit into it. "That's the bottom line, isn't it?" she said between bites, swiping a strand of hair out her eyes with the back of her hand. "Worried about getting sued. Not really worried about protecting bears, or people for that matter."

Shane sat at the kitchen table across from Harking and pushed his Stetson to the back of his head. "I'm not gonna sugar coat it, Harking. That is the bottom line for management. But you and I both know what it really means if someone gets hurt."

"A bear dies," said Harking.

61

"Exactly. And neither of us want that."

"So...?" Harking raised her palms and shrugged. "What do you want me to do about it?"

"I want you to stay off those trails," said Shane, scrunching his face as if to say that much was obvious. "And I want to know who else is back there."

"I can't say for sure," said Harking, getting up and placing her plate in the sink.

"But you've had your dad's camera out there, I take it? So you have an idea?"

"I do. But I need to follow through on it myself."

"That's my job, Harking." Shane's tone became more serious as he leaned across the table.

Harking nodded. "I know, but I need to try first. I don't like ratting out people, especially when I'm not sure it's who I think it is."

"Fair enough," said Shane. "But I need to know if you don't make any headway. And I need to know sooner rather than later."

Harking nodded again. "I understand. If they don't listen to me, you'll be the first to know."

Shane's face tightened. "Before Marion?"

Harking nodded again.

"Because you know," Shane continued, "if Marion tears another strip off John, I'll be the first to hear about it. Well, maybe the second, after the chief park warden." Frowning, Shane stood up and pulled his Stetson back in place. "After all, shit still flows downhill, in case you didn't know."

"I know," Harking said as she followed him to the door.

"And you'll get that camera out of there?" Pulling on his cowboy boots and straightening up, Shane looked at her for confirmation.

"ASAP." Harking nodded.

"I'll take that to mean right away," said Shane. He was about to leave when he turned back.

"You got some good pictures?"

"Amazing," Harking confirmed.

"Bears?"

"A grizzly sow and three cubs."

Shane clenched his teeth. "Yeah, I don't like that."

"And there was a pretty big male. He looked mean."

Shane hesitated and looked Harking square in the eyes. "There's been a male griz hanging out around the pony barns. I think he's a young bear that hasn't quite figured everything out. They're usually the first to get into trouble."

"I know," said Harking. "Like teenagers, dad always said. Male teenagers. Lots of testosterone and little brains." She smiled at the memory of his exact words. *Small dicks and a smaller brain*, he'd said, adding, *Don't tell your mom I said that*, obviously embarrassed he'd mentioned it in the first place.

Shane nodded. "I should probably go back there with you to get that gear. I don't like how this picture is starting to develop."

"I'll be fine," said Harking.

"You sure? I could ask Megan Weaver to go with you."

"The warden from the North?"

"Huhuh. She's more the mountain biker type."

Harking had seen Jasper's newest park warden on the trails from time to time and knew she was a capable rider. Still, she shook her head. "I'd rather go on my own."

"You sure?"

"Yeah." Harking nodded and held the door open for Shane. "I'm sure."

CHAPTER 15

Unconvinced Match and his buddies would listen to her, Harking decided to leave the camera and recorder for a little while longer. Despite her promise to Shane, she thought it would be a good idea to give it a few more days to make sure no one was using the trail.

In the meantime, she had something else bugging her; she wanted to try and make sense of the directions recorded in her father's field notes. She'd made a few feeble attempts previously using topographic maps to tease out his routes on paper, but had been frustrated when they hadn't worked out, confused by her lack of familiarity with his "system". Finally she figured the best thing to do was to literally follow in his footsteps, using the directions in his notebooks to see where they took her.

Picking what she thought would be one of the easier sites to get to, she convinced Simi to come along and together the pair rode out of town, headed south along the river trail, wearing hoodies to fend off the cool morning mist, tossing barbs of gossip back and forth between them as they navigated their way along the trail.

"So do you think he's into her?" Simi almost shouted the question to reel Harking in as she pedalled hard up a steep section of trail.

"Who, and who?" Harking looked over her shoulder then braked slightly to let Simi catch up.

"Match." Simi panted as she pulled alongside. "Do you think Match is into Brianna?"

"If not, he'd be the only guy that isn't," Harking snarled. "She's such a bag."

"But I don't think of Match the same way," Simi countered, sliding off the pedals and straddling her bike to force Harking to take a breather. "He's better than that." Pulling out her water bottle she took a sip.

"Maybe." Harking didn't seem enthused about thinking about it, one way or the other. "Anyway, I've got better things to think of. C'mon, let's go."

"Okay, okay," said Simi, shoving the bottle into its holder and rushing to catch up.

When Harking figured they'd gone as far as they could, they hid their bikes in the bushes and set their sights on the day's objective, a site high up on the treed slopes of Signal Mountain.

Pulling a compass from her pack Harking slowly turned the compass dial until it lined up with the bearing recorded in her father's notes.

"Wow, that's kind of old school," said Simi as she looked over Harking's shoulder.

"Huhuh. But it was Dad's go-to device anytime we went hiking."

"Not even a handheld GPS?" said Simi, incredulously.

"Nope," Harking replied, referring to the tattered notebook. "At least not when he made these notes."

Simi smiled as she cradled her phone in her hand. "Then I guess a smartphone app would have been out of the question?"

"Yup."

Just as her father had shown her, Harking unfolded the mirrored lid of the compass over the dial and sighted through the lid's small notch to line up the compass needle with the bearing she'd set.

By his account, it would take them to an old wolf den that had been inactive for some time.

By Harking's reckoning, it was going to be an uphill slog.

"Might be more of a grunt than I thought," said Harking.

Simi pocketed her phone and adjusted the straps on her daypack as she looked up at the mountain. "Thank God Signal isn't that steep."

Pulling out her GPS, Harking recorded a waypoint at the edge of the trail then slid the unit into her pack. "In case we need a backup."

"Good idea," said Simi.

Picking a large Douglas fir some distance upslope, Harking looped the compass around her neck and tucked it inside her hoodie.

"Ready?"

Not waiting for Simi to reply, Harking made her way through the underbrush, pushing away buffaloberry and alders as she kept her eye on the large fir. Stopping under its massive canopy until Simi caught up, Harking then slid around to the uphill side of the veteran tree and took another compass shot. Sighting on the largest trees they could see as their objective, the pair leapfrogged their way through the forest.

As the route led them into steeper and steeper terrain, the Douglas fir giving way to an expanse of open lodgepole pine, they stopped and surveyed for possible targets.

"How about that?" said Simi, pointing to a small ridge in the distance.

"Looks good," said Harking.

Picking their way steadily toward the ridge, Harking and Simi cursed as they negotiated a small boulder field, scraping their legs on the sharp edges of the rocks. Finally pulling themselves hand over hand through the rest of the boulders, they crawled up and over the last one, high-fiving each other as they stood on top of the ridge

Looking around, Harking was surprised to see a shallow dip in the topography, otherwise hidden by the ridge they'd just conquered. A small wetland was nestled in the middle of the hollow with what looked like a gravel bank buttressing the uphill side.

"I wonder if that's where the den is," she said, digging her father's journal out of her pack. Flipping through his dog-eared notes, she found the reference and smiled as she read. "The den is dug into a gravel bank overlooking a small wetland."

The notes also included a small pencil sketch with a series of numbers written down the side of the page.

"What do the numbers refer to?" said Simi, scanning the page.

"I don't know," Harking said with a shrug. Like in the other journals, the numbers seemed to have been added at a later date she explained. "But not every entry had a number, almost as if Dad only wanted anyone using his field notes to go to specific places."

"And what's that a reference to?" Simi pointed to the final part of his entry where he referred to a thick stand of young pine as "pecker pole pine," or "P³".

"P cubed." Harking laughed. "He could be such a nerd sometimes but that's what he was referring to." She pointed to what looked like an impenetrable barrier of trees. "I wonder if there's a way around it."

Harking wiped the sweat from her eyes, pulled the water bottle from her pack and took a long drink as the midday sun beat down upon them. "It's getting warmer," she said, taking off her hoodie and stuffing it into her pack.

"I'm keeping mine on in case that comes our way." Simi pointed to a band of dark cloud slowly pushing its way in from the west then took a drink from her own water bottle.

"Hope it holds off long enough for us to find the den and get back down the mountain," said Harking. Returning the bottle to her pack she stood up and took another compass shot.

Opting to find a way around the pine, the pair dropped down into the hollow and picked their way along the edge of the thicket, only to come up against a deep ravine cutting its way downslope, blocking their way.

"Damn," said Harking, searching the slopes unsuccessfully for another way around. "We have to go back to the ridge to see if we can pick a better route."

Back on the ridge top, Harking once again referred to her father's directions, frowning as she noted his warning of "tough going" penciled next to the sketch, with an arrow pointing to the band of trees. Sighing, Harking retrieved her hoodie from her pack and put it back on.

"No point getting scratched to rat shit in that mess."

"Or eaten," she added, pulling a canister of bear spray from her pack and slipping it into her shorts pocket.

"Better safe than sorry," said Simi.

Putting the journal away Harking sighted down the compass once again and took a shot across the wetland. Reluctantly, she dropped back into the hollow with Simi tight on her heels.

"Hey, bear," Harking called out. "Comin' through."

Slowly, the pair eased their way into an opening, crouching and twisting to avoid becoming ensnared in the web of dead branches that threatened to shred their clothes and packs, not to mention arms and legs.

It was tortuous going, the trees thick and unforgiving, standing straight and firm like the bristles of a stiff brush. Every now and then both young women were forced to duck under the lowest branches and crawl on hands and knees, pushing their packs ahead of them as they squirmed through narrow openings.

Harking gripped the bear spray tightly in one hand, passing it back and forth to Simi whenever she needed another free hand to clear a way through the trees.

As the pine gave way to scrubby spruce, Harking called out again, "Hey, bear," her lone voice in the wilderness unable to settle the gnawing in her gut.

Close to the ground, the rich, deep stench of decaying leaves and grasses wafted into her nostrils and Harking sensed she was close to the wetland.

Almost on cue, she shoved one arm into black, muddy ooze, her hand finally finding purchase in the elbow-deep quagmire.

Harking groaned as she extracted herself from the mess and struggled to stand upright. "Watch out for that." She pointed to the spot as Simi followed behind on her knees. As Harking wiped her arm, she peered through the small band of low spruce lining the wetland and could see the gravel bank almost directly across from her.

"This way," she said, shouldering her pack.

Picking her way around the edge of the swamp, Harking finally located a small tunnel through the underbrush, the outer branches sporting small clumps of hair she assumed were left behind by bears or wolves or both as they navigated around the wetland.

"Through here," Harking said when Simi had caught up.

"Seriously?"

"Yup, seriously." Without further explanation Harking half-walked, half-crawled into the entrance. "Hey, bear," she called out again, her voice barely penetrating the tangle of vegetation as Simi reluctantly followed her into the maze.

Suddenly, somewhere to her left, Harking thought she heard a shuffling sound, the swish of dried leaves, the crunch of small twigs. "Did you hear that?" she said, speaking over her shoulder to Simi.

"Hey, bear," Harking called out again. The shout was half-hearted as she closed her eyes and held her breath while Simi repeated the call.

"Hey, bear!"

Listening intently, Harking tried to tease apart the sounds in the bush from the beating of her heart. She knew from experience that something as small as a squirrel or bird could play tricks on your hearing in close quarters, but she figured whatever this was, it was big.

As she tried to stand up and take another step forward, her hair snagged in the overhanging branches.

"Shit." Harking groaned and dropped the bear spray as she slid her fingers through the tangled mess, trying to escape the embrace of tentacles that had halted her progress just as Simi pushed into her from behind.

Somewhere to their left, Harking could still hear breaking branches and what sounded like a muffled grunt.

"Shit, shit, shit," Simi muttered as she also became ensnared.

Stooped over and mud-covered, with their hair caught in the branches, both young women were trapped.

"What are we supposed to do now?" Simi's voice sounded panicked.

Turning her head as much as she could, Harking held a finger to her mouth. "Shssh."

Harking was positive she could hear something breathing. Heavily.

She held her breath to be sure.

"What is it?" Simi whispered.

"Shssh."

Slowly, Harking reached down to grab the bear spray. She was just straightening up as the trees around them exploded.

Harking and Simi screamed simultaneously then charged through the last few feet of thicket just as a large bull moose came crashing out of the bushes, missing them by inches.

With her heart pounding in her ears, Harking collapsed on the ground next to Simi as they watched the massive animal barrel downhill, its long hind legs splayed to the side as it tried to navigate the tricky slope.

"God," Simi sighed heavily, "that was crazy." As she tried to catch her breath, she inspected her hands. "I'm still shaking."

Sitting back against her pack, Harking took stock of their situation, wincing as she tried to smooth out her hair, tugging small pieces of wood and leaves from the long strands. As she straightened out her legs and leaned forward to gently run her hands over the new scrapes and bruises, she noticed the blood-stained tear in her hoodie.

"Ouch," she whimpered as she rolled up her sleeve and surveyed the cut on her arm, the edges angry and swollen.

"That doesn't look good," said Simi, momentarily distracted from her own self-inspection as Harking gently pulled off her hoodie and tossed it on the ground.

Taking a small first aid kit from her pack, Harking spilled the contents onto the hoodie and retrieved several gauze wipes, ripping them open and lightly dabbing the cut to clean up the blood and dirt.

Turning her full attention to Harking, Simi assisted, picking out a large butterfly bandage and gently placing it over the gash, smoothing it into place.

"Thanks," said Harking. "That should work until we get home."

Reassembling the first aid kit, Harking stuffed everything into her pack and put her hoodie back on while Simi pulled herself together. Making their way to the base of the gravel bank, they found a large log and sat down and took a long drink of water from their water bottles.

"So, no to Match?" Simi glanced slyly at Harking.

"Will you give it a rest?" Harking snapped.

After an awkward moment of silence she apologized and looked around, taking stock of their surroundings.

"We came up here to find something," she added. Looking over her shoulder she noticed a large hole, dug into the sidehill. "And I think that's it."

Harking winced as she stood up and made her way to the den. A few large bones lay strewn around the entrance but otherwise the site looked abandoned. Getting down on her hands and knees she poked her head into the entranceway and looked into the shallow cave.

"Surprisingly clean and empty," she said as Simi knelt down next to her and peered inside, just as the sun slid behind the clouds, further darkening the hole.

"Doesn't look like it's been used for awhile," Simi said as Harking pulled back from the den's entrance.

"Not this year for sure," said Harking. Looking skyward she pointed at the heavy clouds reeling in from the west. "I think the weather's going to turn on us."

Kneeling back on her heels, she pulled out her GPS and quickly recorded a waypoint. "For future reference," she said as Simi crouched down beside her. Scrolling to the waypoint she'd collected when they started their hike, Harking pressed the GO TO button and checked the distance back to their bikes.

"2.4 kilometres."

"Yeah right ... 2.4 kilometres, of hell," said Simi as they both stood up and considered their options. "I don't want to go back that way," she added, pointing to the tangle they'd just extracted themselves from.

"No way," said Harking, agreeing not to retrace her father's bearing. "Let's try cutting across the mountain. If we can get past all of that mess, it'll be an easy hike back to the trail."

Harking smiled to herself as she put the compass back in her pack and thought about her father's insistence that it was so much better than the new technology.

I'll take the GPS over that anytime.

Looking at the GPS then around them to find the best way down the mountain, Harking picked what she thought would be the easiest path. "This way," she said.

As the pair started downslope, the skies opened up.

CHAPTER 16

Harking was a drowned rat when she crossed the threshold into the house, unable to escape the observations of her overseer as Marion assessed the rivulets of bloodstained water sliding down Harking's scratched and bruised legs, dripping onto the floor.

"My goodness, what in the world have you been up to?"

"We went looking for that wolf den Dad always talked about," said Harking, bending over to wipe bike chain grease from her calves.

"We?"

"Simi and I."

"Goodness. Does she look anything like you?"

"Pretty much," said Harking, standing up and picking small pieces of twigs from her twisted locks. "Although the chain didn't come off her bike on the way back, so she's not as greasy."

"Hmmm, I see." Marion shook her head. "And which wolf den did you go looking for?"

"The one on Signal."

"The one on Signal ... Mountain?" Marion's frown stretched across her face.

Harking nodded.

"But it hasn't been used for years," said Marion. "I was up there in the spring."

"*You* ... were up there this year?" Harking suspected that Marion was losing track of time, the years especially.

"Yes, just after the snow came off the side hills."

"And you ... hiked up from the trail?"

"God, no. That way is much too rough."

"So ... which way did you go?"

"I took the fire road as high as I could, then cut across the slope, following the contour lines."

Harking slowly pulled off her pack and let it slip to the floor, still suspicious.

"And you did that *this year*?" Wide-eyed, she pointed both index fingers at Marion.

"Yes. The den was still empty but I did run into a massive bull moose. Scared the living daylights out of me."

"Hmphh," Harking grunted and bent down to untie her hikers.

"Don't tell me you followed your father's compass bearing up the side of Signal?"

"Huhuh."

"God, that would lead you right into that quagmire of a wetland and that damned stand of pecker poles. What was it your father called it? P cubed or some such silliness."

"Yeah," said Harking, pulling her feet out of the sodden boots and tugging her socks off. "P cubed." She sighed. "Or some such silliness," she murmured under her breath.

"The apple does not fall far from the tree," Marion chuckled. "Why in the name of God's green earth did you follow that bearing? You know as well as I do that he didn't always follow the easiest path."

Harking knew Marion was right. Her father, despite being a self-professed explorer, investigator and seeker of things, of anything, was also a notorious wanderer.

"But his compass bearing led us right to it," Harking explained. "I just wanted to see for myself." She pulled the journal out of a small plastic bag and opened it to the sketch of the wolf den. "See the bearing is right there."

"I don't doubt it." Marion took the book from Harking and thumbed through the pages. "He was always recording points of interest and how to get to them. I don't know why he never learned how to use that GPS I gave him?"

"You mean this one?" Harking pulled the GPS from her pack.

"Yes, exactly. It was Malcolm's. I gave it to your father after Malcolm died, after he led me on a particularly roundabout hike to one of his 'secret places.'" She laughed. "I thought he was going to kill me."

"But Dad never used it."

"It appears not. All I see here are compass bearings." Marion flipped through the pages.

"But what about these numbers in the margins?"

Marion pondered the numbers for a moment then shook her head. "I don't know. They could be GPS coordinates."

"I don't think so," said Harking. "I plotted some of them on a topo map but they didn't line up with the location in Dad's notes."

"Hmm," said Marion. "Go get me the map you were using."

Harking disappeared upstairs and came back with a worn and tattered map from her father's collection.

"Just as I suspected," said Marion as she spread the map on the coffee table and read the fine print in the map legend. "When Malcolm and I first started using GPS, everything was recorded based on mapping done in 1927, like this one." She retrieved a newer version of the same map from a pile of maps sitting on a bookshelf and laid it on top of the first. "Since then, all mapping has been upgraded to 1983. So your father's coordinates just need to be converted. It's actually quite easy."

Flipping through the notebooks, Marion smirked. "Not unless he had his own system. You know your father."

Harking smiled, recalling how he had his own way of doing everything. "He did. But you know, I think he was usually right. He had a way of explaining things that made more sense to Col and I than what someone like Ms. Peacock might say."

Marion laughed. "He certainly did. And I think in many ways he was ahead of his time. Kind of funny, don't you think, for someone who had a keen interest in history and tradition? David Thompson was always top of mind when we hiked anywhere in Jasper with him. Still your father was always keen on the next best gadget to come on the market. Except for some reason he never seemed to take to using a GPS." She smiled at the memory. "He said if David Thompson could get around using a sextant and the stars, then he should be fine with a map and compass."

She handed the journal back to Harking.

"Now go on and get cleaned up," she added. "I'll look after this mess and get dinner going. You can tell me more about your exploits then."

Harking was about to make her way upstairs but had an afterthought.

"Marion."

"Yes?"

"Why did the wolves leave that den?"

"I don't know. They'll often use a site repeatedly but they do move around, maybe because of better hunting ..."

"Or did they abandon it because of us?" said Harking.

"Possibly," said Marion. "Biologists are only just beginning to understand how our activities displace wildlife. It doesn't take a lot of people to displace them."

Harking pondered the last point and thought about how much use there was in the valley around the town of Jasper.

"So, are we literally forcing them out of the valley? And will we do the same thing to the bears?

"I don't know." Marion hesitated. "I don't know if anyone knows. But I think if we give them space and room to move around on the landscape, if we try to co-exist with them, hopefully things will work out."

CHAPTER 17

After the adventure on Signal Mountain and her discussion with Marion, Harking figured it was time to finally keep her promise to Shane and pull the camera. Leaving town on her bike, she headed for the lake. Hoping to be as inconspicuous as possible she was surprised to see yellow caution tape stretching across the main trailhead, along with an official closure sign, including a map showing the extent of the closed area.

Great, she thought. *At least they didn't waste any time shutting things down.*

Hesitating, she wondered now if she should go back to retrieve the camera or leave it until the closure was lifted.

But knowing Parks, that could be weeks or months from now.

Deciding to take a chance, Harking hid her bike and slipped under the caution tape, looking around to ensure no one saw her.

As she headed down the trail, paying attention to any wildlife sign she encountered, Harking heard what sounded like a raucous quarrel of crows and ravens and assumed the corvids had found a resting owl, torturing it as was their custom by dive-bombing the bird into submission, forcing it to move on to another haunt.

Closing in on the frenzy of grating calls, the croaks and caws suggesting a battle was afoot, Harking stopped short as the stench of death wafted up the trail toward her. Thinking she'd probably stumbled on a kill site Harking expected to find the remains of a deer, elk or even a moose, all common prey of the park's wolves, cougars and bears.

Bear spray in hand Harking cautiously rounded a turn in the trail and spotted the body.

Unsure at first what to make of the mound of fur, she stepped closer, peering into the surrounding forest before approaching the carcass. Certain it wasn't one of the ungulates she'd initially suspected, she now hoped it also wasn't the sow grizzly or one of its cubs.

"God, what happened to you?" she said as she stood over the body of the black bear, holding a hand over her nose and mouth as she investigated the remains.

All around her, the vegetation looked as if it had been mauled to death, not unlike what was left of the body at her feet, decapitated and torn apart, aided no doubt by the usual suspects, the myriad scavengers that usually benefitted from the efforts of larger predators: coyotes, fox, marten and weasels along with their avian counterparts, now squawking in defiance as Harking used a stick to pull the remains of the black bear off the trail and into the surrounding forest.

Checking the area, trying to decipher what had happened, Harking found a set of larger tracks belonging to a grizzly and speculated how the black bear had met its demise. According to her father, the two species rarely occupied the same piece of ground. When a black bear did find itself in grizzly country, it often paid the price. Considering the absence of smaller grizzly tracks, Harking figured the male grizzly in her photos was probably responsible for killing the black bear.

Noticing the stripped buffaloberry branches and the piles of fresh bear shit loaded with partially digested berries, she imagined how things might have gone down ... the black bear finding this berry bonanza and gorging on the windfall, the grizzly picking up the scent of an intruder and moving with purpose through the forest.

While the black bear would have been distracted, the grizzly would have been stalking it, lifting its nose to catch any scent, quietly pushing through the understory, easily climbing over deadfall as it made its way through the forest, each heavy step swallowed by the thick moss.

Harking suspected the grizzly attacked before the black bear could even react, shooting across the narrow opening, catching its smaller cousin by surprise, using its size advantage to pin the intruder to the ground.

Although outmatched, the trail of trampled vegetation leading away from the initial point of contact suggested it wasn't over quickly.

Fighting for its life, the black bear probably did some damage of its own, taking advantage of the momentary lull in the attack to break free. But as it tried to escape, the black bear only managed to get a short distance through the tangle of downed trees bordering the trail, the speed and strength of the larger bear being too much.

As she interpreted the extent of destruction, Harking imagined the grizzly grasping the black bear in its powerful jaws, shaking it vigorously from side to side, tossing it around like a rag doll, destroying the surrounding patch of shrubs and mosses before dropping the carcass at its feet.

At first Harking couldn't decide on the aftermath, whether the grizzly would have left the carcass to the scavengers, or eaten some of the black bear itself. But considering the extent of damage to the black bear, its body literally ripped apart, she concluded the grizzly must have been responsible.

However it ended, Harking knew it wasn't pretty.

Hopefully this particular grizzly would move on to other parts of the park and wouldn't do the same thing to the mother grizzly or her cubs, something male grizzlies were notorious for.

Taking a final look at the remains, Harking thought about reporting the carcass, but decided against it. If she did, park staff could then warn others about its presence and prevent someone from walking down the trail and running into another predator feeding on the black bear's carcass. But considering the area was now officially closed, and since there wasn't much left of the black bear for other animals to feed on, Harking figured it was a moot point.

Satisfied that she'd pulled the remains of the bear far enough into the bush, Harking headed back to the trail and continued on her way.

She was happy to find the camera setup untouched and, considering her earlier discovery, decided to download whatever photos it held but leave it for a few more days to see what else it might capture. *Shane won't be happy about it, but hey, what he doesn't know won't hurt him.*

But she would also have to keep it from Marion and that was something she was less keen to do.

Oh well, Harking thought. *Same, same. What she doesn't know ...*

CHAPTER 18

"Area closed by order of the Park Superintendent," Tyson said, leaning across his handlebars, reading aloud from the new closure sign. "Hmph," he muttered, looking at the other three boys. "We going or not?" He directed his attention to Match.

"We probably should stay out of there."

"Because of that?" Tyson scoffed. "No one will ever know we're in there."

"But it's officially closed now," said Match.

"Right," said Tyson. "We all know the wardens don't get out of their trucks so how will they catch us? Or are you just too scared your old man will find out?"

Match's stare drilled into Tyson. "I'm not scared of anyone."

"Then let's go," Tyson ordered. "And tighten that lid." He smirked at Match's newly acquired bike helmet, laughing along with Col and Grayson. "Wouldn't want you to hurt your precious head."

With Col Thompson being a couple grades behind the others who were graduating this year and still had provincial finals to contend with, school for him had already finished for the summer. With Grayson's parents offering him room and board, which Paige Thompson happily accepted to pay for, Col had returned to town for a summer job cleaning stalls at the horse stables. Paige figured the hard work would do him good and although she didn't know Grayson very well, she knew his parents personally and sensed their son was a "good kid" for Col to be around.

For his part, Col hadn't yet connected with Harking, but he suspected she'd be happy to know he'd broken free of their mother's grasp, cutting the apron strings at least for a few months, surprised that she actually agreed to let him return for the summer as long as he promised to buckle down at school come fall. Ignoring his mother's other advice about who to hang out with, and with a few days before work started, Col picked up where he left off and along with Grayson tracked down his old buddies for a celebratory ride, unaware of Harking's concerns about this particular trail.

Without another word, Match hopped on his bike and rode past the sign as Tyson watched with a smirk on his face.

"You next," Tyson said to Col and Grayson, motioning for them to follow Match down the trail.

Riding in single file, the four stuck to the trail, hopping their bikes over downed trees, grunting through the uphill stretches and hooting on the downhills. A few kilometres along, as the trail approached the lakeshore, the boys descended a slight hill and stopped for a minute. Straddling the mountain bikes, they took a drink from their backpacks, sucking and pulling water into their mouths.

Wiping the sweat from his brow, Match turned to the others. "I will be in deep shit if my old man finds out we were in the closed area again." He looked at Tyson. "Just sayin'."

Tyson snickered and let the drinking tube fall to the side. "Scared, Match? Want to turn back?"

Match knew backing out would mean losing face, but he'd been unable to convince Tyson to go anywhere else. And with the trail legally posted as being closed, poaching some single track now offered even more street cred.

Still, after Harking had talked to him, Match wondered if she'd removed the camera or if it would catch them riding the trail. Luckily for him, Col had shown up back in town and was with them for the ride. Harking's younger brother could be his ace in the hole. If nothing else, he'd be able to use it against Harking if she threatened to out them.

Stretching his tired muscles, Match noticed an odd shape etched into the moss, leading from the trail toward a large gnarled pine tree several feet away. Recalling seeing the tree the last time they'd been on the trail he got off his bike to take a closer look. "Wait here," he said to the others.

Realizing he was looking at the footprint of a large bear, Match followed the tracks toward the tree where they stopped abruptly, lost in the heavy mat of pine needles surrounding the base of the old pine.

Clumps of fine hair stuck in the globs of resin oozing from the smoothed trunk of the pine and there was also a series of claw marks coursing down the tree. Looking around the other side, he noticed that the tracks led back to the trail.

For all the time he'd spent biking, Match had never seen a grizzly and wondered how recently the tracks and claw marks had been made. Old or new, he wasn't really keen to find out. He wanted to get off the trail as fast as possible. Walking quickly back to the group Match got on his bike and turned to Tyson.

"Let's get going."

"What's the rush, dude?" said Tyson.

"I just want to get going," said Match, pulling on his helmet. "You guys stay close behind."

Tyson snickered. "Worried your old man...?"

Before he could finish, Match reached out and grabbed Tyson's arm, squeezing hard. "Fuck off, Ty."

"Okay, okay, chill," said Tyson, his faced flushed. "Jesus, I was only joking." Brushing Match away he slid on to the bike seat.

Match looked sternly at Col and Grayson to reinforce the message. "Stay close behind. Dog it and it'll be the last time you ride with us."

Col flipped his chin and nodded as Match turned around and started down the trail, moving quietly as he slipped out of sight.

"Jesus, what's with him?"

"Don't worry about it," Tyson snapped, still smarting from Match's response. Pointing his nose, he directed Col and Grayson to catch up to Match then watched as the trio disappeared around a corner before following them down the trail.

■ ■ ■

Some distance away, toward the opposite end of the trail, the sow grizzly bear was feeding on fresh shoots, working her way through the riparian area where the trail closely followed the lakeshore.

Having circumnavigated the valley over the last few days, she had brought the cubs back to the area behind the lakes, an area free of the people and traffic in the main valley, where all she had to contend with were the advances of the young male grizzly.

As she gorged on the succulent plants, she lifted her head occasionally to sniff the air and check on the whereabouts of her cubs.

Since showing up at the lake, the young male had made several attempts to drive off her cubs, but each time she'd been able to thwart his efforts. It wasn't uncommon for larger males to kill cubs and the young mother seemed to have a sixth sense for when he was in the area.

Vigilant and wary, the sow lifted her nose into the air and sniffed. She grunted as she looked around for her cubs and gave two quick huffs as the young male came barrelling out of the bushes toward them. Without hesitating, the sow charged the young male and drove into his side as he made a beeline for the slowest cub, grazing the small bear's backside with his claws as he toppled sideways into the buffaloberry.

Finding refuge behind their mother, the cubs sidestepped in unison with her every movement as she tried to keep her body between her young and the determined male.

Shaking himself, the young male circled the female as the quartet slowly moved its way upslope toward the trail. With his every feint, the female countered with an aggressive bluff charge, stopping just short of making contact.

84

As they approached the trail, two cubs scurried to stay with their mother leaving the third cub momentarily vulnerable to the advances of the large male bear. As the male honed in on the injured cub, the female found the trail and stopped in her tracks, backing her young up against the trunk of a large fir.

She was about to make another charge when two mountain bikers suddenly raced around the corner, their speed and silent approach catching her off guard.

At any other time, and given enough warning to assess an oncoming danger, the sow would have collected her cubs and led them into the security afforded by the thick underbrush. But the threat of the male grizzly looming and with her already in a defensive mode, there was no time. Without hesitating the sow grizzly reacted and charged toward the bikers, her sudden outburst knocking the bikers down as their screams sent the young male grizzly scrambling to escape.

Before the sow could do anything else, a third biker careened around the corner, losing control and flying into the bushes. Reacting, the mother grizzly bluff charged a final time then gathered her cubs and disappeared into the forest.

CHAPTER 19

Jumping off her bike and rushing into the hospital, Harking spied Marion standing with a group of people at the end of the hall in the emergency ward.

"How is he?" she blurted, pulling Marion away as she surveyed the others: Match and his parents, Grayson with his, as well as Tyson and his father Andrew, all in an animated discussion with Shane Ross and Richard Odili.

"We'll know pretty soon," said Marion, putting an arm around Harking.

Harking looked up into her eyes. "I didn't even know Col was back in town."

"I'm just finding out myself," Marion said. "Apparently your mother agreed to let him spend summer in the park as long as he took his studies seriously when he went back to school in the fall. He's staying with the Moberlys," she added, nodding toward Grayson and his parents.

"The least he could have done was come by and let us know he was here," said Harking. "Or texted me."

"I think he was planning to come by but hadn't had the time yet."

"Right," Harking mumbled. "Does Mom know he's in the hospital?"

"Yes. I expect she'll be here soon." Marion hesitated. "They were biking on the trail behind the lake. In the closed area."

Harking nodded but said nothing.

"Did you take your father's camera out of there?" Marion whispered, looking serious.

When Harking didn't reply, Marion sighed. "Oh, Harking."

"It wouldn't have made any difference," Harking said, looking past Marion at the group. Catching Shane's eye, she turned away as he broke from the gathering and made his way slowly toward Marion and Harking.

"Howdy, ma'am," he said, automatically tipping his Stetson to Marion before being caught in Harking's crosshairs. Blushing, he pulled the hat off his head and held it at his side. "Sorry about young Col." He glanced back at the group before turning back to Marion and Harking. "Inside the closed area," he said, raising his eyebrows as he focused on Harking.

"I know," Harking replied sheepishly.

"Had you talked to them about the bears?"

"I did. I thought they'd listen."

"I don't know if that Tyson kid would listen to anyone."

Harking nodded.

"He's a bit of shitrat like his old man," Shane added, looking over his shoulder before quickly turning back to Marion. "Pardon my English."

A narrow smile creased Marion's face. "They all can be at times."

"Absolutely," said Shane. He turned back to Harking. "Did you take your Dad's gear outta there?"

Harking shook her head. "Not yet."

"Well," said Shane, once again turning to Marion. "This might be one of those times when *not* listening pays off."

"How do you mean?" said Harking.

"Well right now, Tyson's old man wants the supe to have that sow killed on the spot," said Shane, motioning to the large, barrel-chested man standing with the others.

"He can't do that."

"Can so," said Shane. "If the supe's forced into a corner, that griz is a dead bear."

Harking held a hand to her lips, lightly biting her finger-nails as Shane explained.

"Tyson claimed they didn't see the closure sign because they accessed the trail from somewhere other than the fire road. He says the bear attacked them for no reason. And his old man is all over John about not doing a better job of signing the closed area when a dangerous bear is on the loose."

"Asshole," Harking muttered under her breath, her eyes misting over.

"But if your camera picked them up," Shane continued, "we'll know if they're telling the truth or not. We might also be able to figure out which bear it was exactly. From what I can figure out, it sounds like the little sow and cubs but we can't be sure. We know there's other bears back there." He looked back at the group. John Walleski had broken away from the others and was motioning for Shane to join him off to the side.

"I'll be back in a minute," said Shane.

Harking nodded and turned to Marion. "They'll want to destroy the bear," she said, her anger starting to simmer as she watched Shane and the park superintendent. Shane motioned toward her at one point, but then turned back to John Walleski when he saw that Harking was watching him. Concluding his discussion with the superintendent, Shane returned to speak with Harking and Marion.

"John wants me to get statements from the boys and from you," he said, focusing on Harking. "He also wants Richard Odili present when I take them."

"I'm confused," said Harking. "Why?"

"In case it goes to court," said Shane. "This could turn into a criminal or civil matter," he added, speaking directly to Marion.

"Court?" said Harking.

"This is serious stuff," said Shane. "A lot depends on what happens to your brother."

"What do you mean?" Marion demanded.

Shane shook his head. "I'd rather not get into it, but let's just hope Col is not seriously injured." He was about to leave but turned back to Harking. "I have to go help secure the area back of the lake. I'll get back to you later about the interview. And the camera." He paused. "You'll have to tell me where it is and I'll go get it. I don't want you back in there."

Before Harking could protest Shane rushed away, just as a doctor appeared in the hallway and approached the other group. When Match's mother pointed toward Harking and Marion the doctor made his way toward them.

CHAPTER 20

Leaving the hospital, Harking quickly rode to Marion's and bounded up the stairs, having already made up her mind to ignore Shane's warning. The doctor had said Col suffered a concussion but only minor cuts and bruises. Yes, he was unconscious but his condition was stable. He suggested there was no point sticking around and would let them know if things changed. Harking figured she should stay until her mother arrived, but when Marion offered to wait, Harking took it as her cue to escape.

"Be careful," Marion had told Harking before she left, no doubt suspecting where Harking was headed.

Collecting her pack and a light, she was about to run out the door when she remembered the bear spray. Grabbing the canister, she bolted outside and jumped on her bike, using back alleys and side streets to get to the edge of town.

As dusk settled over the valley, Harking followed a series of back trails to avoid the dragnet of park wardens and RCMP officers busy turning traffic around as people hearing the news were drawn toward the scene of the bear attack. Harking knew the wardens would be combing the area back of the lake for a grizzly, any grizzly, and decided to take a roundabout way to the lake trail.

She knew it wasn't wise to ride the trail at dusk, but she had to get to the camera before it—or she—was discovered. As she approached the camera location she could hear voices in the distance but hoped she wouldn't run into anyone as they scoured the area, before darkness forced them to end their search.

Jumping off her bike, she ran to the large pine, its silhouette easily distinguishable in the fading light. Her hands shaking,

Harking fumbled with the strap holding the camera to the tree as thoughts of the past few hours raced through her head. Despite the doctor's assurances, she was worried about Col and dreaded meeting her mother. And although the fate of the grizzly was back of mind, she couldn't shake the idea that she was somehow responsible for everything that had happened.

First the avalanche and now this.

Fighting off her emotions, Harking grabbed the camera and quickly shoved it into her pack.

Suddenly a series of shouts broke the stillness, followed by a shotgun blast, its reverberations cascading off the mountain and echoing across the lake.

Startled, Harking dropped to her knees and held her breath, her heart pounding in her ears as her entire body shook.

Realizing there was no way she'd be able to collect the sound recorder that night she decided to leave and come back at another time.

Riding down the lake trail, taking care not to be seen, Harking picked her way toward town, sliding quickly down the rear alley and entering Marion's through the backyard gate, cringing as the squeaking of its rusty hinges threatened to give her away.

Safe within the confines of her bedroom, she pulled the camera from her pack and extracted the memory card. Her hand was still shaking as she pushed it into the computer and scrolled through the most recent photos, beginning with the last images taken.

Surprisingly, there was an excellent shot of each of the boys as they rode past the camera setup.

Must have been going slow for some reason, Harking thought.

When she realized Match was wearing a helmet she smiled to herself and wondered if he had finally heeded her warning about grizzlies on the trail and the need to be careful.

But obviously they weren't careful enough.

Reviewing the order the boys rode past, Harking could see Match was in the lead, followed by Col and Grayson with Tyson some distance behind.

That's funny.

For all his tough talk she thought Tyson would have been out front or at least right on Match's tail.

As Harking scrolled through the other pictures, she saw the usual suspects including a moose and calf as well as numerous photos of elk and coyotes. There was also one earlier sequence of photos showing the sow and cubs.

When a photo of a black bear turned up, followed immediately by a grizzly she suspected was the lone male, Harking figured this was the same black bear whose remains she'd found. Surprisingly there were several images of the lone grizzly as he travelled back and forth along the trail over a period of several days but there were no other photos of the sow and cubs.

That didn't necessarily mean anything, other than they might have been avoiding the adult male and not using the trail when he was around. Or they might simply have been somewhere else in the valley.

She'd heard reports of a sow with three cubs across the river and Harking figured it had to be the same quartet of bears, considering it unlikely that there was another female grizzly with that many cubs in the area.

Satisfied she'd gone through all the photos, Harking opened her database and recorded the information then made a copy of the images and saved them to a thumb drive she kept locked in her dresser drawer.

As she shut things down, Harking's phone buzzed with a text from Simi.

Where r u?
Home
How's Col?

Okay but unconscious
Can I come by?
Sure

Within minutes Simi was at Marion's house and knocking.
Come up, Harking texted. *Door's unlocked.*
She listened as Simi's footsteps mounted the stairs.
"You okay," Simi said, embracing Harking as she entered her bedroom.
Harking nodded. "Yeah." She pulled Simi over to the bed and the two sat down. "So what have you heard?"
"Only gossip. Brianna is all over Instagram. Talking like she knows something."
"Figures." Harking scrolled through the social media site on her phone.
"Saying Col almost died," said Simi.
"Well he could have." Harking seemed lost in her own thoughts as she read the scuttlebutt making its way around town. "But the doctor thinks he'll be fine. He took a pretty good whack on the head from a fall but it doesn't look like the bear touched him." She paused and looked up at Simi, trying to keep it together. "He's lucky."
"What's he doing back here anyway?"
"Here for the summer apparently. I guess I'll get the scoop when Mom shows up. She's on her way."
"Is that a good thing?"
Harking sighed. "Doesn't matter. She has to come. She's our mother after all."
"You gonna be okay?"
"I have to be. This could go sideways you know."
"Huh?"
"The whole story and all. He says, she says and all that. The boys were in the wrong, but I'll bet the story will get twisted."

"Well I'll let you know if my dad lets anything slip. Although he doesn't usually talk a lot of cop stuff around me."

"Still though," said Harking.

Simi nodded.

"But I might have to talk to him about it anyway," Harking admitted. "Shane Ross said they want to interview me."

Simi put a fist to her mouth. "Will she crack under pressure," she mused, imitating a news reporter. "Simi Odili reporting." When Harking didn't respond she wrapped her arm around her. "Sorry. Just trying to take your mind off your brother."

"He's not the one I'm worried about."

"Seriously?"

"I mean I *was* worried about Col but the doctor says he'll be fine." She looked sheepishly at Simi and shrugged. "I'm almost ashamed to say it ... but I'm more worried about the bears."

CHAPTER 21

After Simi left, Harking collapsed into bed, the adrenaline rush of the day's events playing havoc with her mind as she lapsed in and out of sleep and a series of distorted dreams. Finally unable to close her eyes again, she lay wide-awake trying to make sense of them all.

For reasons she thought she understood, the avalanche was always front and centre in her dreams even if most of the details of those final moments eluded her.

Always, there was the whiteout and an impending sense of catastrophe.

And she was always one step behind, unable to change the outcome.

But tonight the bears took over front and centre, starting with the large male grizzly, stalking its smaller cousin, surprising it, almost playing with it as the black bear battled for its life.

With every deke the black bear made to avoid the grizzly, Harking tossed and turned, held tighter and tighter in a python-like embrace as she twisted into her bedsheets, struggling to free herself, desperate to escape.

When the grizzly finally finished, Harking's heart seemed to stall as she watched it move on down the trail, drawn on by what, Harking couldn't be sure ...

... until she saw the mother grizzly and her cubs.

Crying out, she tried to warn them, but the male grizzly kept coming. It seemed unstoppable.

Looking further down the trail, Harking's heart skipped a beat as a blur of mountain bikes sped toward the mother grizzly and her cubs, engrossed in feeding on the rich patches of berries.

Her cries to warn the mountain bikers were suddenly lost in the chaos as everything and everyone seemed destined to collide.

Just before the point of impact, with the male grizzly ready to strike and the mountain bikes zooming around the bend, the mother grizzly looked up, alert to both dangers.

Suddenly the air around Harking reverberated with a loud *whumph!* and the ground beneath her feet collapsed. As an overpowering force pulled Harking along, she fought for her life as her father called her name, drawing her toward the darkness ...

"... Harking."

CHAPTER 22

"... Harking."

"Harking."

"Get up."

Fighting to get to the surface, Harking gasped for air.

When she opened her eyes Marion was leaning over her, tugging at the quilt as she tried to untangle Harking from its grip.

"My goodness, Harking," she said, breathing heavily.

Finally extracting Harking from the twist of sheets, Marion sat on the edge of the bed. "Shane is here to speak with you."

"Really?"

"And one of the RCMP officers is with him."

Harking looked at the time on her phone. "But it's early."

"Not that early," said Marion. "Get dressed and come down." Retreating from the bedroom she pulled the door closed behind her.

Harking slid out of bed and sat on the edge, running a hand through her hair before standing up and stretching. She quickly pulled on a top and shorts and stood in front of the mirror. Leaning in she rubbed her eyes and stared at her reflection then brushed her hair and tied it back with an elastic.

Going to the bathroom she ran water in the sink and splashed it over her face, towelling off before making her way downstairs to the kitchen. Hesitating in the doorway, she looked around the corner.

Shane and Simi's father, Richard Odili, were sitting at the table as Marion fussed over them, pouring tea and offering muffins from a plastic container.

"Thanks, Marion," Shane said, tipping his head as Marion filled his cup.

Nodding his thanks as well, Richard suddenly noticed Harking and motioned for her to come in. Although she'd met Richard many times before at Simi's house, this was the first time Harking had to deal with him in his official capacity.

"Good morning, Harking," Richard said finally. Sounding formal and more than a little intimidating, he seemed to size up his daughter's best friend. "Have a seat."

Harking pulled out a chair and turned it around, then sat with her arms folded over the back.

"Your brother was lucky," Richard started.

Harking looked to Marion.

"Col was awake this morning," Marion explained. "Your mother is with him. His memory of what happened is a little foggy but he seems fine otherwise."

Harking nodded and looked at Shane, who seemed to be trying to match the serious look on Richard's face.

"Warden Ross says you may have information that can help us sort this mess out," Richard continued.

"The camera photos," Shane chimed in.

Harking nodded.

"Tell me about them," said Richard, recording Harking's responses in his notebook.

Harking bit her lip and regarded Simi's father. "Just some photos from the trail back of the lake."

"Photos of what?" Richard took a sip of his tea and leaned back in the chair.

"Wildlife mostly."

"What kind of wildlife?"

"All kinds."

"Bears?"

"Yes."

"Grizzly bears?"

"Yes. A sow and cubs from a few days ago but mostly a male that's been hanging around back there."

"And you have some photos of the boys, the four boys involved in the incident yesterday?"

Harking nodded. "I do now," she replied, avoiding Shane's puzzled stare.

"Where do you keep the photos?" Richard pressed on, oblivious to their body language but sounding more serious.

"On my computer."

"Can we see them?" Richard pushed his chair from the table and stood, not waiting for Harking's response.

She looked at Marion, who nodded. "Yeah, I guess," said Harking, slowly rising to her feet. "They're on my laptop. I'll go get it." Disappearing momentarily Harking returned with the laptop and sat down at the table.

"I'll leave you three to go over them," said Marion, retiring to her bedroom.

"What's going to happen to the bears?" Harking asked as she fired up the laptop and navigated to the folder of trail camera pictures.

"Not sure," said Shane, looking over her shoulder at Richard.

Harking paused and looked up at Richard.

"The bears weren't at fault," she stated flatly, her voice showing no emotion.

"But your brother or one of the others could have been seriously injured," said Richard. "Or killed."

"Because they shouldn't have been on the trail," said Harking, sounding flustered.

"The area was closed."

"They claim they didn't see the sign."

"That's bullshit," said Harking, her face gaining a crimson hue. "They would have passed right by it."

"They claim they got on the trail another way Harking," said Shane.

"Whatever way they went," Harking countered, "Match for sure would have known it was closed."

Richard held up a hand. "Can we see the photos please?" he asked, sounding agitated.

Returning her attention to the computer Harking brought up the digital files from the trail camera.

"Do you mind?" said Richard. Getting up from the table he motioned to Harking's chair and switched seats. With Shane and Harking looking over his shoulder he scrolled through the images, stopping at the photos of the boys to identify each one.

"The lead rider is the superintendent's son, isn't it?"

"Yeah, that's Match," Harking confirmed.

"And your brother is behind him?"

Harking nodded silently.

"What was that?" Richard looked over his shoulder directly at Harking.

"Yes sir, that's Col," she admitted.

Richard smirked and looked at Harking. "You can call me Richard, you know. I don't bite when I'm working."

Harking nodded silently.

"And Grayson?" Richard continued to the next photo.

"Yeah."

"And finally Tyson ... Tyson Griffin." The tone in Richard Odili's voice changed, sounding more resigned as he said the last name.

"Yeah," said Harking, imitating the officer's tone.

"He's the one who seems to be saying the most about what happened," said Richard.

"No doubt," said Harking. "He can be all mouth sometimes."

"But other times not so bad?" Richard asked.

"Yeah, I guess," Harking conceded. "Although when he's with his buddies he sees himself as the alpha male."

"But he's at the back of the pack in the photos?" said Shane.

"Exactly," said Harking. She nudged Richard in the shoulder to get his attention. "What has he told you?"

"That the bear attacked them for no reason," he said without turning around, scrolling through the images showing the other wildlife, and pausing at the grizzly and black bear. Looking back and forth between the laptop and his notebook he recorded dates and times from several of the photos.

"He's lying," said Harking, giving Richard a chance to finish writing. Then she leaned across the officer's shoulder and grabbed the mouse and scrolled through the full series of photos. "See." She turned toward Shane then back to the computer screen. "The bears have been using the trail on a regular basis. First it was the sow and cubs, but then this male showed up and he's been a regular. I think he killed the black bear." She paused again and looked sheepishly at Shane. "I found a carcass on the trail," she admitted. "Or what was left of it. I pulled it off into the bush."

"You didn't report it?" Shane frowned and shook his head.

"There wasn't much left to report. By the time I found it, the crows, ravens and eagles and whatever else, had pretty much cleaned it up. Besides the trail was closed. So what was the point?"

"Fair enough," Shane shrugged, "but you still should report that stuff."

Harking turned back to the images.

"The sow and cubs do show up earlier but recently it's just been the male." She scrolled back and forth between the last pictures of the bears.

"The male could have been giving the sow and cubs some grief and pushed them out of the area," said Shane, piping up to explain one possible scenario to Richard. "But if the sow and cubs came back and ran into the male ..."

"Exactly," Harking interjected. "And if the boys rode into the middle of it."

Shane nodded. "If you look at the time stamp, they do pretty much overlap.

If that was the case I could see why a bear might react like it did."

"Makes sense." Richard rubbed his chin and looked at the pictures again. "Can you give me a copy of these?"

Harking hesitated.

"Just so I don't have to seize your computer as evidence."

"You don't have to do that." Harking sighed. "Give me a minute," she added, and ran back upstairs. Returning to the kitchen she handed the thumb drive holding the copied photos to Richard. "But I'd like it back. You *will* give it back? Right?"

Ignoring the request, Richard pocketed the drive and turned to Shane. "I think we have all we need." Turning back to Harking, he asked "When did you place that camera on the trail? And is it the only one you have?"

"You didn't answer *my* question," she replied.

Richard sighed and rolled his eyes. "Yes, yes. I'll get it back to you when this is all over."

Harking rolled her shoulders and nodded. "This camera is the only one I have. It was my dad's. I've only had it out for a couple of weeks." Harking was grateful he didn't ask about the recorder. Although she suspected Shane might have mentioned it to Richard, she didn't offer the information.

Escorting the two men out of the kitchen, Harking showed them to the door.

"Are you off to school?" Shane asked just as they were about to leave.

"I don't know. There's not much going on other than review for finals, and I only have a couple exams next week."

"Nice," said Shane. "Okay, well I guess we're out of here."

"We'll be back if we have any more questions," Richard said as they left the house.

"Sure," said Harking. She watched as Shane and Richard spoke to each other for a moment on the sidewalk before getting into separate vehicles. As she watched the RCMP cruiser pull out onto the street and drive away, she realized Shane was motioning for her to come to his warden truck.

Slipping into a pair of sandals she walked to the passenger side of the truck and opened the door, expecting some sort of scolding from Shane for obviously having gone back to the camera.

Instead he was grinning. "Thanks, Harking."

Harking shrugged. "I just had to get those pictures."

"I know."

"So what do you think will happen to the bears?"

"Not sure." Shane turned away and gazed through the windshield as he pondered the most likely prospects. "Tyson's father is kicking up quite the stink. I don't know how well you know him, but he can be a regular shit disturber when he doesn't get his way."

"Like father, like son," said Harking.

Shane raised his eyebrows and muttered something unintelligible.

"What was that?"

"Oh nothing. Just seconding your motion."

"I won't be happy if the Park goes after that sow and cubs, or any of those bears for that matter." Harking's stare was unsettling.

"You know you're sounding more like Marion every day?" said Shane, returning the stare.

"Whatever." Harking blew off the comment. Consciously trying not to imitate Marion she cursed, "Jesus, you know better than anyone, Shane. The boys were at fault. The bears were just reacting."

"I wish it was always that easy, Harking."

"It is," she growled under her breath. "But people just make it so much harder."

CHAPTER 23

Harking was torn about what to do after the men left but knew she should probably go to the hospital.

Reluctantly conceding to Marion's suggestion, she put on some clean clothes, and with Marion nudging her toward the door, donned a jacket and walked the block and a half to the hospital, pausing again at the entrance before finally walking inside past the nursing station and making her way to Col's room.

Hesitating outside the door, she peered through the small window and saw her mother sitting at Col's bedside, holding his hand. Her brother appeared to be sleeping, so Harking opened the door slowly and slipped inside the room.

Her mother looked up and acknowledged her with a nod then motioned for Harking to sit with them. "He's asleep again," Paige said as Harking joined her, lightly grasping her mother's hand. Paige used the contact to pull her daughter into an embrace. Relinquishing, Harking wrapped an arm around her mother for longer than she expected she would, then eased away and stood at the foot of the bed.

"How is he?"

"He'll be fine," said Paige, looking somewhat relieved. "He has a concussion and will need to rest for the next several days, but the doctor says there'll be no lasting effects."

"That's good to hear," said Harking, smiling at Paige before her look turned serious. "I didn't even know he was in town."

"It was a last minute thing," said Paige. "I've been meaning to call you and Marion but hadn't gotten around to it." She looked at her son. "I certainly wasn't expecting this. I was hoping you'd keep an eye on him."

"But ...."

Before Harking could launch into an attack her mother quickly cut her off. "I mean once you knew he was in town. I'm not blaming you for this. This is no one's fault."

"But their own," said Harking, bluntly.

"What do you mean?" Paige sounded testy.

"They were biking in a closed area. I warned Match about the bears."

"How would *you* know about that? The bears, I mean." Paige's tone was accusatory.

"I had Dad's camera on the trail they were using."

Paige Thompson closed her eyes and shook her head.

"What?" said Harking.

"Following in your father's footsteps. I should have known."

"What's so bad about that?"

"Well at least you didn't follow in Dan's footsteps that day." There was a hard edge to Paige's voice.

Harking bit her lip. Suddenly reminded of the avalanche she felt a wave of guilt wash over her.

"I'm so sorry, Harking," said Paige, wringing her hands. "I didn't mean anything by it." She paused, looking down before making eye contact again. "But your father could be reckless sometimes."

"Oh my God," Harking blurted. "It was totally an accident. It could have been either of us."

"Or *all* of you."

"I'm not getting into this again," said Harking. "It's taken me long enough to get this far." She turned to leave.

"Harking." Paige's voice was desperate as she clung to the edge of the chair. "Please don't."

"Don't what?" said Harking, turning back to face her mother. "Don't defend Dad's judgment? Don't speak up when people spread rumours and lies? You weren't there," she blurted. "You don't know what happened." Tears started to roll down

Harking's face as she realized her own truth; she also couldn't recall what happened.

"No, I wasn't," Paige conceded. Sounding apologetic she turned away for a moment. When she turned back, there was a look of anguish on her face. "Maybe things would have been different if I had."

"Maybe they'd have been worse," said Harking, giving her mother no quarter. "But like I said, I'm *not* getting into it. I came here to see how Col was doing, not to fight with you."

Her mother ran a hand through her hair, forcing a smile. "I'm sorry." She turned back to Col and held his hand. The contact seemed to arouse him from his sleep as he gazed first at his mother and then Harking.

"How you doin', sis?" He winced and closed his eyes.

"More like how're you doing?"

"My head's throbbing." Col opened his eyes briefly then closed them again.

"They said you took a pretty good fall. You're lucky."

"I don't remember much."

"Do you remember anything?" Harking pressed. "Did you see the bears? Did you give them any warning?"

"Harking." Her mother held a finger to her mouth.

"What?" She turned to face her mother. "Parks and the RCMP are going to want to know if the bears were provoked or not. If the boys rode into them, I suspect the bears were just reacting normally, defending themselves."

"We didn't see them," Col interjected.

"But you did see the closure sign?" said Harking.

Col shrugged and looked away.

"You rode right by it," Harking continued. "You *have* to admit that."

"Let it go, Harking," her mother scolded. "He's not up to it."

"Well he better get up to it soon, otherwise Tyson Griffin's father will get his way and Parks will shoot those bears."

"Why?" said Col, turning back to Harking, looking surprised.

"Why? Because they need a scapegoat and if no one accepts responsibility for their actions," she added, glaring at Col. "The bears will take the fall."

"Harking, you're overreacting," said her mother.

"Am I?" Harking challenged.

"I'm sure Parks will do the right thing," said Paige.

"They'll do whatever they're pressured to do," Harking countered. "Shane Ross told me as much." She dropped her head and closed her eyes for a moment then looked at Col. "I'm glad you're okay. And I'm glad you're here," she said to Paige. "But I have to go. I'll check back later."

And with that, Harking left.

CHAPTER 24

She didn't need to be there, she had good grades and expected to ace the exams, but Harking decided to drop by the high school anyway to pick up her study notes, hoping she might also run into one of the boys and see if she could worm the truth out of them about what happened on the trail.

She figured Tyson in particular might be there, cramming to just get a pass.

He wasn't the sharpest tool in the shed.

But then again he didn't put in the effort.

Cruising the halls, the place seemed deserted, though a few of the classrooms Harking looked into had small groups of students listening attentively to teachers reviewing material.

She finally found Tyson and Match in the last class she checked and decided to wait for them, avoiding eye contact with a couple of her teachers as she leaned against the wall, pretending to read through her notes.

"I didn't expect to see you here." The unmistakable accent caught Harking off-guard, her notes scattering to the floor. "So sorry," said Ms. Peacock. "I didn't mean to startle you." She bent down and helped retrieve the papers, passing them to Harking before regaining her stiff British posture. "Again. Sorry."

"No worries," said Harking as she organized the pages. "It's all good." She forced a smile.

Ms. Peacock raised her eyebrows. "I heard the news. How's your brother?"

"Fine, fine. He just has a concussion. Otherwise he seems okay."

"It's terrible really, though," said Ms. Peacock, seemingly

stuck on one line of thought. "We live in such an amazing place, but you never know what dangers lurk around the corner."

"Hmm, yeah well, not really lurking," said Harking. "The boys rode right into those bears."

"You don't say? That's quite different than the story I heard ..."

"From Brianna Smith." Harking scowled.

"Well yes. But how did you know?"

Harking waved off the comment, somewhat incredulous that a supposedly objective science teacher like Ms. Peacock would pay anything more than lip service to the likes of Brianna Smith. "I should really be going. Just thought I'd check in." Harking turned to find another spot to wait for the boys, but Ms. Peacock placed a hand on her shoulder.

"You know I wanted to mention to you, there are several university scholarships you should be thinking about. You're a shoo-in for at least one of them and I'd be happy to provide any letters of reference required."

Harking blushed. "Thanks. I'm just not sure of next steps." Out of the corner of her eye, Harking noticed Tyson and the others getting up from their seats. "I might just take a year off and figure out what I want to do."

"Well a gap year is a splendid idea, but my advice is not to let it go longer than that. Once you get away from school, it's hard to get back into learning mode."

Harking didn't say what she wanted to say, how she was sick of school and figured time away, maybe a long time, would be the best thing for her. Instead she smiled, her attention focused on the emptying classroom.

"I appreciate the advice, sorry, I've got to run." Without giving Ms. Peacock another opening, she set her sights on the boys, who were now joined in the hallway by Grayson.

Harking was certain Tyson saw her when he came out of the classroom, but if he did, he didn't let on to the others as the trio high-fived each other and walked down the hall with Harking tight on their heels.

As soon as they exited the school, Tyson suddenly turned to confront her.

"What do *you* want?" he sneered.

His comment seemed to catch Match and Grayson by surprise as they turned to see who Tyson was speaking to.

"The truth," said Harking, her fists clenched to her side.

"The truth about what?" said Match, stepping between them.

"Seriously?" Harking fumed. "My brother is in the hospital. And I want to know the truth about what happened on the trail." Confidently, she staked her claim. "I think you rode into those bears and surprised them. They didn't do anything other than react in self-defence."

"Bullshit," said Tyson. "They attacked us."

"I don't believe it." Harking turned to Match. "I know you and Col were in the lead. Col told me as much," she lied. "And Grayson, you were right behind them. You would have seen what happened." For a split second she sensed Grayson wanted to say something, but when he hesitated, Harking turned back to Tyson. "And *you*. You weren't even near the front. *You* were at the back." She jabbed a finger into his chest. "Probably shitting your pants."

"Oh yeah?" Tyson pushed himself into Harking.

"Yeah." Harking pushed back before Match separated them.

"Okay you two. Give it up." He pushed Tyson away and turned back to Harking.

"So what? What does it matter who was in front?"

"Duh! Whoever was in front would have the best idea of what happened. And what matters is the truth. If you guys don't fess up ..."

"What?" said Tyson. "What'll happen to us?" He shrugged his shoulders.

"Not to you, asshole." Harking fumed.

"What? Those bears?" Tyson ranted. "They're as good as dead. My old man will make sure of that."

"Shut up, Ty." Match glared at him.

"But he's right," said Harking, turning to Match. "Those bears *will* die. Parks will have to destroy them. But it wasn't their fault."

"No?" Tyson smirked. "Whose fault was it then?"

Harking could feel her face turning red and her blood begin to boil. She wanted to rip Tyson apart then and there, but Match stood in her way as she lobbed insults instead. "You're such an asshole, Tyson." She locked eyes with Match. "You and I both know what happened. And you and I both know what will happen to those bears if you don't tell your father how it all went down. Do the right thing."

"Do the right thing," Tyson mimicked as Harking fought to control her anger.

"Arghhh," she growled. She wanted to punch him in the face but instead, turned and walked away.

"Yeah, that's it," Tyson continued with his barbs. "Get outta here, girl."

Although she didn't look back, she overheard Match say, "Shut the fuck up, Ty."

Or I'll shut you up myself, Harking thought as she stormed off.

She was unsure what her next move might be, but first she needed to find out the latest on the bears.

CHAPTER 25

It didn't take Harking long to track down Shane Ross, knowing he frequented the bakery every morning for coffee. As soon as he saw her walk in, Shane said goodbye to the local outfitter sitting with him then quickly switched out of cowboy mode, ditching the toothpick hanging from the corner of his mouth and losing the trademark Western drawl.

"Morning," he said as Harking dropped into the empty chair next to him. "How's Col?"

"Good." She nodded and looked around the shop, avoiding eye contact as she sussed out the place.

"So, what's up?" said Shane, sitting back and rubbing his chin.

Harking pulled the Crankworx ball cap lower across her forehead then leaned in close, both arms on the table. "What's the latest on the bears?"

Shane detoured before meeting her stare. "We baited and set the trap this morning," he said finally. "We also set some snares."

"Fuck." Harking mouthed the word, barely able to contain her emotions, her bottom lip quivering.

"Now calm down," said Shane his voice almost a whisper as he leaned forward. "The boys all say it was the sow and cubs. They didn't see any other bear."

Harking's eyes bored into Shane but he held firm.

"It's for the best. Hopefully we'll catch the sow first. With her in the trap, the cubs will stay close and end up in the snares."

"*Three* cubs, Shane." Harking held up three fingers. "What's the chance you'll catch all three cubs?" she asked, her voice breaking. "Slim to none," she added, before Shane could answer. "You'll separate the family. How is that for the better?"

"We'll catch the whole shootin' match or we'll let the sow go," Shane said. "It's all or nothin'."

"And then what? You'll move them and they'll come right back. Isn't that what happens?"

"Could," said Shane. "But at least it shows Parks taking some action."

"Shows who?" Harking was unrelenting, her voice rising. "Tyson's father?"

"He'd be one," Shane conceded, matter-of-factly. "But not just him."

"Who else?" Harking pressed, lowering her voice again and looking around.

"Doesn't matter. The trap's set. And I've got work to do." Shane stood and caught himself, almost tipping his Stetson to Harking. "I'll let you know how it goes." Before walking out, he paused. "Aren't you supposed to be in school?"

"I was already there. There's nothing much going on other than review for finals." She didn't bother to mention accosting Tyson and his buddies.

"Then maybe you should go spend some time with your brother. Your mother said she wasn't going to be able to spend so much time with him today."

"And how would you know that?"

"I saw her briefly this morning. Ran into her ..." Shane stumbled for words before regaining his composure. "Anyway, that doesn't matter. Go see him. I got work to do."

"I just might," said Harking, realizing it was going to be hard to get anyone to come clean and tell the truth about what happened.

Or what was going to happen.

CHAPTER 26

Harking slipped into the hospital unnoticed and made her way to Col's room. Checking first to make sure Paige wasn't around, she eased his door open and went inside. Standing over his bed she had second thoughts about waking him.

Although she hadn't noticed it before today, she could see her father's features in him, the dark hair and square jaw among other things. Even though his eyes were closed, she was familiar with them, brown and intense like Dan's.

She also sensed Col was filling out, finally putting some weight on his lanky frame, probably from eating crap, she thought, knowing he craved burgers and any red meat just as she had herself before she started paying more attention to her diet and its impact on the environment.

As she regarded him sleeping peacefully, Harking knew that whatever did happen on the trail, none of the others got more than a few scratches. Col had taken the brunt of it. And she felt sorry for him in a way.

But not that sorry.

"Col," she whispered. "Col. Wake up."

"Huh?"

"Col, it's me. Wake up."

Col opened his eyes and right away, there it was, the intensity. "What do you want, Harking?" He slid up on an elbow and searched the room. "Where's Mom?"

"She's gone but will probably be back later. How are you feeling?"

"I've felt better," Col sighed and fell back on his pillow. "What do you want anyway? I told you what happened."

"You told me almost nothing."

"Whatever."

"But I know what happened."

"You do?" Col sounded sceptical.

"Yeah, I do. And I have pictures to prove it." She had his attention now.

"So what do you want from me?"

"The truth. God, didn't Mom and Dad teach you anything?"

"Yeah ... but."

"But nothing, Col. You guys rode right into those bears and the sow reacted like any bear protecting her cubs would. If she wanted to really hurt you do you think we'd be talking now?"

Col hesitated. "Probably not."

"*Absolutely* not."

"So?"

"So, you need to come clean with Mom and you need to get her to speak to Shane and Match's dad. Otherwise those bears will be trapped and destroyed. And there isn't any time to lose."

"I don't know."

"Don't know what?"

"Don't know if I can."

"Why not? Why are you protecting a shit like Tyson Griffin when you know you guys were in the wrong?"

" 'Cause it's not just Tyson. It's Grayson and Match as well."

"But nothing is going to happen to either of them. They might get a slap on the wrist and a talking to, but that's it."

"And then what?" Col propped himself up again on his elbows.

"Then the bears stand a chance. But only if you tell the truth."

"But it's not just me. Match or Grayson can speak up. Hell, Match's dad is the park superintendent."

"Exactly. And that's exactly why he might not say anything. He's caught in a way. But you're not." Harking poked Col in the chest.

"I don't know," said Col, wavering.

"Christ, Col. You *do* know. And you better figure it out fast."

"Or else?"

"Or else, you'll have to deal with me. And if anything happens to those bears, those wrestling matches we used to have when we were kids," Harking grinned, "they'll be nothing compared to the thrashing I'm going to give you if you don't tell the truth. A concussion will be the least of your worries."

"Is that a threat?"

Harking laughed. "Seriously? You have to ask that?" She whacked him lightly on the side of the head.

"Hey."

"Hey nothing, you're fine." Harking leaned in. Squeezing his arm she whispered, "Do the right thing."

CHAPTER 27

Leaving the bakery, Shane Ross made his way out of town and headed to the lake to check the bear trap. Not expecting to have caught the bears this quickly, he was more interested in keeping an eye on things to ensure people stayed out of the area while the trap was set.

It always surprised Shane how humans had an innate attraction to tragedy. It seemed to draw people to closures or accidents, or anything involving sirens and emergency vehicles. Ambulance chasers, some called them, but Shane had his own more disparaging term for people who got in the way of first responders: idiots.

He knew Harking was right and the grizzly sow was going to take the fall for doing what came naturally to her when threatened: defending her cubs.

The boys were in the wrong and lucky to be alive.

The mother grizzly and her cubs might not be so lucky.

But Shane was bound and determined to do whatever he had to do to give her and her family the best chance at making it.

Harking's pleas only served to reinforce his commitment to do right by them.

Driving up to the area closure signs, Shane unlocked the gate to the fire road then pulled the truck ahead and locked the gate behind him. Continuing along the fire road to within sight of the culvert trap, he stopped the truck and pulled out his binoculars.

"Holy shit," he said as he focused the glasses, realizing the trap door was down; a sure sign something had already tripped the release. Scanning the area around the trap, he also saw a dark-faced bear cub pacing back and forth, its gaze trained on the large metal culvert trap.

Grabbing his radio, Shane contacted Jasper's radio dispatcher and asked her to send another park warden to the lake to give him a hand.

"Yeah, Val. Looks like we might already have somethin'," he said, not wanting to say too much over the radio in case anyone scanning the park frequencies was listening.

As he waited for backup, Shane prepped the tranquilizing drugs and darts, wanting to deal with the sow and cubs as quickly as possible and get them out of the area.

If, as he suspected, the mother grizzly was in the trap and the other two cubs were in the snares, it would be easy to dart them and place them with the mother. The third cub might be more of a challenge but as long as the others were in the trap, Shane knew it would stick around, giving him an opportunity to dart it. Once they were all together he'd transport them to a release site.

Shane was happy when he heard a truck making its way up the fire road toward him and pleased that Megan Weaver was at the wheel. The daughter of a park warden who specialized in wildlife work in Wood Buffalo National Park, Megan had earned a Masters degree in conservation biology and along with her extensive experience handling everything from bears to bison, she had what Shane figured to be the best combination to make a great park warden; she was smart but also very practical.

And they worked well together.

With her education, work background and striking appearance, tall and lean with high cheekbones indicating her Dene heritage, Shane figured she could be a poster girl for recruiting women into the outfit, certainly as capable as any man he'd worked with and more capable than most.

"Whatcha' got, Shane?" Megan asked as she jumped out of the warden truck, brandishing the park issue .308 Winchester rifle.

118

"Not a hundred percent certain, Meg, but I think the sow's in the culvert trap and at least two cubs are snared. I also saw a third cub at the edge of the bush. Looks like it might be injured." He pointed to where he had seen the cub pacing back and forth.

"We'll deal with it last," he added, passing the immobilizing rifle to Megan.

"If we've got the sow, I'll give you the thumbs up. I'll use the jab stick on her and dart the cubs with the pistol."

"Sounds like a plan," said Megan, slinging the immobilizing rifle across her back.

With the pistol and jab stick in hand, Shane headed up the fire road with Megan tight on his heels, rifle at the ready.

On Shane's cue Megan stopped and waited as he quietly approached the trap and peered inside. Moving toward the back of the trap he raised two fingers in the air, indicating two cubs were caught in snares.

Giving a thumbs up, Shane backed off slightly to make sure the jab stick was all set. He motioned for Megan to stay put then approached the trap again. Shielding his eyes from the direct sunlight he peered through a small portal cut into the side of the trap. As his eyes adjusted to the darkness he could just make out the mother grizzly, sitting in the dark shadows at the very back of the trap.

Seeming to sense something, the female grizzly met Shane's gaze, her dark eyes staring right through him, piercing in their determination.

"Hello, girl," Shane said calmly. "You're going to be alright."

As Megan watched him from a distance, Shane slowly inserted the jab stick through another cut-out in the side of the trap. Suddenly he made a quick thrust and stood back, removing the jab stick instantly as the mother grizzly threw herself against the trap door with a huge crash, testing the metal welds holding it together.

119

Her sudden response set off a chain reaction with her snared cubs as they bolted to the end of the snare's safety cables and were brought up with a solid thud. Hoping to prevent the cubs from hurting themselves, Shane quickly darted the first cub, then reloaded. Momentarily disappearing from view behind the culvert trap, he resurfaced a few seconds later and motioned for Megan to approach.

"Got 'em both," he said, sounding happy with the outcome. "We'll give them a few minutes to let the drug take effect."

"That's great," said Megan, scanning the forest around them. "But there's still the third cub." She motioned toward the forest.

Partially hidden near the base of a large pine, the dark-faced cub peered out at them, seemingly curious about the fate of its mother and siblings.

"Why don't you take a crack at it?" said Shane. Cradling the jab stick and pistol, he took the .308 from Megan and stood back as she loaded a dart into the immobilizing rifle.

Slowing down her breathing, Megan took careful aim, waiting for the cub to expose more of its flank. She was about to shoot when the sound of a vehicle approaching sent the cub bolting through the trees away from them.

"What the hell?" Shane yelled as the superintendent pulled up beside them in his Parks vehicle. When John Walleski exited the vehicle, Shane launched into him. "Christ, John, what're you doin' here?"

"Whoa, Shane." John held up a hand as he strode toward them. "I heard you caught those bears and I just came to check for myself. I wanted to make sure nothing goes sideways with this."

"Well you couldn'a come at a worse time. Megan had clear shot at the third cub but you scared it off." He looked toward where the cub had disappeared into the trees, hoping it would resurface.

"Well, that's too bad," said John, only now acknowledging Megan with a nod of his head. "I've got lawyers and townspeople crawling all over my ass. If you got the sow and at least some of the cubs, I want them out of here."

"No can do," said Shane. "The third cub is close by so let us do our job. It's all or nothin'."

"I beg your pardon?" said the superintendent.

"It's important that we get them all," Megan interjected calmly. "If we don't, the last cub's as good as dead."

"I understand how you feel." Walleski directed the comment at Megan before he turned back to Shane. "But that's a minor concern for me right now."

"Well it's *my* biggest concern," said Shane. "That and not wanting to leave these bears too long."

"Well I hate to pull rank," said John, unwavering, "but I want these bears out of the park right now, Shane."

"Outta the park?" Shane began to protest. "C'mon. Outta the area, yes, but outta the park means into the province and I'd have to get approval from Fish and Wildlife. Jesus John, we don't have time for that. If we have to fly them into the backcountry let's do it, but ..."

"But nothing, Shane. I want them out of the park," John repeated, his face turning red. "Get whatever approvals you need from the province but I won't take no for an answer."

Shane was about to square off with John when Megan stepped between them. "Shane," she said calmly. "We'll load the cubs and you can drive them out. Leave the immobilizing gear with me and while you sort out a release site with the provincial folks, I'll get the third cub." She sounded confident.

"When I do," she added, "I'll meet up with you."

"But what if you don't?" said Shane. "With the mother gone you might never catch that third cub."

"Maybe not, but I'll give it my best shot." She nodded toward the trap. "But right now, let's deal with *these* bears. And we'll cross that bridge if we get to it. If we have to, we'll reset the trap and snares and try again. If we can catch it right away, we can drop the third cub where you drop the others. Hopefully they won't have gone too far."

Shane knew that taking the bears out of the park opened up another can of worms. He also knew Megan was clutching at straws and the likelihood of the sow sticking around the release site was low. But he saw the intensity in her eyes and knew she would do whatever she could to break this impasse and reunite the bears

"Fine," he said. He motioned toward the trap. "Let's load 'em so I can get going."

"Thanks," said John, softening his stance. "I'll get out of your hair."

Shane waited until Walleski was out of earshot and muttered something under his breath. Then, as the superintendent pulled his vehicle around in the road, Megan and Shane quickly removed the cubs from the snares. As Shane manned the trap door, keeping a careful eye on the sow, Megan gently lifted each cub into the opening.

"A male and a female," she said as she laid them inside next to the sow.

"They're beauts," said Shane, stopping for a second to admire the cubs, their lighter faces distinctive from the darker-faced third cub he'd seen.

"Absolutely," Megan said, before turning her attention to the mother grizzly. "Aren't we going to ear-tag her?" she asked as Shane latched and locked the door.

Shane shook his head. "No way. I hate ear-taggin' animals. Besides, this bear didn't do anything wrong. She doesn't deserve to be a marked bear for the rest of her life."

"But ..."

"No buts," said Shane. "And the clock's tickin'. We don't have a lot of time."

"Fine," said Megan.

"I'll grab the truck," said Shane. "Guide me back, will you."

Megan stood by the trap as Shane ran to his vehicle. Turning the warden truck around, he backed up to the trailer hitch as Megan guided him. Hooking the trap to the truck she gave him a thumbs up.

"Keep me posted on the other cub," said Shane, leaning out the window as he was about to drive away.

"Ten-four," said Megan. "Where do you think you'll end up taking them?"

"I honestly don't know but it won't be out of the park. I've got a couple of other locations in mind."

"Geez, Shane, I'm not sure about that." Megan shrugged and winced. "The supe won't be happy if he finds out the bears are still in the park."

"What he doesn't know won't hurt him," said Shane. "But we gotta give these bears a chance to get back together. You know that."

"Yeah, I agree with you, but what if he asks?"

"Leave that to me," said Shane. "If I have to, I'll take one for the team."

"Okay then. You're the boss." She smiled and nudged Shane on the shoulder. "Get on outta here then. Time's wasting."

Without another word, Shane put the truck in gear and pulled away, moving slowly down the potholed road, trying to make the ride as smooth as possible for the bears. At the fire road gate he quickly went through the motions of pulling the truck and trap through then locked the gate again and headed for town and the highway. Rounding the first turn on the paved road he was surprised to see Harking Thompson pedalling her way toward the lake on her mountain bike. When she saw him, she motioned to get him to stop but Shane kept driving.

Looking in the rear-view mirror he saw her throw her hands in the air.

"No time for you right now," Shane muttered as he watched Harking turn her bike around and follow him back toward town, disappearing from sight as he powered around the next turn.

CHAPTER 28

Harking was out of breath by the time she reached town, never catching another glimpse of the warden truck and bear trap as she raced along the road, all the while hoping Shane might pull over for a moment so she could find out what was happening.

Judging by Shane's determined look as he drove past her, and by the speed he was going, Harking figured the bears had been caught and he was on his way to release them. She would have liked to press him, to push for keeping the bears well within the boundaries of the park, but she suspected he'd been given strict instructions to take them as far away as possible to reduce the likelihood they'd make it back anytime soon.

Hopefully he was transporting the entire family of bears, increasing the cubs' chances of survival, but if they ended up outside of the park, she wasn't sure it would matter anyway. With all of the coalmines, forestry cut blocks, and oil and gas sites that covered the foothills bordering the national park she figured the bears would have a tough time surviving.

Only last month, Mrs. Peacock had brought a local grizzly bear biologist into her science class to talk about the fate of wide-ranging species such as grizzlies. His assessment of the bears' poor prospects for survival in much of the province as they tried to navigate all of the human use and development was sobering.

Taking the opportunity to ask some pointed questions Harking was disappointed, but not surprised, when the biologist suggested the future of grizzly bears in Alberta was tenuous at best. Unless the province started to enforce stricter regulations about where people could and couldn't go, he figured it was only a matter of a few years before grizzly bears were pushed out of some of the best habitat remaining outside of the national parks.

Right now, access to the backcountry in Alberta was pretty much a free-for-all, with quads and other ATVs tearing up the landscape at a record pace. The province was notorious for its Texas-like attitudes about people having the right to go pretty much wherever they wanted by whatever means they wanted. And despite the best efforts of provincial biologists and conservation officers, poaching grizzly bears was still a major factor keeping their numbers well below what many figured was necessary for a naturally sustainable population, even though the legal hunt had ended years before.

Frustrated at not being able to talk to Shane, Harking raced home, hoping to catch up with Marion and encourage her to speak with John Walleski. Wanting to find out what they planned to do with the bears, Harking knew Marion could be like a dog on a bone once she tackled an issue she was passionate about, and the fate of the grizzlies represented a line in the sand that Marion would probably die for before crossing.

Dan Thompson had had a similar worldview and Harking could see why he and Marion had become such good friends, allies on so many issues. Paige had also been in the same camp during their younger years, but for some reason, had softened her stance over time, often throwing up her hands and admitting she was tired of fighting whenever Harking confronted her on the issue.

As Harking leaped up the back stairs to the house, she knew she wouldn't get the same response from Marion.

"My goodness," Marion said as the screen door slammed shut behind Harking, who was doubled over, panting for breath. "What's got you all worked up?"

"The bears," Harking gasped. "I think they've trapped them."

"How do you know?" Marion asked as Harking caught her breath.

"I passed Shane coming from the lake, towing the bear trap. I tried to get him to stop to tell me what was up, but he just drove past."

"And where do you think he's headed?"

"I don't know," said Harking. "Out of the park I think. I thought you could try to talk some sense into Match's dad. Maybe get them to at least release the bears in the park."

"But you don't know *for certain* they're taking them out of the park?" Marion pressed.

"No. But it's just the way Shane acted when I caught up with him this morning at the bakery. He was avoiding telling me something I'm sure of it."

CHAPTER 29

Shane Ross made quick time as he headed east on the highway, weighing his options as he approached the turnoff to the Palisades and Snaring Campground. With only two of the cubs captured, he knew taking the bears all the way out of the park was a death sentence for the last cub, unless by some stroke of luck Megan was able to dart it and bring it to him right away.

But she hadn't called on the radio so he assumed she hadn't had any luck yet.

Deciding to stick to his guns and to buck the orders John had given him, Shane turned off the highway at the Palisades. He planned to take the bears down the Snaring Road as far as he could and release them somewhere on the north side of the Athabasca River within the boundaries of the park.

If she wanted to, the female grizzly could make it back to town within a few days, but Shane hoped she might stay farther out in the Athabasca Valley and avoid returning. And if Megan was able to catch the third cub and they could reunite it with its mother, he felt confident the sow might stay away from town altogether after the negative experience of being trapped and drugged. That would give her a better chance of avoiding people and successfully raising her cubs.

The further she stayed away from town the better, so Shane planned to make the sow's release as unpleasant as possible. With any luck she'd want to avoid a similar experience in the future.

After driving several kilometres down the Snaring Road, Shane made a quick stop to make sure the bears were still drugged. Seeing no sign of movement he continued on his way, finally pulling the truck and trap into a large clearing at the end of the road. He thought about continuing along the Celestine Lake Road toward Devona Flats, but reasoned that the further he went reduced Megan's chances of catching up to him. Then he'd be forced to release its mother and siblings on their own, something he really didn't want to do.

Choosing to avoid using the park radio so the rest of the world wouldn't know what he was up to, Shane called Megan on his cell to see if she'd caught the third cub. Although cell coverage was spotty on the east side of the park, Megan answered right away. "It's in the back of my truck and I'm headed your way. What's your twenty?"

"Just drive down the Snaring Road as far as you can," Shane replied. "You'll see me."

"I'll get there as fast as I can."

When Megan finally pulled in behind him Shane quickly jumped out of his truck and trotted over to meet her. The sow and her other cubs were still drugged but Shane knew it would only be a matter of minutes before all three would start to come around.

"Well isn't this a beaut," he said, admiring the dark-faced cub as he opened the tailgate on Megan's truck and pulled the little bear toward him. "Let's reunite this little gal with her brother and sister. It'll be cramped but at least they're all together."

"Careful," said Megan as she lifted the cub out of the truck. "This little one does have a bit of a gash on its hind end. I managed to clean it with hydrogen peroxide and put some antibiotic ointment on it but I guess we'll see how it does. Hopefully it'll help."

"Great," said Shane as he opened the trap door.

Together they slid the small bear inside with the rest of its family.

"I'll lock the trap open," Shane said as he secured the heavy door and took one last look at the four bears. Without another word, he grabbed a handful of bear bangers from his truck and motioned toward Megan's. "Let's move your truck back and we can watch from there. When they come around I plan to give them a taste of some bear bangers. Hopefully that'll remind mom to stay away from town."

As they watched from the edge of the clearing and waited for the effects of the immobilizing drugs to wear off, Shane pulled a tin of snuff from an inside pocket and stuffed a pinch in his mouth. He looked at Megan as if to offer her a taste, but thought twice about it.

"Nah," he said to himself as he caught the look on her face, and put the tin away.

"I'm still thinking we should have ear-tagged them," Megan said as they watched for any sign of the bears coming to. "Just so anyone else who might have to deal with them in the future knows they've been handled."

"And then what?" said Shane. "If that someone sticks to the policy of three strikes and you're out, these bears would already have one strike against them." He stared at Megan. "No way," he said resolutely. "I hate taggin' every friggin' animal we deal with. Besides, I'd rather tag those little shitrats that caused all this."

Megan chuckled as she turned her gaze back toward the trap.

"Looks like we've got some movement," she said, motioning toward the trap as the sow came into view, nuzzling the cub closest to the entrance.

Stepping over the cub, the sow dropped to the ground and stumbled slightly.

"The drug's not worn off yet," Shane said as the mother grizzly clumsily manoeuvred around and slowly pulled the cub out of the trap with her mouth and laid it on the ground. Stepping up on the edge of trap and leaning inside, she pulled a second cub out just as the last cub appeared in the doorway and looked around, finally tumbling out on its own and clumsily rolling over its siblings.

"They look like partiers spilling out of the Atha-B at one in the morning," Megan chuckled.

"Pretty much," Shane replied, smiling at a memory of crawling out of Jasper's iconic bar in a similar state himself.

As he and Megan waited for all four bears to come around, Shane kept track of the time it took for the drugs to wear off, a kernel of information he would add to his notes for future reference. It was always a good reminder that no two bears reacted the same to being immobilized.

When he was confident the bears had fully recovered, Shane opened his side door to get out. "And now for the *piece de resistance*," he said with a butchered French accent.

"Pièce de résistance," Megan corrected, holding back a laugh.

"Whatever." Shane shrugged and stood by the truck door.

Loading a bear banger in the pistol, he took aim and fired just in front of the sow, startling her and the cubs. Expecting she would hightail it and take the cubs with her, instead, the grizzly took one look at Shane and charged, covering the short distance in a split second before stopping abruptly a few metres from the warden truck, her hind end lifting noticeably as she dug her front paws into the dirt. Scrambling, Shane jumped back into the truck and slammed the door, as Megan doubled over laughing.

"Pièce de what?" she said, barely able to get the words out as they watched the sow pace back and forth in front of the truck before rounding up her cubs and disappearing into the bushes at the edge of the clearing. "That worked well."

"Yeah, well, at least they're together," Shane gasped. Breathing heavily, he exited the truck as Megan squirmed in her seat, desperately trying to keep from laughing again.

"Why don't you make yourself useful and get back to work?" Shane scowled. "I'll see you back at the warden office."

Still feeling the weight of embarrassment, he slunk back to his truck.

"Ten-four," Megan called out, smiling as she watched Shane wheel his truck around and head back toward town with the bear trap bouncing crazily along behind.

CHAPTER 30

John was no sooner in his office when Marion Seawell walked in. Shaking his head and heaving a sigh, the park superintendent pulled out his chair and sat down.

"Your secretary wasn't at his desk," Marion offered by way of apology, "so I thought it was okay to come in."

"When has that ever stopped you before?" John said, throwing up his hands as if already conceding defeat. "How can I help you, Marion?"

"What's happened with the grizzlies your wardens trapped?" Marion asked, getting to the point immediately.

"God, Marion." John sounded exasperated. "How did you find out so quickly? They were only just caught."

"I have my sources," said Marion, her eyebrows raised.

"Scanning the park radio frequencies, are we?"

"Never," Marion scoffed. "I have better things to do with my time."

"Like riding the superintendent?"

"John, John, John. I'm merely here to see what you did with the bears. I'm assuming Shane was able to catch them all?"

John Walleski's silence provided an opening for Marion's next assault.

"Surely, John, you know how critical it is to keep a family of bears together. Did Shane catch all three cubs or not?"

"He only caught two ..."

"John ..."

"Please let me finish, Marion. Megan Weaver was going to stay behind and try for the last cub while Shane dropped off the sow and the other cubs."

131

"Dropped off where?" Marion insisted.

Again, the park superintendent was silent and avoided looking directly at Marion.

"John, please don't tell me the bears were taken out of the park? You know as well as I do that would be a death sentence for them!"

"Really, Marion? A death sentence? Being a little melodramatic aren't we?"

"Absolutely not. That sow and cubs represent four bears out of how many in the park population, as few as fifty? Maybe a hundred bears ... at most?"

She paused to calculate the numbers in her head then continued.

"You're talking about removing as much as eight percent of the park's grizzly bear population in one fell swoop. Not to mention at least one of the cubs might have been female as well. If so, the park population loses one breeding female and a potential breeding female. That's devastating."

"Devastating?" Walleski slammed a fist on his desk and stood up to face Marion. "Jesus, Marion." He was seething.

"Now who's being overly dramatic?" Marion chided.

"I'm not being overly dramatic when I say what's really devastating is to have a grizzly bear kill someone, Marion. What would you be saying if the Thompson boy had been killed by that bear?" John leaned across his desk. "Now *that* would be devastating," he said, dropping back into his chair as if all the wind had been taken out of his sails.

"But Col wasn't killed," Marion calmly replied. "And if he wasn't following *your* son into a closed area, none of this would have happened. If you allowed your wardens to actually *enforce* closures, likely no one would get injured or killed."

"Here we go again," said John, his voice almost a whisper as he slumped back into his chair.

132

"Yes. Here we go again," said Marion. "And we'll return here again and again, until we get it right."

John sighed heavily as he regarded his opponent. "Marion, do you have any idea of the pressure I'm under when things like this happen?"

"I can well imagine," said Marion, her tone softening slightly. "Which is why my previous point is so valid. You've closed the area, which is great. Good for you, John. Now enforce the closure. It's simple." Marion paused to take a breath. "Now, where outside of the park was Shane Ross going to release those bears?"

"That's not your concern."

Sensing she'd probably got as much as she was going to, Marion turned to leave, but stopped short. "And what's going to happen to those boys?" She glared at John Walleski. "Do you plan to remove them from the park as well? Do *they* face any consequences?"

"Seriously, Marion. Don't you think the boys have suffered enough already?"

"Suffered?" Marion looked perplexed. "You think they've suffered?" Shaking her head she muttered, "Oh John," and walked out.

CHAPTER 31

Shane was parked outside of the coffee shop making a few notes, when Harking opened the truck door and quickly slid in next to him.

"Harking, what the ...?" he stammered, almost spilling his coffee as she closed the passenger door and slid an arm across the top of the bench seat, leaning toward Shane.

"You *said* you wouldn't break up the bears."

"I ..."

"But you only caught two cubs," she added, cutting Shane off, her voice elevated as she continued.

"True," said Shane. He turned away and looked out through the windshield of his truck before turning back to face Harking. "I only caught two."

"But you said ..." Harking started, but Shane cut her off, turning the tables on her and giving her a taste of her own medicine.

"But nothing. *I* only caught two." He chuckled as he watched Harking stew. "And Megan caught the other one."

"What? She did?"

"Huhuh."

"But Marion said ..."

"Said what?" Shane cut Harking off again. "What did Marion say?" He pushed Harking's arm off the back of the bench seat and leaned across to within a few inches of her face. "If you don't watch it, Harking Thompson, you're going to end up like her. Going off half-cocked before you know the whole story."

"Marion doesn't do that."

"No?"

"No." Harking was emphatic.

134

"Well maybe not most of the time," said Shane. "I'll give her that." He pulled his arm back and sat upright. "But I told you we'd keep the cubs and mother together and that's what we did." He was proud.

"Where'd you take them?"

"Can't say."

"Can't or won't?" Harking pressed on. "Did you or didn't you take them out of the park? You know Marion and I won't be happy if you did."

Shane could barely hold back a grin.

He shook his head. "Listen to me, Harking." He leaned back across the seat. "You need to understand I don't work for you, or Marion, for that matter."

"I know. You work for the superintendent."

"*Wrong* again." Shane poked his chest with his thumb, "*I* work for the park." He paused to make his point. "For the park." Shane was adamant.

"How is that any different?" Harking asked.

"Because it means I work for what this park is all about," Shane explained, his brow furrowed. "If I was to say I worked for anyone, or anything, it would be for those bears."

Harking settled back in the seat and looked away for a moment.

"Do you understand the difference?" Shane asked before waiting for Harking to turn and face him before continuing. "Yes, I take orders from the supe and there's certain things I can and can't do according to my job description and the outfit's code of conduct. But believe me, Harking, when push comes to shove, those bears and what happens to them is just as important to me as it is to you and Marion."

Harking was silent for a moment. "So where'd you drop them off?"

Shane shook his head and grinned even wider. "All I can tell you is they are in a safe place with a great view of the river and the mountains."

"But where exactly?" Harking persisted.

"Can't ...," Shane started to reply then stopped. "Listen, Harking, I can only tell you if you promise to keep your mouth shut about it. Understand? You can't go blabbing to Marion or Col or your pals from school. If word gets back to the superintendent, I'd be in deep shit."

He peered at Harking waiting for a response.

"I won't tell anyone."

"Promise?"

Harking nodded.

"Ah hell," Shane said, looking at his watch and back at Harking. "You got time to go for a ride?"

"Sure."

"Throw your bike in the back if you want."

She turned and pointed to her bike sitting in a bike stand on the sidewalk. "It's fine. It's locked," she said, turning back to Shane, looking curious. "Where are we going?"

"Back to where Megan and I dropped off the bears. I just want to see if they're still around." Pulling himself back into the driver's seat, Shane started the truck and wheeled it around in the road and headed out of town. "Duck down, would ya," he said to Harking as they drove down Jasper's main drag. "You're not even supposed to be in a government vehicle with me."

Harking leaned forward until Shane indicated they were through the busiest part of town, then sat up as they drove east on the highway. When Shane turned onto Snaring Road she looked at him and smiled.

"What?" he said with a grin.

"You didn't take them out of the park. I'm proud of you, Shane."

Harking's compliment brought a smile to Shane's face. "Why, thank you, ma ...," he was about to tip his Stetson toward Harking but caught himself before the cowboy took over.

"But not that proud," said Harking.

Rebuffed again, Shane silently turned his attention back to the road, his driving noticeably more aggressive as he sped up, gunning the truck on straight stretches and careening around corners, sending up a rooster trail of dust.

"I'm sorry," said Harking, clenching the armrest.

Lifting his foot slightly off the gas pedal, Shane remained focused on the road.

"I do appreciate you sticking to your word though," Harking added, breaking the impasse and offering an olive branch.

"Why thank you," Shane said finally, motioning to a clearing to their right as he pulled off the road. "We let them go here," he added, stopping the truck and scanning the open forest at the edge of the clearing. "Looks like they didn't stick around."

"You figure they're on their way back to town?" Harking asked.

"I hope not. It's not far but with any luck she'll stay away. Hopefully there's enough food to hold her and the cubs around this side of the park until the berries are ripe. There's a pretty good crop, so with any luck it'll be enough to keep them occupied for a while."

As he wheeled the truck around and headed back, they searched the forest along both sides of the road for the family of bears.

"No sign of them," said Shane as they approached the intersection with the highway.

"Yeah. Hopefully that's a good thing."

"Hopefully." Shane looked at her and smiled, then pulled back onto the highway and turned toward town. "It's been awhile since we've really chatted. How are things?"

"Okay."

"I'm worried your living with Marion is going to turn you into a raging environmentalist." He laughed.

"I don't think so." Harking smiled. "She's amazing. Too bad more people don't listen to her."

137

Shane nodded. "I agree. She's a tough old bird, but her heart is in the right place and she has a helluva lot more balls ..." Shane stalled as if choking on his last words. "Sorry about that. I should watch what I'm saying."

Harking raised her eyebrows. "Seriously? As if I haven't heard worse."

"I guess. Anyway, like I was saying, she's a gutsy lady."

"I know," said Harking, smiling and turning her attention to a collection of vehicles gathering on the road ahead of them. "Looks like something's got them interested."

"Huh, oh, here we go again," said Shane. "Third bear jam this week. Hopefully it's not our bears already."

"I don't think so," said Harking, her face pressed to the side window. "There's a mother black bear and cubs in the ditch," she added, pointing down the steep slope.

"And a father and kids trying to get some pictures," said Shane as he turned on the truck's emergency lights and pulled up behind the last vehicle. "Stay in the truck," he ordered, then checked behind to make sure there was no other traffic coming before getting out. "And keep your head down, would ya."

Shane shut the truck door and made his way toward the family while Harking tried to stay hidden, sneaking a peek over the dash every few seconds to see what was happening. She imagined Shane laying down the law, telling bystanders how dangerous it was to approach a female bear and cubs as he herded people back to their cars, all the while keeping an eye on the bruins.

Gradually Shane made his way down the line of vehicles, waving people on as more traffic began to block the driving lane.

Harking was impressed with how professional he looked in his warden uniform and Stetson, calmly dealing with the tourists.

Keeping one eye on Shane and the other on the bears, Harking watched as the female and cubs slowly picked their way along the edge of the trees, munching on grasses and the occasional clump of dandelions.

As the last car pulled away, Shane turned toward the bears and loudly clapped his hands, walking downslope a few steps.

"Yo, girl. Get outta here. Go on!" he called out.

The mother bear casually regarded Shane then edged into the bushes with the cubs following loosely on her heels.

"Keep going," Shane called as Harking watched him wait near the top of slope while the bears morphed into the trees, gradually disappearing in the underbrush.

Striding back to the truck, Shane tossed his Stetson on the seat next to Harking and climbed in behind the wheel. Brushing a hand through his greying hair he looked at his passenger.

"Some folks never learn," he sighed. "That guy had a bag of treats and was planning to get as close as he could."

Harking parroted the sigh and shook her head. "I don't get it. Why do they even stop? Don't they know they're in a national park?"

"Oh, I get that part," said Shane. "And I don't have a problem with it."

Harking looked at him curiously.

"Hey, people come here to see wildlife. And seeing a bear ... wow. You can't fault them for wanting to stop."

"I guess," Harking conceded.

"They just need to stay in their vehicles and move on once they've had their look." Shane picked up his Stetson and placed it back on his head. "No, it's the stupid things people do that drive me crazy. Like a dad trying to impress his kids by feeding the damn bear. How dumb can you get?"

Harking nodded. "Yeah, that's not too smart."

Checking over his shoulder, Shane started the truck then pulled back onto the highway while Harking took one last look for the bears.

"No sign of them," she said as Shane slowly drove past the spot where the mother bear had led her cubs into the bush.

"Good," said Shane. "Hopefully they stay away from the highway."

CHAPTER 32

Leaving the culvert trap, the sow gathered her cubs and headed for the thick band of willow bordering the opening where they'd been dropped off.

Somewhere in the distance, a train horn sounded as the steady hum of tractor-trailers, cars and recreational vehicles sped along the valley bottom.

On the other side of the railway the river beckoned.

Moving through the bushes, the mother grizzly made her way around the edge of a small wetland, the cubs tight on her heels. Continuing in the direction of the river, the sow dropped down into a narrow ditch and climbed back out, picking her way up the steep embankment and stepping over the railway track.

As the three cubs followed her lead, the dark-faced female trailed behind, limping slightly. As its siblings crossed the tracks it suddenly veered off toward a small pile of spilt corn, ignoring the sow's attempts to call it back. Sniffing the pile, it was about to taste the rotting grain when the sow reacted, charging quickly toward the cub and pushing it off the tracks. Nipping its ear, she shoved the little bear ahead of her as the other cubs followed quickly behind.

For the next several kilometres the bears followed the river westward until their path merged with the adjacent highway. Initially giving it a wide berth, the bears continued west, gradually funnelled into an ever-narrowing strip of willows between the railway and highway. Continually assessing their route, the female finally made a beeline for the highway, dropping down into a shallow ditch separating them from the asphalt corridor.

Ensuring the cubs were with her, she moved quickly up the gentle slope and started across the road toward the river as the outline of an approaching transport truck loomed in the distance.

Suddenly an air horn echoed loudly through the valley, sending the cubs skittering across the pavement. Quickly rounding up her panicked offspring, the sow pushed them toward the other side of the busy highway as the screeching tires of the large rig blasted past, barely missing the older bear as the rig suddenly swerved into the oncoming lane and sped by, the air horn bellowing as the driver regained the right hand side of the road.

Making their way quickly across the remaining stretch of highway, the bears dropped down into a patch of willows and followed the river upstream. Without losing momentum, the sow led her cubs along the riverbank toward a shallow riffle where the family could safely cross toward the far shore.

With the ebb and flow of the highway fading in the distance, the bears continued upstream, stopping from time to time to feed on pockets of horsetails as they crossed gravel flats and sandbars, navigating toward the stone-grey range of sharp-edged mountains that defined the valley's western boundary.

As the valley continued to narrow, the sow followed a well-worn trail of elk tracks up and over the steep riverbank and into a forest of young fir, finally settling into the soft cushion of moss as her cubs snuggled in at her side.

CHAPTER 33

"Hey, Marion," Harking called out as she closed the front door behind her. "Great news." She barely stopped to hang up her jacket as she bound into the living room. She wanted desperately to tell Marion about Shane not taking the mother grizzly and her cubs out of the park but remembered her promise.

Noticing no movement from Marion who was seated in her favourite chair facing away from her, Harking tiptoed to her side and whispered, "We saw a mother black bear and her cubs today. God, they were adorable."

Creeping around to the front she nudged Marion as she repeated herself.

"Marion. We saw some cubs today."

"Marion?"

Inspecting her closely, Harking watched for Marion's chest to rise and breathed an audible sigh when Marion finally opened her eyes.

"Oh, it's you," Marion said groggily, pulling herself upright in the chair and peering at the clock on the fireplace mantel. "My goodness. What time is it?"

"Almost six o'clock."

"Goodness," said Marion as she began to get up. "I must have dozed off. I have to get supper ready."

"You stay." Harking gently placed a hand on Marion's shoulder and eased her back into the chair. "It's my turn to cook."

"Well this is new," said Marion.

Harking smiled. "I'm just in a good mood." She gave Marion an overdrive play-by-play of everything that had happened at the bear jam then waltzed off into the kitchen. "And Shane kept his word," she called out above the rattle of pots and pans, unable to contain her enthusiasm despite the promise. Hearing no response, Harking briefly reappeared in the living room. "Did you hear what I said?"

When Marion didn't show any signs of movement a look of concern came across Harking's face.

"Marion?" Harking nudged her awake again.

"Goodness, I can't keep my eyes open."

"Are you feeling okay?"

"Not entirely. I think I feel a cold coming on."

"Well, I'll make some soup," Harking offered. "Chicken noodle, your favourite."

"Hmm," Marion mumbled, closing her eyes.

"You're falling asleep again," said Harking. "Maybe you should go to bed and I'll bring some to you." She worried Marion's condition might be more serious and recalled how Marion had been complaining recently about having *spells*.

"Yes, I think I'm going to," said Marion. Rising slowly to her feet she shuffled along the hallway to her bedroom as Harking monitored her effort.

When Harking went to check a short time later, carrying a tray with soup and crackers, Marion looked too peaceful to disturb. Returning to the kitchen Harking poured the soup back into the pot.

I'll feed it to her tomorrow.

Sitting alone at the kitchen table, Harking devoured her share, then after washing up the few dishes, decided to call it a day.

Locking the front and back doors, she closed the hallway window and headed upstairs to get ready for bed.

Tired but still excited about the day's events, Harking lay beneath the covers, unable to fall asleep. Reaching for her father's notebooks, she began to randomly flip through the pages, stopping here and there to ponder the numbers in the margins. Still convinced there was something in her father's notation similar to the symbols and style used by David Thompson, she put the notebooks aside and reached for one of her father's historical reference books about the great explorer.

Unsure what she was looking for exactly, Harking flipped through the pages, initially checking out the photocopied samples of Thompson's original journal entries inserted at the beginning of each chapter. Scouring the notes, comparing them to her father's, she seemed to be pulled along, guided by an unknown force. But finding little to support her theory, her attention shifted to the scattering of details around the explorer's personal life.

Despite his copious notes, Thompson made few references to his family. All Harking knew was that he married a Métis woman named Charlotte Small, and together they had several children.

Unlike others from that era, Thompson made no effort to hide his wife's existence from a potentially critical public that frowned on mixed marriages. But there was little in the pages to tell Harking much about the woman or her heritage.

Pausing, Harking couldn't help but think things may not have changed much in the century or more since Thompson travelled west, considering no one she asked could tell her much about the history of Métis and First Nations in the Jasper area. If it wasn't for her own discoveries and subsequent questioning of her father, she probably still wouldn't know anything about Jasper's early days and the mistreatment of Indigenous families forced out of the valley in 1910 just after the park was established.

Her own initial discovery had been a fluke, stumbling on what was obviously some sort of sacred site near the Palisades, what she assumed to be a more recent prayer offering consisting of a small leather pouch tied to a poplar sapling along the trail and marked with a square of red cloth moving easily in the slight breeze.

Concerned she might be walking over an old gravesite, Harking didn't investigate further and continued on her way, intent on quizzing her father that evening.

Dan Thompson knew what Harking was referring to the moment she mentioned the coloured flagging and went on to give her a brief history of the park's early days and attitudes toward the Métis in particular, a group he seemed intent on identifying with.

"I think they've always felt caught in the middle," he'd explained. "And to make matters worse, in the early days of white settlement, it didn't help people with Métis roots, or First Nations roots for that matter, to let people know their ancestry. In many ways, they became invisible to the rest of us. That's pretty sad considering their rich history here before we came along. Thankfully Parks seems to be trying to right that wrong."

Harking couldn't help but think it was all about fitting in. As a bit of an oddball herself, she knew how cliquish people could be, ostracizing anyone who was different. Even her interest in history had left her on the outside looking in with peers at school when she'd mentioned some facts about David Thompson, who was known to the Indigenous peoples as Koo Koo Sint or "Stargazer."

When she'd mentioned the name in history class, Brianna Smith quickly bastardized Koo Koo to "Cuckoo" and was relentless in tormenting Harking with the nickname.

Trying to follow her parents' advice to ignore Brianna, Harking endured the taunts for as long as she could until finally, totally fed up, she confronted Brianna in the hallway after school. Eventually separated by Principal Stellar before anything physical happened, Harking made it crystal clear she'd "break Brianna like a matchstick" if she ever heard the slur again. And although she never did hear it outright, the murmurs and whispers whenever she walked by Brianna and her clique reminded Harking of her status with some of her cohort.

"Screw them," Simi had said. "You're not honestly worrying about what that ho and her little gang of sluts say about you?"

Harking chuckled thinking of Simi's comment. Coming from the daughter of a cop and a person of colour to boot, Harking knew the cuckoo comment was trivial compared to the abuse Simi had endured when she first arrived in town.

But together they'd settled a few scores outside of school and still smiled to themselves whenever Brianna and her entourage turned tail and scurried away at the first sight of Simi and Harking in the school hallway.

As Harking thumbed through the journals, she suspected it would have been even tougher for Indigenous people, with family names like Rattlesnake and Crowfoot acting as fodder for the taunts and jeers from some of the white kids in school.

Thankfully Col hadn't been sucked into that mindset.

I would have tuned him up if he had.

I'm sure Mom and Dad would have as well.

Especially Mom.

Paige Thompson did not suffer fools easily and Harking knew that despite her differences with her mother, Paige was fundamentally a good person and together with their father had given both her and Col a solid foundation.

If only she wasn't so controlling.

But then again, maybe, as Marion kept reminding her, their relationship was pretty typical of mothers and daughters at that stage of their lives. Harking didn't particularly agree or like the comment, but she also didn't dare talk back to Marion. She knew Marion cared for her, but she also suspected it wouldn't take much to set her off. Having seen Marion tackle some of the pro-development forces in town, there was no way Harking wanted to be on the receiving end of her fury.

The thought brought a smile to Harking's face as she fought off sleep and turned her attention back to the Thompson journals. Maybe tomorrow she'd do a little exploring and visit some of the places where he'd actually stood back in the day. She might even follow some of his directions to see where they took her.

The exercise would put her on the ground, literally following in the explorer's footsteps, and might shed more light on her father's notes ... yes, her father ... somewhere, out there in the whiteness ... she could hear him calling her name ... pulling her along ... toward the abyss.

"*... Harking.*"

CHAPTER 34

The next morning, slow to get rolling, Harking lay in bed, once again exhausted by the recurring dream about the avalanche. Wracking her memory, she tried in vain to recall the details, and while some seemed to be getting clearer, large segments of the story still continued to elude her.

By the time Harking got up, Marion was already gone but had left a note outlining her plans for the day and saying she'd see Harking at dinner.

Good, she must be feeling better, Harking thought, knowing Marion spent a ton of time doing her own thing, looking for bears and elk and other wildlife in the valley, keeping a finger on the pulse of the park.

Or being a pain in the ass.

Harking knew how some people viewed Marion, especially when she spoke out about new developments in the park or the need to manage human use.

At the bottom of the note Marion had scratched a quick message to say Paige had called. Col was going to be released from the hospital today. By all accounts he was fine.

Hopefully he'll stay away from Tyson, Harking thought. *Then again, I'm not his babysitter.*

Happy she didn't have to go back to the hospital and chance running into her mother, Harking pulled together some of the Thompson reference material along with a couple of her father's notebooks and rode out of town toward Old Fort Point. She figured it was a good starting point considering its prominence in Jasper's early history.

Leaving her bike locked at the bottom of the rocky knoll, she quickly climbed the lower stairs two at a time, stopping briefly at the large monument to once again read the plaque detailing the historical significance of the Athabasca River, serving Indigenous people for millennia before David Thompson and other early explorers made their way to the mountains.

Here, near the town of Jasper, where the Athabasca, Miette and Maligne Rivers converged, the confluence of their valleys provided a critical juncture for wildlife, connecting the park east and west as well as north and south.

It's like the beating heart of the park, Harking thought.

And the rivers are the arteries and veins.

Harking knew this area of low-lying montane forest and grassland represented some of Jasper's most critical wildlife habitat, but comprised less than ten percent of the entire national park, the largest portion of Jasper and the other mountain national parks being made up of rock and ice that held little value to most wildlife.

Except climbers, Harking thought, as she bounded up the cement stairs past the monument, closely skirting a quartet of foraging bighorn sheep as the sparsely treed hillside gave way to an expanse of thin grasses.

"Good morning, ladies," she said as she passed the four ewes, staring blankly as she walked by.

Continuing upslope, Harking followed the narrow trail through a copse of Douglas fir to the top of the ridge and sat down. Looking around she was intrigued by the shades of green blanketing the landscape, the lighter patches of aspen behind Old Fort Point reinforcing the darker green swaths of fir and pine blanketing the lower mountain slopes, the subtle differences hinting at past forest fires or outbreaks of insects that shaped the tapestry of colours.

Even now she could see a sheen of red as mountain pine beetle tightened its grip on the pure stands of lodgepole pine dominating the valley, the recent warmer winters unable to stop the beetles' westward spread throughout the park.

Pulling out her water bottle, Harking paused to think about what the park might look like in a few years but accepted the fact that fire and beetles and other natural disturbances were all just part of the natural evolution of the landscape and had been forever.

We just need to get over thinking this place has to look a certain way, she thought, recalling some of the discussions in science class when others argued that the effects of forest fires and insects detracted from the park's beauty.

Harking took pride in facing down those arguments, likening them to some of her classmate's efforts to emulate the latest looks and styles, conforming to whatever fashion was in vogue at the time.

Smiling to herself at the memory of putting Brianna in her place, in particular, Harking took a long drink and scanned the slopes of Pyramid, Roche Bonhomme, Signal, and the Whistlers; the four mountains bordering the valley bottom habitat around the town of Jasper.

As Harking watched trains shuttle in and out of the railyard and a steady flurry of traffic making its way through the town's busy streets, she realized just how much human activity was concentrated in this one small part of the park.

There's not much of it, but we all want a piece of it.

Looking across the valley at the benchlands below Pyramid Mountain, Harking could better appreciate their importance as natural corridors for wildlife, providing a safe route around the town, highway and railway.

And according to her father, the benchlands stretching behind her along the base of Signal Mountain served a similar purpose, allowing wolves, bears and other wildlife to avoid people and not become habituated.

Finding the right balance between protection and use meant keeping wildlife "wild" and people safe, he'd often said.

Closing her eyes, Harking took a deep breath and recalled how her father often turned their observations into a "teachable moment", as he would call it, never lecturing, but encouraging her and Col to ask questions about the natural world around them.

Smiling at his memory, Harking lay still, listening as songbirds flitted through the branches of the Douglas fir while overhead a lone eagle rode the currents.

For a moment Harking was reminded of her quest to find the Lewis's woodpecker, realizing that lately she'd been distracted from adding to her life list.

Oh well, I'll get to it eventually.

Returning her attention to the morning's chorus of song-birds, Harking tried her best to identify each call. When one of her favourites, a white-throated sparrow, sang nearby, she pursed her lips and tried to duplicate the call, which her father described as sounding like *Oh sweet Ca-na-da*. Surprisingly the response was almost immediate and for the next few minutes Harking and the small songbird shared the airwaves.

She was basking in the moment when something else dis-tracted her.

Was that someone calling out?

Drawn by the sound, she got up and made her way toward an overlook that provided a clear view of the Athabasca River. Below her, a series of dry, braided channels stretched along the river, strewn with masses of woody debris from this years' runoff. As Harking watched, a small group of hikers picked their way upstream along one of the channels, pausing from time to time to take pictures or wait for slower members of the group.

Suddenly, out of the corner of her eye, Harking noticed a large black bear making its way in the opposite direction, for-aging on riparian vegetation along the river's edge as it headed downstream, adjacent to the group.

Harking was about to call out to warn the hikers but thought better of it, figuring they wouldn't hear her anyway.

150

Besides, she thought, they were separated by bands of wolf willow and conifers, and far enough from each other that the likelihood of them running into each other was slim.

Still, as Harking watched, she noticed the bear lift its head frequently and sniff the air, as if keeping tabs on the hikers as they passed by. While it was obvious that the hikers were totally oblivious to its presence, Harking wondered if the bear had modified *its* route to avoid *them*.

She also wondered how often a scene like this played itself out as wildlife and humans occupied the same landscape.

Even though it's probably worked well for thousands of years, with everything that's happening here, can humans and wildlife really coexist in places like this?

Can both survive?

Harking wasn't quite sure.

CHAPTER 35

Over a span of two weeks, reports from hikers placed the mother grizzly and her cubs further out in the Athabasca Valley, leaving Shane Ross to think he'd made the right decision. The family of bears were together, staying out of trouble and avoiding the area around the Jasper townsite. And John Walleski was none the wiser.

Shane was now back to his regular routines including moving any elk that had wandered into town overnight back to the surrounding forests. Parks's patented technique of wildly waving a hockey stick emblazoned with streamers of yellow tape to move the ungulates garnered lots of laughs from the locals but ultimately it worked, keeping the elk out of Jasper's unfenced green spaces,

Out of sight and out of mind, Shane thought.

At least until nightfall brought them back into the security offered by humans, deterring wolves and other predators from an easy meal.

With the elk moved, Shane's next few hours were spent making routine patrols south, east and west along the highway, stopping in at the gateways and campgrounds to chat with the park attendants and wave the flag. Often he'd take a side trip to The Range, the park's horse barn and corrals, and if things were slow, he'd continue along the Maligne Road, keeping an eye out for bears, wolves and moose or any other wildlife.

This morning's cooler weather had thankfully kept most tourists off the road, giving Shane a chance to slowly pick his way up to Medicine and Maligne Lakes, enjoying the stunning scenery on his own terms.

Returning from the lakes, he approached the intersection with the main highway and watched as a group on mountain bikes popped out of the bush on the other side and coasted down to the blacktop. After they'd crossed and disappeared down a trail, Shane was surprised to see Harking Thompson ride out of the bush just after them, alone and obviously not part of the group.

She's a bit of a different cat, he thought.

Not really a follower.

She'd probably make a good park warden.

He chuckled, recalling an expression from an old chief park warden who used to say, "Park Wardens wouldn't follow anyone unless it was uphill, through four feet of snow."

He was pretty much bang on, Shane thought, reflecting on the usually A-type personalities the Warden Service attracted, men and women with an over-abundance of confidence tempered only by the stark realities of some of the situations they ended up in; a challenging mountain rescue during a blizzard that no *normal* person would have attempted or venturing *solo* into a late night party in the campground that would have needed several RCMP officers to break up, real-life experiences that tended to rein in even the most stubborn amongst them, if they wanted to enjoy a long career in the outfit.

"No sense getting' older if you don't get a little smarter," that same boss had reminded Shane on more than one occasion.

Wanting to get Harking's attention, Shane flipped on the truck's red and blue emergency lights. When she raised a hand in recognition Shane turned off the lights and waited until there was a break in the traffic and she could cross the blacktop. "Where you off to?" he said, rolling down his window as she rode up to his truck.

"Overlander," said Harking, referring to a strip of single track on the other side of the river that paralleled the highway. Hikers often walked the trail one way or the other, positioning a

153

vehicle at the opposite end, while most bikers usually turned the ride into a loop, returning via the highway or vice versa.

"Throw your bike in the back if you want and I'll drop you off at Twelve Mile," he said, referring to the far end of the Overlander where the highway crossed the Athabasca River.

"You sure?" Harking's eyes lit up.

Shane nodded. "No point riding the highway shoulder if you can avoid it. And I'm headed that way."

After Harking placed her bike in the back of the truck and jumped in the cab, Shane turned on to the highway and headed east.

"No sign of the grizzlies?" Harking asked.

"Nope," said Shane. "Sounds like they're spending time on the other side of the river."

"That's good. Hopefully they stay away from town."

"Knock on wood," said Shane, lightly tapping his head with a fist.

"So what have you been up to?" Harking inquired.

"The usual," said Shane. "Movin' elk, keepin' folks out of trouble. Tryin' to stay outta trouble myself." He grinned.

Harking smiled and peered ahead, her eyes slowly drawn to a collection of vehicles pulling over on the shoulder of the highway, overlooking the river.

"Something's got their attention," she said, as they approached the end of the line of cars.

"Hmm," Shane muttered. Pulling in behind the last car in the line, he flipped on the truck's emergency lights to warn oncoming traffic, all the while searching the grassy highway right-of-way for whatever had caught people's attention.

Just then a trio of bears, a sow and two light-faced grizzly cubs, appeared at the edge of the pavement.

"Jesus, here we go again," Shane said, as the female grizzly made several attempts to start across the blacktop, only to turn the cubs back. Seemingly agitated by the traffic and the

154

challenge of keeping her cubs by her side, she paced along the gravel shoulder, forcing several of the onlookers back into their vehicles.

As Shane and Harking watched in horror an oncoming transport truck swerved to avoid the bears' next attempt at crossing, its horn blaring. Almost at the same time, the driver of one of the cars stopped on the shoulder decided to pull back into the eastbound lane, further congesting traffic on the narrow highway.

When a third, dark-faced cub limped into view, hobbling as fast as it could to catch up to its family, Shane could see the impending disaster unfolding.

"Watch out," Harking screamed as the little masked grizzly barely avoided the first oncoming vehicle.

Successfully dodging the next car, it was almost across the road when it was clipped by a pickup truck, the sickening thud audible above the confusion.

"Fuck," Harking screamed.

Flinging open the truck door, she was about to jump out when Shane grabbed her arm.

"Stay put and close the door," he yelled, pulling Harking back inside.

Giving a blast of the siren Shane powered the warden truck across the lane of oncoming traffic to prevent the cub from being hit again.

"Stay there," he yelled at Harking as he jumped out and hurried toward the injured cub, a hand held aloft signalling the oncoming traffic to stop.

Oblivious to Shane's command, Harking jumped out of the truck, her open door almost clipped by a driver trying to avoid hitting her and the other vehicles parked on the shoulder, the cars' screeching brakes adding to the chaos.

"I told you to stay in the truck," Shane yelled, trying to keep his eye on the traffic, the bears and now Harking.

"But the cub ..." Harking started toward Shane but he waved her back.

"Stay there and direct traffic," he yelled, realizing he had to keep her occupied to prevent the shit show from worsening.

Watching the sow, Shane cautiously approached the cub lying at the side of the road and knew right away its injuries would be fatal.

Rearing up on its hind legs, the mother grizzly stood at the edge of a line of trees bordering the far side of the ditch, seemingly trying to catch a scent or sight of her cub, her reluctance to leave obvious as the other two cubs cowered at her feet.

"Get back in your vehicles and get out of here," Harking yelled as a bevy of onlookers jumped out of their cars to get a better look, quickly returning to their vehicles at the sight of an enraged Harking.

"Get the hell out of here," she yelled again as she directed traffic past the warden truck, brushing away the tears and verbally threatening anyone who hinted at stopping.

Worried about Harking, but satisfied that people were moving along, Shane stood over the injured cub and directed his attention to the sow.

"Go on," he called out, walking into the ditch toward her. "You get out of here too."

The mother grizzly dropped to its feet and slowly started toward him.

"Go on, get out of here," he yelled, picking up a rock and hurtling it at the bear, missing her by mere inches.

The mother grizzly stopped and hesitated for a moment, seeming to regard Shane and weigh her options. Slowly, reluctantly, she returned to her other cubs and with one last glance over her shoulders, pushed them into the bush and disappeared.

Shane sighed heavily and walked back to the cub then past it to his truck.

"Get in," he ordered Harking, who was standing at the

tailgate, waving the last of the vehicles by. "Get in the truck," Shane repeated, jumping in behind the wheel as Harking finally slid in on the passenger side.

"What a fucking schmozzle," Shane growled as he started the vehicle and spun it around in the middle of the highway, glancing over at Harking as he pulled onto the shoulder next to the cub.

Slowly opening her door, her body shaking from the heavy sobs, Harking tumbled out of the truck, falling to her knees next to the dead bear.

Waving the last of the traffic past him as he exited the truck, Shane walked around to Harking and put a hand on her shoulder.

"Well this is the shits," he said, kneeling down next to her and smoothing a hand over the cub's ruffled fur. He couldn't bring himself to look at Harking but knew she was devastated. Still, he didn't want to linger.

"Let's get her outta here," he said finally, working his arms under the bear and taking the weight. "Can you open the back?" His tone softened as he cradled the cub in his arms and got up. Gently, he slid the cub in the back of the truck and closed the tailgate, leaning his body against it until he heard it latch.

"Where are you taking her?" Harking mumbled almost incoherently.

"You'll see," said Shane as he moved toward the driver's door.

"Not to the freakin' landfill," Harking blurted, her eyes on fire as she glared at Shane and climbed into the cab of the truck.

"No way," he said softly, his hangdog look exaggerated by the rim of red around his eyelids. "Give me some credit, for Christ's sake."

"Then where?" Harking demanded between heavy sobs.

"You'll see," said Shane. Turning off the emergency lights he started the truck, checked over his shoulder for oncoming traffic, and pulled onto the highway. As he drove away, Shane picked up the radio mic and contacted Dispatch, recounting the details of what had happened. When he'd finished he radioed Megan.

"Did ya catch all that?" he asked when she answered.

"Ten-four, Shane."

Keeping their on-air discussion to a minimum he asked her to check the accident scene as soon as she could to make sure the other bears were gone.

"Ten-four," Megan replied.

"I'll fill you in when I get back," said Shane, returning the mic to its holder and driving away.

CHAPTER 36

Driving into town and turning toward the benchlands, Shane headed for the lake. Stopping at the gated fire road, he unclipped a key ring from his belt and selected one key from the collection.

"Can you open the gate?" Shane asked, passing the mass of keys to Harking who sat stone-faced, staring forward. Sliding out of the truck, she wiped a sleeve across her nose and stumbled to the gate.

"It's a bit finicky," Shane called out as Harking wrestled with the lock. Finally solving it she pulled the gate open, closing and locking it again once Shane had driven through. She was about to climb back in the truck when Shane interjected.

"Just a second," he said as he slid out and pulled a blanket from behind the seat.

As Harking watched zombie-like, Shane lowered the tailgate and lifted the small cub onto the blanket. Carrying it to Harking's side he motioned for her to open the door and get in.

"It's going to be bumpy," he said, gently placing the cub in her lap.

Carefully closing her door, he walked to the rear of the truck and closed the tailgate then slid back into the cab.

Still a train wreck, he thought as he looked over at Harking.

Although her tears had dried, her face was blotched and flushed.

Bumping along the pot-holed road, Harking tightly held on to the cub as the truck clawed for traction, pulling itself up and over the weathered ruts and exposed boulders.

As they gained altitude, the road was increasingly over-grown with alders and young pine that scraped against the sides of the truck.

At an obscure fork in the road, Shane turned off and picked his way down a narrow track, only stopping when a massive deadfall blocked their route.

"I guess this is as far as we can drive," he said to Harking.

Exiting the truck, Shane pulled his pack and a fire shovel from the back and opened the side door for Harking.

Taking the weight of the small cub, she eased her feet onto the ground and stood up, blowing the hair out of her face as she embraced the small bear. Looking into its face she forced a smile, barely holding back the next round of tears.

"She was a cutie," said Shane. He ran a hand over the cub's head and regarded his partner. "You okay?"

"Yeah," said Harking, choking back the lump in her throat.

"Do you want me to carry her?" Shane offered.

Harking shook her head.

"Follow me then." Shane picked his way around the downed tree and regained the narrow track as it wound its way toward the skyline. "It's not far to the spot I'm thinking of."

Harking followed, carefully stepping over and around exposed roots, trying not to trip.

At the edge of the trees, Shane stopped and waited for Harking.

"Quite the view, eh?" he said as she sidled up alongside.

The river valley spread out below them and a series of ridgelines faded off into the distance, interspersed with mountain peaks rising in every direction.

Shane looked around then walked along the edge of the ridge toward a large Douglas fir, motioning for Harking to follow. "I'll try digging here," he said, when Harking had caught up.

Cradling the cub in her arms Harking knelt and waited as Shane probed the ground, finally finding a spot where he could easily sink the fire shovel into the duff. Scraping away the uppermost layer of needles and small bits of wood, he stepped on the shovel and repeatedly drove it into the earth, methodically tossing shovelfuls of soil to the side. When the hole was deep enough, he stood the shovel against the tree and pulled out a pocketknife. Harking watched as Shane made his way into a small thicket of fir saplings and returned with an armload of freshly cut boughs. Kneeling next to Harking, he carefully placed them in the bottom of the hole.

"What d'ya think?"

"Looks good," said Harking, gently laying the cub on the mat of green boughs.

Shane placed the remainder of the boughs over the cub then took a handful of soil from the pile. He motioned for Harking to do the same.

As large tears rolled down her face, Harking lightly sprinkled a handful on the grave.

"Goodbye, little bear," she said. "I'm so sorry."

"Goodbye, little bear," Shane added, his eyes brimming as he added more soil on top of the boughs. He placed an arm around Harking and drew her close to quell the shaking, his own tears rolling onto Harking's tangled hair. "I'm sorry, too."

Relaxing his embrace, Shane collected himself and reached forward, pulling handfuls of soil on top of the bear. Harking did the same. Looking around they collected any rocks within reach and placed them on top.

"I'll get some more," said Shane, as he stood up with a groan. "God, I must be getting old," he said, arching his back. He grimaced and walked away, returning with a small armload of stones that he carefully laid by Harking's side. As she placed them on the grave, Shane made another trip to the edge of the escarpment, returning with another load.

Finally satisfied that the cub's body was well covered, Shane and Harking stood side by side and surveyed their work.

"That should keep any scavengers away," said Shane.

Harking nodded then wiped the back of her hand across her eyes to dry the tears.

"C'mon," said Shane, putting an arm around her. "Let's grab a drink and something to eat."

"But I didn't bring anything," said Harking.

"No worries. I've got lots." Shane led Harking to the edge of the escarpment and sat down. He opened his pack and pulled out two cans of pop and two sandwiches, tightly wrapped in clear plastic. He handed one of each to Harking who reluctantly accepted the gift.

"D'ya like tuna?" Shane asked,

"Is it Ocean Wise?" said Harking. Carefully unwrapping the sandwich she scrutinized the middle layer.

"Yeah, right," said Shane. "Should I remind you we're in Alberta?"

Harking forced a smile and sunk her teeth into the sandwich before opening the pop. "I don't usually drink this stuff. It's not good for you."

Shane feigned a frown. "If *you* know what's good for you, you'll shut up and eat."

Harking laughed and drank, pretending not to like the sugary sweet pop.

They sat quietly for several minutes, each immersed in their own thoughts before Shane broke the silence.

"You know," he said, looking out over the valley. "This was always one of your dad's favourite spots." He paused and looked at Harking. "Mine too."

Harking scrunched her face. "You came up here together?"

"Well, not exactly," said Shane. "There used to be a fire tower at the top of the ridge and part of my job was to make sure the tower was well supplied. If the towerman needed anything, he'd call into town and I would pick things up and drive up here to drop it off. Whenever I had the chance, I'd take my lunch break or coffee break right around here."

Harking listened intently.

"One day I met your dad hiking up the road so I offered

him a lift. I'd seen him around town and heard he was a bit of an explorer, but we'd never really met before, officially. We hit it off and had a good chat about different trails in the park. He seemed intent on hiking them all and getting to know the lay of the land."

Shane laughed and looked over at Harking.

"He took an awful lot of notes. I don't think I ever met anyone who wrote things down as much as your father did."

Harking smiled.

"Anyway," Shane continued, "we certainly covered a lot of ground together. Then over the last few years we seemed to lose touch. The next time I met him I could tell something was different. He seemed lost. Not like his normal self. He finally told me he and your mother weren't getting along."

Shane was silent for a moment.

"Oh, there wasn't anyone else in his life or your mother's. It wasn't that kind of thing. It just seemed they were growing apart and for the life of him, he couldn't figure out what to do or if he could do anything at all. All he talked about was you and Col and what would happen if he and your mother didn't stick together. Even though some of the happiness seemed to have disappeared from their marriage, you were both top of mind for him, and he hoped you both knew that."

Shane looked away as he struggled with the last words, thinking back to some of his own challenges growing up on the Prairies.

He knew he'd disappointed his family when he told them he had no interest in farming, that he didn't think some of their practices, like draining and filling in wetlands and their widespread use of pesticides, were good for the environment.

And his opinions didn't always garner him any favours in the farming community, his outspoken nature often landing him in trouble, even with other members of his family.

None were surprised when Shane went to university to study biology and fewer still blinked when he landed a job in

Prince Albert National Park with Parks Canada, an organization whose values Shane figured were about as close to his own as he could hope for.

Leaving the farm behind was a way out for him and his family, but still he missed them. And although they didn't share his opinions, he knew they loved him and when push came to shove, they always had his back, coming to his defence whenever someone else slighted him or his name.

Recalling an incident where his brother Cade had hung a lickin' on someone who'd been criticizing Shane as a 'no-good tree hugger', he smiled to himself then turned to Harking.

"Family is everything," he said.

"I guess," Harking replied.

They sat in silence for a moment longer, listening and watching a flock of siskins hopscotch through the pine tree.

Finally Shane stood up and stretched. "C'mon. I'll take you home."

CHAPTER 37

Harking leaned against the vanity, squinting through red-rimmed eyes at her reflection in the mirror. Having snuck into the house to avoid letting Marion see her in such a mess, she hid out in the bathroom, exhausted from the emotional outpouring of the past several hours.

Fighting to hold back the tears, she pulled the brush through her hair, wincing as she untangled knot after knot, beginning a head-to-toe assessment to try and forget the chaos of the day.

It's nice that it's not so red anymore, she thought, recalling the taunting from the boys in elementary school that led to her first fights, never willing to back down no matter how mismatched the battles might have been.

But at least the physical fights with the boys her age, more rough and tumble scuffles than full on fisticuffs, were a way to get rid of her frustrations, and earned her a degree of respect with her male peers.

The fights with the girls were actually worse, though not so much physically; Harking's size usually gave her a distinct advantage.

But the taunts and name-calling were another matter.

Sticks and stones, yeah right.

The names did hurt.

Even though her parents tried to make light of it all and suggested she laugh it off.

Mom especially.

Harking shook her head then smiled at the memory of how hard her mother tried to be her friend and influence her choices.

Maybe she tried too hard.

She grinned thinking about how Paige had dyed her own hair to try and make a point with Harking about how silly her own hair looked at the time, "bluer than the sky" her dad had said.

Even though her mother's efforts hadn't worked, Harking had to finally concede that her natural colour was more to her liking.

Now everyone's kind of jealous about my hair.

Combing out the last knots she stood back and admired the result, then frowned as she surveyed the rest of her body.

But they're not jealous about that.

"Big-boned," her mother would say, "like your grandfather." ... Not flattering, but probably true.

Harking was solid and in shape.

Five-foot ten barefoot, five eleven if she focussed on standing tall.

Mountain biking, competitive mountain biking in particular, had helped tone muscles developed in her early years when she'd taken Tae Kwon Do, but she also had to give credit to skiing, snowboarding, hiking and other aspects of a healthy lifestyle, including diet.

Rarely a day went by when she and Marion didn't munch away on carrot or apple slices. And they always ate a large salad with dinner, loading it with avocado, tomato, peppers and feta, among other ingredients. Harking was getting hungry just thinking about it all when a gentle rapping on the door brought her back to the moment.

"You okay in there?" Marion's voice dripped compassion. "I heard what happened."

The door opened and they were standing face to face, the battle-weary elder warrior and the young combatant, the emerging soldier.

Marion's worried expression softened on seeing the look of defeat in Harking's eyes. Before she could say anything, Harking fell into her arms, sobbing.

"I hate this park," she blurted as she clung to Marion. "The bears don't have a chance."

"Now, now..." Marion began, but Harking pulled out of her grasp.

"It's true," she cried, slumping to her knees, head bowed. "This place is supposed to protect them." She looked up at Marion." We're supposed to protect them. But instead we're killing them. One by one."

Gently kneeling down by her young charge, Marion leaned back against the wall and drew Harking into her, soothing the shaking as she silently stroked Harking's head.

"But I promise you one thing," said Harking, pulling away from Marion and wiping a shirtsleeve across her face to dry the tears. "I'm going to do whatever I can to make sure the others survive."

"You and I both," said Marion, pulling Harking back into her embrace. "You and I both."

CHAPTER 38

After the loss of her cub, the mother grizzly was increasingly protective as she navigated her way back to the familiar territory behind the lakes, quickly scolding the two remaining cubs when they strayed too far from her.

When the male cub resisted her urgings to keep moving, she tore into him, her teeth sinking into his hind end enough to make a point without seriously injuring him.

Slinking to her mother's side after watching the encounter, the smaller female hurried past, trying to keep up with her sibling as the sow voiced its displeasure from the rear, her efforts all the more critical as an approaching train's horn tore through the stillness, pushing her and the cubs up the steep slope on the other side of the tracks.

Cresting the ridge top, the mother grizzly stopped for a second as the train passed below, the overwhelming sound of metal on metal striking fear and panic in the cubs, sending them bolting for cover.

Gathering the pair, the mother led them through the forest, putting distance between them and the maelstrom of noises in the Athabasca Valley.

Finally out of earshot, she led them non-stop down a series of loosely connected wildlife trails, away from the stresses of the valley. Gathering the cubs as she neared the lake, the grizzly was acutely aware of the scent of humans on the other side and moved the cubs further back from the shoreline.

The mix of fir, pine and aspen forest stretching several kilo-metres between the lake and the alpine slopes of the mountains provided security and food, including a variety of berries, forbs and grasses. Coupled with the potential to hunt deer, elk and moose, especially their calves, this habitat could easily sustain the family of bears for the summer.

If the grizzly kept her family's movements restricted to this area, the only serious risks they faced was the presence of the male that moved through from time to time and any people who ignored the closure signs, putting pressure on the mother bear to move her family into poorer, less secure habitat.

The challenge for the grizzly and her cubs was to avoid them all.

CHAPTER 39

Shane Ross didn't expect to be called into John Walleski's office quite so soon after his last meeting with the superintendent, but was pretty certain it had to do with yesterday's mayhem on the highway. And although he could never figure out how word could spread so fast, people in town were already talking about the return of the grizzly and her cubs.

Thinking back to yesterday, Shane figured someone passing through the accident scene must have recognized the bears and spread the word, but try as he might, he couldn't recall any familiar faces.

He'd been too busy juggling balls to pay attention.

Maybe releasing the bears inside the park had hastened their return to the benchlands behind town, but that was a moot point now.

It really didn't matter.

He'd done what he felt he had to do, and would deal with the fallout.

If John Walleski tore a strip off of him, so be it.

Even though he thought that, deep down, the park superintendent was on his side, Shane was sometimes at a loss to explain decision-making in the outfit. Often it seemed totally in line with what he understood to be the park's main purpose: to protect this incredible part of the country and the wildlife that called it home.

But at other times, the decisions seemed to be contradictory. *Totally unpredictable, like a coin toss.*

Shane was pretty certain it had more to do with satisfying the squeaky wheel of some local businessman who had the superintendent's ear, or a developer who was politically connected at higher levels of government, but Shane had little time for either.

Although he knew John's job was probably more of a balancing act than he would have liked, Shane felt it would be more black and white if it was up to him.

Protection of the park and its wildlife would come first.

Everything else was secondary.

Walking through the administration building to the superintendent's office, Shane convinced himself that was the stand he was going to take with John, but was thrown off guard by the silence of the administration staff. Looking up from their desks with drawn faces, acknowledging his presence with a simple nod or a faint smile, Shane wondered what side of the coin they were on.

Unsure what to expect, Shane knocked and entered John's office.

With the windows closed and a solitary desk lamp barely compensating for the lack of natural light, the extent of the spacious office was largely lost in the shadows, giving the room a feeling of apprehension.

The look of foreboding on Walleski's face added to the effect as he sat silently at his desk.

"Close the door would you, please," he said finally, speaking in a low voice and motioning for Shane to take a seat. "Sorry to hear about the grizzly cub," he added as Shane sat across the desk from him, expecting to get reamed out not only for having released the bears inside the park, but also for having Harking with him the day before.

"I ...," Shane began to speak but John raised a hand.

"I don't want to know the details, Shane. The less I know the better at this stage of the game. Marion has already taken a chunk out of me today and I don't want to argue with you."

Shane nodded and waited for the shoe to drop.

"I just need you to deal with those bears and get them out of here for good." Before Shane could protest, John continued. "It

171

doesn't have to be outside of the park. Christ, this park is huge ... more than ten thousand square kilometres. And the neighbouring parks butting up against us are almost as big. There has to be somewhere to take them, down the Parkway, wherever. I just need them out of *here*." Motioning to the broad expanse of valley outside his window, he sounded uncompromising.

But so was Shane.

"What if we try something else," he said when he finally got an opening.

"Christ ...," John started, but this time Shane held up a hand.

"Wait. Hear me out." He paused. "I know the park is big, but no matter where I take those bears, they'll either come back or get killed trying. Marion's right. *This*," Shane pointed out the window at the Athabasca Valley, "is *their* home."

"Shane...wait," John tried to interject.

"No, *you* wait John," Shane continued, intent on saying his piece. "You've closed the area back of the lake and that's great. And that family of bears is back there now. What happened yesterday probably wouldn't have happened if we left them there in the first place and aggressively enforced the closure. I say we do that, and make this work *for* the bears."

Shane paused to let his words sink in.

"That sow is the kind of griz we want here. The valley is part of her home range and it'll become part of the cubs' home ranges. That's how it works. She'll teach her cubs how to survive here, without getting into trouble *with us*." Shane pointed a thumb at his chest.

Arms folded, John Walleski sat patiently and listened as Shane articulated his plan.

"We just have to give them some space," Shane concluded, unsure if he'd convinced John, who fidgeted in his chair, sighing heavily.

"Okay," John said, sounding somewhat reluctant. Relaxing his position, he nodded his head. "We'll try it your way. You and the other wardens can aggressively enforce the closure and I don't care who you catch. I'll back you up."

He paused before adding with grim hope, "Maybe it'll shut Marion up as well."

Shane waited for the 'but', there was always a 'but'.

"But if that bear runs into trouble again," John continued, "you know I'll be forced to order you to put it down."

"Fine," said Shane, knowing in his heart it wasn't. "But as long as we keep people out of the closed area, I'm convinced she won't get in trouble again."

"She better not," said John.

There was a moment of awkward silence before Shane spoke up.

"Thanks," he said.

John nodded and waved him off.

Shane was about to leave but turned back.

"What is it?" said John.

Shane shuffled his feet as if to kick dirt.

"You do know Match is one of the kids who's been using that area."

"I know," said John. "We've talked about it again and this time I think he got the message."

"And if he hasn't?"

"Then that's his problem. He's eighteen. If he hasn't figured it out by now, then he'll have to learn the hard way."

CHAPTER 40

Having spent most of the afternoon riding up Pyramid Mountain on the fire road and now on their way back home, Match, Tyson and Grayson were drawn to the new and improved "Area Closed" sign near the lake. Adorned with even more yellow caution tape than before and spanning the trail entrance, it seemed to present itself as a challenge, waiting to be violated.

"Let's just ride home along the road," Match suggested, suspecting what Tyson was thinking, knowing how his buddy's mind worked.

"Screw that," said Tyson, never one to play by the rules.

"But it'll be faster along the road," Grayson offered.

"Fuck off, Gray," said Tyson, motioning to the trail. "The trail is way more kick-ass."

"I guess."

"C'mon. Let's ride," Tyson goaded.

"I don't know," said Match. "My old man sat me down and read me the Riot Act. Parks is serious about the closure this time. He said it's going to be enforced aggressively by the wardens."

"Yeah, right," Tyson howled. "Whatever."

"Whatever yourself," said Match. "Besides, people are saying the grizzlies are back. Why don't we just ride the road home today?"

"No way," said Tyson. "You can chicken out if you want. Grayson and I will ride it on our own. Right, Gray?"

"Ahhh, I'm not sure," said Grayson. "I caught hell after Col's accident and promised my folks I'd stick to the main trails. Think I'll just hang with Match."

Tyson hesitated slightly then gave them both a dirty look. "Suit yourselves, pussies. I'll go by myself."

Grayson looked to Match who shook his head.

"You're gonna get us all in shit, Ty."

"Whatever."

"But what if you run into a bear again? You don't even have any bear spray."

"Right. Bear spray. As if that would've helped."

Straddling his bike Tyson hesitated. "Comin' or not?"

Match and Grayson looked at each other and shook their heads.

"Suit yourself." Without looking back, Tyson ducked under the caution tape, hopped over a log lying across the trail and sped off.

When he was out of sight of the others, he stopped to see if they would follow.

Screw them, he thought, realizing he was on his own.

Slowly he continued along the trail, taking time to confirm that every dark shape in the forest was nothing more than an upturned stump or a dark patch of vegetation.

Looking down the single track, Tyson carefully navigated some of the rockier sections but sped along when the going was good, wanting to get to the other end where the trail emerged onto a main road as quickly as possible. When he figured he was out of earshot of Match and Grayson, he gave a few war whoops to warn any animals that might be around, his memory of the encounter with the grizzlies gnawing at his nerves.

Only ever having ridden the trail a couple of times, and never in the lead, Tyson wasn't entirely certain of the way. The only feature he remembered was the old pine tree with the bear tracks worn into the moss that Match had pointed out on their earlier ride. Beyond that, nothing looked familiar.

At the first major fork he came to, he was forced to dismount and figure out which branch of the trail seemed most

175

likely, walking each until he found an old tire track or some other clue suggesting the way to go. As much as the trail was well used by wildlife, there were places where merging trails forced him to make a choice, both paths similar in appearance with little to indicate which was the branch he needed to follow.

Halfway around the lake, his war whoops louder now, he encountered a particularly confusing stretch of trail and began second-guessing himself, wondering if he should keep going.

But turning around meant he could run into Match and Grayson and lose face for having high-tailed it back to the fire road.

He wasn't prepared to do that.

Ditching his bike, Tyson walked what he thought was the most likely route. As he searched for some sign to confirm a gut feel he'd been down this section of trail before, he stumbled on a huge set of bear tracks and suddenly felt out of his element.

Daylight was fractured under the thick canopy of trees and even though he knew it was not that late, Tyson sensed the day slipping away. When a bank of cloud blocked the sun, adding to the dusk-like feel of the surrounding forest, Tyson felt a shiver run down his spine.

Somewhere off to the side he could hear the rustling of leaves and suddenly a branch snapped. Startled, he jerked his head around to see where the sound had come from and stumbled over a downed log.

Quickly picking himself up, Tyson hurried back the way he'd come.

Just then he heard the unmistakeable huffs of what sounded like a large animal, followed by a series of grunts and more snapping branches.

Quickening his pace, Tyson tried to stay ahead of the sounds, scanning the forest as he hoofed it back to his bike.

Looking over his shoulder as he rounded the last corner, Tyson was certain he could see a dark shape paralleling him through the undergrowth.

Suddenly, a loud roar broke the relative silence of the day and Tyson fell forward, slipping on a downed log next to his bike.

As he scrambled to get up, his legs covered in mud, sweat beading down his face, a high-pitched laugh brought him around to face his assailant.

With her hands on her belly, Harking bent over in the middle of the trail, roaring with laughter. As she straightened up, she pointed at Tyson and smirked, barely able to suppress a huge grin. "God, I think you pissed yourself."

Looking down at his soiled pants, Tyson's expression changed from one of absolute fear to unbridled anger.

"You fucking bitch," he swore, leaping at Harking.

Quickly stifling the laugh, Harking sidestepped Tyson and launched a powerful roundhouse kick into his ass that sent him sprawling face down in the trail again. She was about to laugh again but Tyson was back on his feet in an instant, coming at her a second time. Catching her by surprise, he threw a handful of dirt in Harking's face and grabbed her shirt.

"Fuck," Harking yelled as she tried to wipe her eyes, fending off Tyson's blows with her free hand.

But he was too fast.

Outmanoeuvred for an instant, Harking toppled to the ground and before she could fight him off, Tyson was on top of her.

"Who's laughing now, bitch," Tyson yelled, grinding into Harking's chest so hard it hurt.

Cursing, Harking shoved upward with all her might, finally getting a leg around Tyson and forcefully scissoring him off. As she carried through, she rolled on top and tried to pin his arms, but not before Tyson swung and struck Harking in the jaw.

Momentarily stunned, Harking slumped to the side.

Quickly clambering to his feet Tyson was poised to strike again when he was suddenly grabbed from behind and tossed to the ground.

Seething, Match towered over him, clenched fists at the ready.

"Don't even think about it," Match yelled, digging his fingers into Tyson's arm and dragging him to his feet. As his smaller protégé screamed to be let go, Match shoved Tyson backward and turned his attention to Harking, now on her feet and coiled to fend off the next attack.

"Whoa," said Match, standing between the two combatants as they glared at each other, fuming. "You okay?" He pointed to the raised welt on Harking's cheek.

"Is *she* okay?" Tyson whined, pushing closer. "What about me?"

"Screw you," Harking blurted, as her fist shot past Match and caught Tyson just above the bridge of his nose, sending him to his knees.

Reeling from the blow, Tyson clambered to his feet, holding a hand over the darkening hollow around his eye as blood began to drip from his nose.

"I'm gonna fuckin' kill you," he screamed as he tried to shove Match to the side.

"Whoa," said Match, standing his ground. "It's over."

"Besides, you deserved it," said Harking, wiping her eyes. "You're a dirty little prick."

"You'll find out how dirty I am," said Tyson, jabbing a finger into the air as he cupped his other hand over his nose. "And *this*," he added, glaring at Match, "isn't over."

"Just get on your bike and get outta here," Match warned.

"Yeah, right," Tyson growled before turning back to Harking. "You'll pay for this."

"Yeah, right," Harking snickered. "You've got me shaking in my boots, you little dick. Go home and change your diaper."

"Why don't you shut it?" Match growled, his eyes cutting into Harking.

Catching Match's stare, she said nothing else and brushed herself off.

Turning his back on the pair, Tyson grabbed his bike and rode away, cursing loudly.

When he was out of sight Match turned his attention back to Harking.

"What are you doing here anyway? I thought you were the one telling everyone to stay off this trail."

"Yeah, and did everyone listen?" said Harking. "It's more like what are *you* doing here?"

"Just trying to make sure Tyson didn't screw it up for all of us. He wanted Grayson and I to come with him, but we said no. So he came in on his own."

"And?"

"And I figured he didn't really know the way. I sent Grayson home so he wouldn't get in any more trouble, and told him I'd bring Tyson out the other end. I wasn't expecting to run into anyone, especially not you. And I wasn't expecting this." He reached toward Harking's face but she quickly brushed him away.

"I'm fine," she said. "It's swollen a little but it's not as bad as the black eye that little prick's gonna have."

"I don't doubt that, but ..."

"But nothing. He's a dirty fighter. He threw dirt in my face and I couldn't see. Otherwise he'd have more than a black eye."

Match chuckled and shook his head.

"What?" said Harking.

"Nothing. You just don't take any shit, do you?"

"What'd you expect? You think every girl's like goddamn Brianna? Such a prissy little mouthpiece."

"Hey," said Match, raising his hands. "I'm not goin' there." He looked around and turned back to Harking. "Where's your bike?"

"I stashed it," said Harking, pointing a thumb over her shoulder at the trail behind her.

"Well let's go find it and get outta here."

"No," Harking blurted, almost too quickly, not wanting to let on she also needed to retrieve the recorder. "I'll make my own way out."

"I just thought ..."

"You thought what? That I need your help?" Harking shook her head. "I don't."

"What is it with you?" Match challenged.

"What is it with *you*? Your father's the park superintendent and you're out riding closed trails."

"I just told you why I came back here. I wouldn't have if Tyson hadn't. Geez, there's no freakin' way to please you."

"Just stay off this trail," said Harking. "That would please me."

"Yeah, well you should too, instead of being such a hypocrite." Without another word, Match turned and walked to his bike. Shooting one last glance at Harking he shook his head and rode off.

CHAPTER 41

"So you left it like that?" Simi scolded, rolling over to the edge of the bed and looking over Harking's shoulder. "The guy helps you out and you just brush him off." She put her head close to Harking's and whispered in her ear, "You know the rumour was he wanted to ask you to grad."

"Whatever," said Harking, pulling away and turning to stare at her friend. "As if I was going to go to that. Besides, he probably went with Brianna freakin' Smith."

"Actually, he was there on his own. Looks like he and her are done."

"Yeah, well, I don't care."

"I didn't figure you did. I'm just sayin'.'"

"Well you can say whatever you want." Harking glowered. "And I didn't need his help on the trail."

"Kind of sounds like you did." Simi was persistent.

"I can handle Tyson Griffin on my own."

"Huhuh?"

"Huhuh," Harking replied, pulling away and looking at Simi. "Don't give me that look." She sat back as Simi sat up on her knees on the bed. "What?"

"Maybe you should lighten up on Tyson. He's probably got enough to deal with."

"Like what? Coming from a broken home and all? The fact his father is an asshole? Is that supposed to make me feel sorry for him?"

"I'm just saying." Simi pushed her hair out of her eyes. "What are you looking for anyway?"

"Not sure," said Harking, thumbing through one of her father's journals. "I'm still trying to figure these things out." She tossed the notebook on the pile and picked up another.

"What's your plan for summer work?" said Simi, changing the subject.

"Don't know yet," said Harking, flipping pages. "Probably just stay at the bike shop."

"You should have applied for a summer job with Parks."

Harking scrunched up her face. "Not sure if that's for me."

"Seriously? You're made for it."

"How so?"

"Outdoorsy, fit, passionate about the environment."

"Passionate?" Harking scoffed.

"Yeah, passionate. About those bears for sure. And other animals, too. Not many people have a peregrine falcon tattooed down their arm."

"Yeah, well I'm not sure Parks is passionate about the bears."

"No? Not after that story you told me about Shane Ross and the little cub that was killed?"

"Shane's different."

"Is he? My dad says he's never met so many people that give a shit about what happens in their backyard. And not just the wardens he's met. He says pretty well every Parks person he's encountered has impressed him."

"Hmph."

"They all love this place and have their own ways of trying to protect it."

"Right. Whatever."

"Whatever nothing," Simi scolded again. "You think you're the only one who cares about this place?"

"I didn't say that."

"It sure sounded like it. Anyway, all I'm saying is you should give Parks a try. You'd be so good."

"Why don't you? You seem to be such a cheerleader for them."

"Maybe I will. Maybe I won't. I'm probably going to take a year off and just travel. Nice as it is, I could use a break from this place.

"But you want me to stay and work for Parks," Harking countered. "What if I want to travel?"

"Then travel. If that's what you want. All I'm saying is Parks might be a great fit for you. It might also give you a different perspective. Anyway, don't knock it before you try it."

"Hmmm," Harking mumbled.

"Maybe you should chat with Megan what's-her-name," Simi suggested.

"Weaver," said Harking. "Megan Weaver."

"Yeah, her," said Simi. "She's a woman and a warden to boot. Maybe she could give you some advice instead of always listening to Marion."

"I don't listen to everything Marion says."

"No?"

"No."

Simi chuckled.

"What?"

"You don't even realize how much you sound like Marion. You're like a clone."

"Am not."

"Okay, girl. You just keep believin' that." Simi rolled off the bed and danced across the room, singing. "Don't stop believin' ..."

"Oh gawd." Harking shuddered. "Besides, what if I do?" she said. "Marion's got her heart in the right place when it comes to this park. And the bears."

"I don't doubt that," said Simi, prancing back and plopping down next to Harking. "But as my dad reminds me constantly, not everything is black and white." She chuckled as she pointed to herself and Harking.

"Maybe some things are though," Harking countered. "Maybe your dad should just focus on his job and figure out what happened between the boys and bears."

"Ouch."

"Well it's true. I still haven't heard anything about the investigation."

"You mean you haven't heard what you want to hear," said Simi. "Anyway, I'm not getting into it with you. We were talking summer jobs. And like I said, maybe you should talk to Megan Weaver or Shane about working for Parks."

"What are you, some kind of career counsellor?"

"No, but I think it would be better if you talked to someone in the know. Shane or Megan would probably give you a straight answer about what it's like instead of going on what Marion says."

"I told you I don't always listen to Marion."

"Besides," Simi continued, ignoring Harking, "it helps to have someone on the inside when you're looking for work."

"Yeah, right, Counsellor Odili."

"It's true, *Marion*."

CHAPTER 42

Marion had never worried about how others in town felt about the sometimes-abrasive ways she spoke her mind when it came to matters affecting the park. As she often told Harking, she didn't give a rat's ass what others thought. She was going to say what she had to, especially when she knew there were Parks staff who agreed with her views but were reluctant to express them, worried about their jobs.

She had already seen too many good staff moved to other parks when they voiced their objections to some proposed development, replaced by someone less opposed to satisfying some developer's dreams of pulling in more tourists, making more money, park values be damned.

Marion was willing to speak up.

But after seeing how the years of protest had taken its toll on Malcolm, there were times when she wanted to leave the fight to others younger than herself.

Then again, that wasn't a path she wanted Harking to go down, since it could have the effect of alienating her from others her age and possibly limit her options in a small town like Jasper.

For now, with school over and her job at the bike shop keeping her in pocket money, Harking had some stability in her life. It was probably best things stayed that way.

Marion knew Phil Sykes liked Harking and was impressed not only by her work ethic at the bike shop, but her infectious enthusiasm for mountain biking in particular. He likely wouldn't pay much attention to the rumblings in town about Harking's own hardline position on the need for trail closures, dictating where bikers should and shouldn't be allowed to go to keep the bears safe even if it did frustrate some of his customers including the harder-core riders in town.

In fact, he generally agreed with Harking.

Still, Marion was a little suspect when she saw Tyson Griffin's father walk into Syko Cycle late on a Friday evening and couldn't stifle her curiosity as she walked past. Doing a one-eighty as inconspicuously as possible, she slid in through the shop's open door and pretended to browse through the racks of cycling clothes, keeping one ear tuned to the animated conversation that had immediately started as Andrew Griffin approached Phil who was behind the counter.

Straining to hear every word, Marion edged closer, her ears perking up at the mention of Harking's name.

"Damn bears," she heard Tyson's father say as Phil Sykes tried to deflect the comments.

"They're partly why this place is a national park," said Sykes. "And they need a voice."

"A voice," Tyson's father scowled. "That old battle axe, Seawell, is voice enough for every goddamn animal in this park."

Marion bristled at the mention of her name but bit her tongue and slid back between the racks when Phil shot a glance her way.

"Keep your voice down, Andrew," Sykes turned his attention back to Tyson's father. "And watch your language. This is a public place."

Marion was unable to decipher much else other than Harking's name mentioned a few more times along with some reference to the bears. Sensing from Phil's body language that he was about to put an end to the discussion, she slid out from behind the racks and started for the door, but came up short as she almost walked into Tyson Griffin, his bruised and swollen face and black eye giving her a start.

"What are you gawkin' at?" he asked rudely, his voice loud enough to attract his father's attention.

Stepping away from the store counter, Andrew Griffin approached Marion, followed closely behind by Phil.

Momentarily speechless and somewhat embarrassed, Marion was confused about what to do next.

"I, I," she stammered, not used to being caught on the defensive.

"You've got no business eavesdropping on a private conversation," said Andrew Griffin. "You're part of the damn problem with this town."

"Whoa there," said Phil Sykes, inserting himself between Marion and the father-son duo. "I told you to watch what you say, Andrew."

Andrew Griffin appeared to want to challenge Sykes, but thought better of it. Without another word, he grabbed Tyson by the shoulder and pushed him toward the door. "C'mon," he growled as Tyson shot a quick scowl over his shoulder toward Marion. "Let's get outta here."

When the pair had departed, Phil turned to Marion. "You okay?"

"Yes," said Marion, putting on a brave face, even though her body was still shaking from the encounter. For whatever reason, Andrew Griffin's verbal assault left her feeling oddly unsettled and out of sorts. Hearing what she'd always suspected were whispered comments, she felt distinctly unwanted.

"I should be going," she said. Brushing off Phil's concern, Marion made her way slowly to the door. Once outside she stopped and took a deep breath, closing her eyes for a moment then opening them to stare at the fading slopes of Signal Mountain as dusk settled over the town.

With a huge sigh, she turned and began to walk home, but immediately noticed Tyson leaning against a shop window a short distance away, apparently texting someone. Alone, away from his father's overbearing presence, Tyson had the same foul expression on his face when he noticed Marion leaving as he had had in the bike shop.

Unnerved, Marion turned around and walked in the opposite direction, intent on taking a different route home in an attempt to avoid Tyson. When she looked over her shoulder, Tyson was nowhere to be seen and she breathed a sigh of relief.

Regaining her confidence, she walked one block and decided to cut back to her usual route home. But as she turned the corner, Tyson was there again, in the same pose, leaning against another storefront.

Turning back, Marion went two more blocks out of her way and was relieved not to see Tyson when she rounded the next corner.

Picking up her pace, she quickly made her way home, periodically glancing over her shoulder to confirm she wasn't being followed. Finally, at her front door, she found it locked, and remembered that Harking wouldn't be back until later in the evening. Fumbling in her jacket pocket for the keys, she let herself in, once again breathing a sigh of relief as she turned on the lights and hung up her jacket.

Suddenly hungry and thirsty, Marion slipped out of her hikers and went to the kitchen, turning on the kettle before reaching for the tea and crackers.

Outside, the streetlights were just beginning to come on as Marion peered into the evening light before pulling down the shade on the kitchen window. With the tea and crackers on a small tray, she retired to the living room and placed the tray next to her chair. She turned on the television to watch the late news and was about to close the living room curtains when she noticed something outside.

Peering out the window, she could just make out the shape of a person, standing in the shadow of the streetlight directly across from her house. Although she couldn't be certain, she couldn't help but think Tyson Griffin had followed her home.

Slowly closing the curtain, Marion felt chilled as she stood alone in the house and wished Malcolm was still around.

I miss him so much.

Closing her eyes for a moment the memories flooded back; the many adventures they'd had together, the way his presence seemed to fill up the house.

With Susan gone as well, it seems so empty now.

Finally regaining her composure she took charge of her emotions.

But I can go and visit Susan anytime.

And besides, Harking should be home soon.

Hesitating at the window, she slid the curtain apart just enough to peer through the opening. Whoever had been standing in the shadows was gone, but still Marion felt unsettled.

Returning to her chair, she reached for the television remote. As she flipped through the channels, she couldn't help notice her hand was shaking again. For some reason she couldn't ascertain, she sensed something was different, but couldn't put her finger on it. *This can't just be my age finally catching up to me*

Muting the television, Marion strained to hear anything out of the ordinary, but with the exception of the clock on the mantle, all was still.

Turning the volume back up on the television, she settled into her chair and sipped her tea, savouring its warmth between mouthfuls of crackers. Feeling more comfortable than she had all day, she pulled a small quilt over her legs and quickly fell asleep.

CHAPTER 43

Harking was later than she expected as she bound up the stairs to the front door of Marion's house. Surprised to find the door locked, she quietly let herself in and slipped out of her coat, curious that the television was still on at this late hour.

Marion must have fallen asleep in front of the TV again, Harking thought as she kicked off her boots, suddenly feeling an ominous chill. Sensing something wasn't quite right she headed into the living room.

Marion was in her favourite chair, partially covered with her lap quilt.

Yup, asleep again, Harking thought as she walked over to her.

But then she noticed the overturned tray on the floor by Marion's side. A pool of spilled tea sat next to it, holding the shards of a broken teacup.

"Marion, wake up," said Harking, her voice rising as she nudged Marion on the shoulder, causing her head to slump to the side. "Oh, Marion." Her face felt cool.

Kneeling by her side, Harking frantically took Marion's wrist and checked for a pulse.

Only able to feel a very slight pulse, she grabbed the phone from the coffee table and dialed 911, fighting off the tears.

"Send an ambulance," she blurted when the dispatcher answered, rhyming off the address and quickly responding to his questions about the circumstances. "Please, hurry."

Waiting for what seemed like an eternity, Harking knelt at Marion's feet, grasping Marion's hands in her own. When she finally heard the siren and the sound of a vehicle pulling up in front of the house, she went to the front door.

"She's in the living room," said Harking as two paramedics entered the house carrying bulky first aid kits. Hovering over them, Harking held her breath as the first paramedic did a quick assessment, checking Marion's vital signs.

"Well?" said Harking.

"Faint and irregular pulse," said the paramedic, ignoring Harking and speaking to her partner. "We need to get her to the hospital."

At that moment Shane Ross appeared in the hallway and immediately went to Harking's side. "I overheard the call from Dispatch and figured I better get over here," he said, holding her in a strong embrace. "You okay?"

Harking nodded.

"Is Marion okay?" Shane added, speaking to the paramedics as they prepared to transport their patient.

"Not sure." The first paramedic shot a serious look at Shane. "But we need to get her to the hospital ASAP."

Worried sick, Harking watched silently as Shane helped place Marion on a wheeled stretcher, then stepped out of the way as the paramedics took her to the ambulance.

"We can follow them to the hospital if you want," he said to Harking.

"Sure."

Arriving at the hospital just behind the ambulance, Shane escorted Harking inside Emergency and asked her to wait in the sitting area while he followed up with one of the nurses. Worried Shane seemed to be gone a long time Harking breathed an audible sigh when he finally reappeared in the hallway.

"It'll be awhile before we find out anything," he said as he sat down next to her. "They're just running some tests."

"I wonder what happened?" said Harking, her attention split between Shane and texting on her phone. "I know Marion hasn't been feeling well lately but I thought it was just a cold or flu."

"Well, she's not getting any younger," Shane suggested.

"I guess not," said Harking. "Plus she's been getting worked up about the bears. I know she spoke to Match's dad about the boys."

Shane smiled. "Well, she's a fighter and passionate about the park, but for her own sake, maybe she needs to slow down."

Harking scoffed. "You do know her, right?"

"Yeah, I guess that's not going to happen," Shane agreed.

They were sitting together in silence, each seeming to privately mull over the situation, when Simi Odili walked in.

Looking surprised, Shane turned to Harking.

"I texted her," said Harking, pre-empting his question.

"Is Marion okay?" Simi asked, embracing Harking as she stood to meet her.

"We don't know yet," Shane offered. "But thanks for coming."

At that moment a nurse approached the trio, wearing a faint smile.

"How's Marion?" Harking asked, getting right to the point.

"She's conscious but a little confused," the nurse replied. "Sorry, you can't see her right now, but we think she'll be okay. Still we'd like to keep her overnight under observation. The doctor will reassess her in the morning and decide if she can go home at that time. You can see her then."

"That's great," Shane offered.

"Yeah," said Harking. Relieved, she thanked the nurse and pulled Simi and Shane into an embrace. "Thanks for being with me."

"No worries," Shane replied, blushing slightly.

"I can stay with you tonight if you want," said Simi, smiling at Harking.

"That would be great." Harking turned to Shane. "Thanks again for showing up when you did. We can walk home from here. The fresh air will do me good."

"Again, no worries," Shane replied. "I'll check back with you in the morning to find out how Marion's doing." With that he tipped his hat to Simi. "Force of habit," he confessed, looking at Harking with a grin.

CHAPTER 44

The night's dreams seemed especially real as Harking tossed and turned in her bed next to Simi; the first a static-filled kaleidoscope of short scenes with Marion, segueing to a sequence of Harking and Marion arguing over how best to protect the bears and the park. It ended with Harking screaming that if she didn't protect the bears no one would, leaving Marion with a look of deep hurt on her face before her image faded away.

Next Harking was in a howling whiteout, following a track, calling out to her father somewhere ahead of her, skiing in and out of focus, disappearing over the edge as she and the others (there were always others) tried to keep up, the ghostlike figures seemingly luring her toward an abyss.

Her father was the only one she recognized, the other faces hidden in the shadows of hoodies and long hair. But with every recurrence of the dream, more detail surfaced: snippets of information that helped Harking piece together those final minutes, including the moment that changed everything, the loud crack of the cornice snapping, the echo ricocheting off nearby mountains, the sudden gust of wind pushing her over as a river of snow rushed downslope, pulling her along, trees snapping as the snow plowed a path into the valley, her father disappearing into the maelstrom of white, yelling ...

... *Harking!*

Fast-forward through the avalanche and Harking was clawing at the snow, digging frantically.

"Dad!" she screamed, as she cleared the snow from around his head.

She was yelling for him again when Simi snatched her from the dream.

■ ■ ■

"Harking, wake up." Simi prodded Harking's side until she opened her eyes then leaned in, hovering over her friend. "God, what were you dreaming about?"

Without replying, Harking rolled over to look away from Simi as tears streamed down her cheek.

"Harking, c'mon. You okay?" Simi reached a hand across and gently massaged Harking's shoulders and neck. "Your phone was buzzing. Might be the hospital." She reached for Harking's phone on the bed stand and passed it to her.

Harking rolled over, wiped the tears from her eyes and read the text. "Yeah, Marion's already awake. The nurse says she'll be ready to leave in about an hour." Laying the phone aside she stared at the ceiling briefly, then quietly got up and stood in front of the mirror in her underwear.

"What a night," she said, pulling a brush through her knotted hair.

Simi paused and yawned then wiped the sleep out of her eyes. "What were you dreaming about anyway? I had to sleep on the edge just to stay away from you."

"Sorry," Harking bowed her head, trying to recall the dreams. "Everything," she said finally. "The bears, Marion, the avalanche."

"You've got a lot going on up there." Simi tapped her own head then rolled into the centre of the bed.

"Yeah, too much." Harking paused. "But the dreams all feel so real. And with each one I feel like there's more detail. Like I'm remembering more of what happened that day."

"How so?" Simi rolled over and lay staring at Harking.

"Well, I always thought I was right behind Dad. But I remember someone, at least one person, getting past me. They almost knocked me over."

"Well, all I know is there were several people in front of me," Simi replied. "You and your dad, Match and Tyson for sure. I was a little behind so there might have been others."

"Well in the end there were just four of us caught in the slide."

"So maybe Match or Tyson got ahead of you?"

"Hmm, I don't know. All I could hear was Dad calling out, saying to stay back."

"Maybe it wasn't you he was calling to. Maybe he didn't know who was behind him. He just knew someone was."

"Maybe," said Harking. "Either way, I still feel responsible." Harking faltered. "Doesn't matter now, anyway," she added solemnly.

Breaking the moment of silence Simi rolled out of bed and stretched then walked up behind Harking, still standing at the mirror. "C'mon, you can't dwell on what happened. It was an accident. It was nobody's fault, especially not yours. You did what you could. Stop beating yourself up over things you can't change."

"I don't know."

"Besides," Simi continued. "Your dad would be the last one to blame you. And you do know what he'd be saying if he saw you like this." Simi leaned in and whispered, "What's done is done. Time to move on."

Standing tall, all five foot eleven, Harking looked past herself at Simi's reflection and nodded. "You're right. He would."

"Besides," said Simi, trying to maintain the momentum, "it's time to get dressed. Marion will be waiting."

CHAPTER 45

It only took Marion a day to get back to her old self and she was soon busy welcoming friends and neighbours who dropped by after hearing she had been in the hospital. As the gathering in her kitchen ebbed and flowed she was quickly inundated with food, flowers and get well cards, the house bustling with activity until noon. By then, most of the well-wishers had gone back home, leaving Harking and Marion sitting at the kitchen table with Paige, who'd shown up early and stayed for the morning.

"So how long do you think you'll stay with your daughter?" Paige asked Marion, upon hearing she planned to leave town for a while.

"At least until they can figure out what's causing these spells. Susan has been after me for some time to come live with them and I'm actually looking forward to spending more time with my grandchildren. But at some point I will need to get back to my own space and routine." She turned to Harking. "I'm hoping you'll stay here and look after the place for me while I'm gone?"

"Of course," Harking replied.

"Oh," Paige remarked, seemingly taken off guard by the comment. "I was really hoping you'd come live with us." She pulled her chair closer to the table and focussed on Harking. "Now that Col is out of the hospital, you'd be a positive influence, certainly better than those boys he's been hanging out with."

"Right," said Harking, raising her eyes at Paige.

"But I really don't want you staying here on your own." Paige looked from Harking to Marion.

"Why not?" Harking said. "School's almost done and I've got a job that I like. Besides I'll be eighteen in a few days."

"God, that's right," Paige conceded, stalled in a moment of reflection. "I can't believe it's been eighteen years."

"And if it would work," Marion interjected, "Col is welcome to stay here as well." She caught a hard stare from Harking then added, "But only if it would work for you both."

"Col's probably fine where he is," said Paige, saving Harking from a response she might later regret. "I've spoken with Grayson's parents and he's fine there for the summer. And I guess Harking is fine here." Harking knew her mother was offering an olive branch. "Maybe we can revisit it toward the end of summer, or whenever you're thinking about coming back," she added, directing the comment to Marion.

"That works for me," Marion agreed.

"What about you, Harking?" Paige asked, negotiating a settlement.

"Sure," Harking nodded. "As Dad would've said, we'll cross that creek when we get to it."

"Yes, he would say that, wouldn't he?" Paige smiled.

"Well," said Marion, getting up from the table. "I should pull some things together. Susan said she'd be here by early afternoon and would like to get going right away so we can get to her place before dark. I don't want to keep her waiting." With that she left Paige and Harking sitting at the kitchen table, awkwardly silent before Paige broke the ice.

"You look tired."

"Yeah. I'm not sleeping super well."

"How come? Is there something on your mind?"

"Hmph, yeah," said Harking. "Lots." She paused. "I've been having terrible dreams about the avalanche, the bears, the boys, you name it."

Somewhat reluctantly she told Paige a few of the details.

"And now Marion," she added.

"Marion will be missed here," said Paige.

"By some," Harking replied.

"You might be surprised," said Paige. "Marion knows a lot of people in town. Just look at how many showed up here this morning."

"Right," Harking muttered.

"They might not have always supported her outwardly," Paige conceded, "but they were still behind her most of the time."

"That's the problem with this place," said Harking. "People say they support you but sit on their hands when it's time to stand up and be noticed. It's so damn hypocritical."

"Harking," said Paige, pursing her lips.

"What? It's true. Marion never knows where people stand. It still eats away at her."

Paige sighed. "You're probably right. I know there were times your father felt the same way. But still, this is a good community. Remember how many people came to support the Earth Day event you and Simi organized?"

Harking did recall the event, and the overwhelming turnout was a good reminder that people did care.

"Besides," said Paige, interrupting the memory. "We can't be fighting all the time. You have to pick your battles."

"A lot of people say that," Harking mused. "But for some that's just an excuse to never fight for anything."

"Maybe not that you see." Paige closed her eyes and massaged her temples then sat back in the chair and looked around the kitchen. "But there's more than one way to protest." She got up and poured herself a glass of water then turned back to Harking. "And sometimes people are just tired of it all. Tired of fighting. Tired of being on the offensive. It takes its toll you know."

"Believe me, *I* know," said Harking.

"I was thinking more of Marion," said her mother.

"So was I." Harking bowed her head as a momentary silence descended on the house, broken only by the high-pitched trill of a flock of cedar waxwings swarming the blossoms on several ornamental trees in Marion's front yard.

Reflecting on the morning's activity, Harking *was* impressed by the number of people who actually did show up to check in on Marion, most of whom Harking barely knew or didn't recognize at all.

But a few in the crowd gathered in Marion's living room and kitchen had stood out, especially Shane Ross, dressed in his "Sunday best," as he would describe it, an eye-catching dress shirt and spanking new jeans, devoid of any obvious cowboy paraphernalia. He'd even ditched his ropers for a pair of lace-up dress shoes.

He cleans up well, Harking thought, smiling as she'd watched Shane and Paige sharing a laugh.

She couldn't help but notice how her mother looked younger, her eyes glistening as she seemed entranced by Shane's stories. And despite the new clothes, which Shane swore he hated wearing, he looked more at ease than Harking had ever seen him.

Even Simi had noticed the difference in Paige, commenting on it when she caught Harking staring at them in the living room. With no one else her own age showing up at Marion's it was a nice gesture on Simi's part.

Harking was lost in that thought when Marion reappeared and motioned to her. "Paige, if you don't mind, I'd like to speak with Harking alone for a moment."

"Oh, sure," said Paige, getting up from the table. "I should be going anyway. I need to check on Col." Hugging Marion and wishing her well she said goodbye then turned to Harking. "Let's stay in touch. We should do something for your birthday. Go out for dinner perhaps."

"Yeah," Harking nodded, reciprocating with her own olive branch. "That'd be nice."

After Paige had left, Marion sat Harking back down at the kitchen table. "I want you to have this," she said, unclasping the grizzly bear talisman then carefully securing it around Harking's neck.

"But ... are you sure?"

"Of course I'm sure." Marion stared into Harking's eyes. "With everything that's happened I didn't have time to buy you a proper birthday gift. And until I return, you are the keeper of the bears. I have no doubt you'll do your best to protect them."

"I don't know what to say," said Harking, her eyes misting over as she fingered the talisman, centering it on her chest. "Other than thanks."

"No thanks are necessary," said Marion. She smiled. "You've been a joy to have around and I'm the one who should be thanking you. You probably saved my life by getting home when you did."

"Oh I doubt that," Harking blushed. "You're a warrior, remember."

CHAPTER 46

With the area closure seemingly working and the bears less of an issue, Shane debated how he would deal with Tyson having been inside the closed area, a truth he had only managed to worm out of Harking after he quizzed her about the welt on her face.

Shane had toyed with the idea of letting the infraction slide since it could mean implicating Harking as well as the superintendent's son. He had also heard the rumours about Tyson's mistreatment, literally at the hands of his father, and considering he had even less time for Andrew Griffin, Shane thought about cutting Tyson some slack. But when Harking told him about the fight and Shane saw her bruised face, he was hell bent on charging Tyson.

If nothing else, it would let others in town know the park was serious about enforcing the trail closure.

Apart from all of this, Shane realized he also had to think about the other consequences of formally charging Tyson. No doubt Andrew would go ballistic and put a lot of pressure on John Walleski to have the charges dropped, but Shane felt he had to take his chances that John would keep his word and back Shane up when the going got tough.

His biggest concern, though, was not revealing how he'd acquired his information. He didn't want to let on that Harking had told him about the fight or that he'd also conscripted her to put her camera out again, at least until the one he'd ordered for the park arrived. The camera was actually Megan Weaver's idea more than his own but he was game to go along with it.

The date-stamped pictures Harking had been able to get showing Tyson in the area after the closure signs had been erected were clearly all the proof he needed.

Unfortunately, there were also pictures of Match Walleski, and Shane knew that revealing those to a defence lawyer could be a problem.

Unless of course he didn't.

Although he was obligated to disclose all evidence to the defence, Shane didn't want charging Tyson Griffin to backfire and he especially didn't want to paint John Walleski into a corner. John had enough challenges as park superintendent and maintaining credibility with the local community was paramount. Keeping him onside was in Shane's best interest, not to mention in the bears' best interest as well.

Thankfully, the sow seemed to be keeping her cubs out of sight, at least for the time being, but Shane knew there would be hell to pay if she and her cubs got into any more trouble, even if it wasn't their fault.

Weighing everything, Shane decided to go for broke and charge Tyson with entering a closed area.

The good Lord hates a coward, he thought, as he made his way to the Griffin's house with a summons for Tyson.

Thankfully, Tyson was eighteen at the time of the incident, so Shane could avoid all the hassle associated with dealing with him as a youth. Technically, legally, he didn't even have to deal with Andrew Griffin at all. But Shane wasn't so naïve as to think Tyson's father wouldn't get involved. Any parent would. And if Andrew Griffin challenged the charges and insisted on seeing all of the evidence Shane had against Tyson, he'd have to figure out what to do, especially with the pictures.

But Shane would cross that bridge when he came to it.

If he came to it.

Shane wasn't above steering attention away from any of the facts that would lessen his chances of successfully convicting Tyson. He reasoned that was for the Griffin's lawyer to figure out and it wasn't his role to make his opponent's job any easier.

His job was to convince the judge that Tyson had broken the law and that in itself could be a bit of a challenge. Jasper's circuit judge had a reputation for rarely siding with Parks on legal issues, so Shane knew that without enough well-documented evidence charges simply wouldn't stick.

In this case, though, Shane was confident that despite all of the tricks a defence lawyer could throw at him around how he acquired his information, Harking's photos of Tyson would be enough proof to convince any judge.

Pulling up to the Griffin's house, Shane slid out of the warden truck and made his way to the front door.

But before he could knock or ring the bell, Shane heard the door handle turn.

If he had a camera, he would have loved to get a picture of the look on Tyson's face when he saw Shane standing outside.

"Mornin,' Tyson," Shane said, trying to maintain a straight face himself.

"Yeah?" Tyson stammered, looking past Shane at the truck before turning his attention back to the envelope in Shane's hand.

"I've got a summons here for you to appear in court," said Shane. "You're being charged with entering a closed area."

"*Charged with what?*" Andrew Griffin's voice boomed out from behind Tyson before he pushed his son aside and stepped out of the house to confront Shane.

"Entering a closed area," Shane calmly repeated, stepping back when Andrew tried to grab the envelope out of Shane's hand.

"Give me that," said Andrew.

"Sorry," Shane said as he quickly pulled it away and stepped around Andrew. "But this is for your son."

"You've been served," Shane said to Tyson, passing the envelope to him then stepping back to deal with his father.

"He's an adult," Shane quickly explained, staring Andrew Griffin in the eyes. "No offence, but the law requires me to serve the papers to Tyson, not you."

In a fit of rage, Andrew Griffin tore the envelope away from his son and ripped it open, quickly scanning the summons before re-focussing on Shane.

"Seriously? You're charging him with biking ... on a park trail?"

"Not quite," said Shane. "He was on a wildlife trail in a closed area. Tyson is being charged with ignoring the closure."

Before Andrew Griffin could reply, Tyson poked his head out from behind his father. "He has no proof, Dad. It's his word against ours."

Shane was about to respond, but before he could, Andrew Griffin pushed Tyson inside the house. "Shut up, Tyson," he yelled as he slammed the door and turned back to face Shane.

"I don't need this hassle," Andrew said, waving the summons in Shane's face.

"Sorry," said Shane, turning to walk back to his truck. "Just doing my job."

"But Tyson's right," said Andrew, following Shane lockstep back to his vehicle. "It's your word against his."

"Not really," Shane replied. He got in the truck and rolled down the window. "I've got proof." He pulled out the picture of Tyson on the trail, gripping it tightly when Andrew tried to pull it away.

"Yeah, well Tyson says he wasn't the only one there," said Andrew. "If you charge him, you better charge Harking Thompson and Match Walleski as well."

"Don't know anything about that," Shane lied. "This here's the only photo I have," he added, waving the picture in the air again before placing it on the truck seat beside him.

"We'll see about that," said Andrew.

"Guess we will," said Shane. Without another word, Shane tipped his Stetson to Andrew, rolled up the window and drove away.

CHAPTER 47

Forewarned by Shane about Andrew Griffin's reaction, John Walleski sat back holding the phone away from his ear as Tyson's father yelled at him from the other end. When Andrew had finished, John spoke calmly into the phone.

"I don't know anything about that, Andrew. I guess you'll have to do what you have to do. But here's something to think about – by all accounts Tyson and the other boys are lucky they weren't seriously hurt when they were on that trail a few weeks back. The fact that Col Thompson only suffered a concussion is something we should all be grateful for." John shifted in his chair before continuing. "We need to send a serious message about not using parts of the park that are closed to human use. This doesn't just protect the bears. It protects people too. If you want to challenge that in court, be my guest. But I'd advise against it. Tyson clearly ignored the closure. It is my wardens' job to enforce it."

Before Andrew could respond, John politely said goodbye and hung up, satisfied that this time around he had stood his ground with Andrew Griffin and said what he had to say.

"Hopefully he gives it some thought," said John, looking across his desk at Shane.

"You did well," Shane grinned. "Thanks. And hopefully that's the end of it. I'd sure hate to drag Harking and Match into this."

"I appreciate that," said John.

"Besides," said Shane. "I know Match was only trying to get Tyson outta there. Harking said as much."

"Hmm." Walleski raised his eyebrows. "I'm not sure it was a wise move to involve Harking."

"Well, what's done is done," Shane said unapologetically. He pulled a tin of snuff from a shirt pocket and took off the lid. "I figured it wouldn't take much time before someone decided to stick their nose up at the idea of the closure. And Harking's the only one I know with a trail camera."

Plucking a pinch of snuff from the tin he popped it into his mouth before adding, "I didn't want to miss an opportunity. With any luck, the message will get through to everyone in town that we're serious about the closure and Tyson will be the first and last person we have to charge for going back there."

"I hope you're right," said John, motioning to the phone. "Andrew Griffin can be tough to deal with at the best of times. And when your kid's involved, emotions can cloud the issue, especially when family reputation is at stake."

"Reputation?" Shane scoffed. "You do know what Griffin's so-called *family reputation* is, right? Divorced former wife-abuser who now takes his frustrations out on his son."

"I've heard the rumours," John acknowledged. "And I guess Match has hinted at Tyson getting a licking or two from his father."

"Sounds like it's a regular occurrence," said Shane. "It's the one thing that bugs me with charging Tyson. The possibility that Andrew might go overboard on him."

"That's not our worry," said John.

"I kind of think it is," Shane countered. "As much as I hate what he did to Harking, he is only eighteen."

"Eighteen means he's an adult," said John.

"In the eyes of the law," said Shane. "But being guys you and I both know eighteen year old males are still pretty immature. Hell, I'd like to think that growing up on a farm in rural Saskatchewan, I was pretty much a man by the time I turned eighteen. But I wasn't. I was still pretty green and still just a kid. So is Tyson, even more so." Shane paused. "And sometimes, all a kid needs is a break."

John quietly digested what Shane said. "But you still want to go ahead with charging him?"

"Got to," said Shane. "Right now, saving those bears is more important to me. But I'd still like to figure out a way to head off Andrew Griffin if he decides to take it out on his son." He got up to leave but turned back. "By the way, Tyson's first appearance in court is set for later next week. Andrew can decide if it goes past that. If Tyson pleads guilty, this can all be over on the same day."

"And if not?"

"Then it could get complicated," said Shane.

CHAPTER 48

It was the day of Tyson's first court appearance and Harking was up bright and early, intent on getting a good seat in the courtroom, not only for her own benefit, but also so she could give Marion a blow-by-blow description of the day's proceedings. Now living with her daughter in southern British Columbia, Marion still wanted to stay abreast of the happenings in Jasper, at least until she got back to town.

With Marion gone, Harking found the house quieter than she liked, slowly realizing that although she was a bit of an introvert, she missed having someone to bounce things off, someone who provided a counterpoint to her own musings. Not having Marion around added to the loneliness Harking felt whenever she thought about her father, and, for that matter, her mother and Col.

Harking and Col had had a lot of good times growing up in the mountains, hiking and camping in the backcountry, exploring her parents' favourite haunts, soaking in everything they taught them, and learning by osmosis how to travel in places that were, for the most part, still wild, out of reach of technology and days from help if anything went wrong, the types of places that cautioned you to only take calculated risks, since one wrong move could kill you.

Sitting in the kitchen, she was thinking about all of the good times when she heard a knock on the front door.

Answering it, she was surprised to see one of the town's two lawyers, Thadius Grimes, standing outside in the rain, his diminutive frame barely reconcilable with the huge voice that was his trademark.

"Morning, Harking," he pronounced loudly. "Mind if I come in?" He opened the door and slid past Harking into the front porch, the lingering smell of his aftershave almost causing Harking to retch.

"Good morning, Mr. Grimes." She barely managed to choke out the words. "How are you?"

The last time she'd had any dealings with Thadius Grimes was after her father died. As a beneficiary listed in Dan Thompson's will, she had to be present along with Paige and Col when the contents of the will were read out. That had been a very hard day.

This time she had no idea what the visit was about.

But before she could say anything else, Thadius Grimes held out a small package wrapped in brown paper and placed it in her hands.

"I was on my way to the courthouse, but thought I should drop this off first," he said, his eyes betraying the same hint of compassion she'd noticed from time to time during the proceedings to deal with her father's will.

Despite the stories that Thadius Grimes was a tough old bird when it came to practicing law, Harking found him to be mildly amusing and kind of took a liking to his quirky nature. "I'm sorry," he said, screwing up his face and blinking uncontrollably. "It's a few days late, but with everything that was going on with Marion I figured you had your hands full. I thought it best to wait." He smiled. "Happy belated eighteenth birthday by the way."

Taking the package, Harking turned it over in her hands and noted the simple address, *Harking A. Thompson, Jasper.* Immediately recognizing her father's handwriting, she read the inscription: *To be opened on your 18th birthday.*

With everything that had happened in the past few days Harking had completely forgotten her birthday, only now realizing it was a milestone that carried some weight. She was now legally considered an adult.

Thanking Thadius for dropping off the package, Harking nudged him out the door, not wanting to take the chance that opening the package would reduce her to tears and unleash a torrent of emotions she definitely didn't want to share with anyone else.

Especially not a loose-lipped lawyer, she thought, recalling an earlier comment from Marion about Thadius Grimes having a hard time keeping his clients' stories private in local gossip circles, earning him the moniker "Blabbius".

Carrying the package into the living room, Harking curled up in Marion's chair and carefully pulled off the wrapping to reveal a small wooden box with a hinged lid. It was her father's version of a Japanese puzzle box and similar to others he'd fashioned in his garage workshop, meticulously crafting the boxes to open smoothly once the sequence was figured out.

Her mother had used an even larger puzzle box to hold his ashes before spreading them at her father's favourite place in the park, something frowned upon by official park policy, but a last act of respect that Paige figured Dan would have appreciated, more especially since it did have a whiff of protest and an air of defiance to it.

Slowly turning the box over in her hands, Harking explored the cubed shape, lightly pushing and pulling at the six sides to see which one might move first. Some of her father's designs were extremely complicated and required a number of steps before the box's contents were revealed, but this box was a simpler version requiring just two simple steps.

Opening the lid, Harking took the piece of notepaper sitting on top, unfolded it and read:

Dear Harking

If you get this package, then I know I won't be around for you, even though it's the last thing I would ever *want. But if I can't be there in person, please know that I am with you in spirit and I always will be.*

The contents of this package might not make sense to you at first, but you're a smart young woman and I know you'll figure it out.

By now you would have also had the benefit of going through my notebooks. I know you coveted them, so it only made sense to leave them to you. And I expect by now you've made some of the same wrong turns I made, but in one way or another found some of the geocaches I put out for you. You probably know I did most of my route finding with a handheld compass, but I hope you figured out the annotations were waypoints I added later using a GPS.

Sure hope you figured out the GPS faster than I did (and had someone explain the mapping coordinates to you)!

Harking smiled. If only he knew how much his numbering had thrown her off.

In any event, the last thing I'll ask you to do will require going back to the trusty compass (three of them in fact). You'll need your mother and brother to help you, so I hope you're back on speaking terms with them.

Anyway, there's more I could say but I'll leave it at that.

I love you. Always did. Always will.

Dad

Fighting back tears, Harking dumped the contents of the box onto the table and stood back to make sense of it all.

There were three engraved compasses, one each for Paige, Col and herself. There was also a small envelope for each of them, in each of their favourite colours red, blue and green, as well as one larger yellow envelope. It was marked 'Directions' with a series of arrows Harking recognized as being similar to the ones David Thompson used to depict the flow of major rivers on his maps. There were also several photocopies Harking recognized as pages from her father's notebooks.

To complete the arrangement, which Harking immediately recognized, Dan Thompson had also included a traditional white envelope. Inside the envelope was another note that read in part:

> Nothing in here. I just needed a white envelope to complete the colours of the Métis sash.
> But I'm sure you already figured that out!

Harking smiled at the level of detail her father had incorporated into the package. He went on to explain the meaning behind the colours, which Harking once knew but had forgotten—red for the blood shed fighting for Métis rights, blue for the depth of the Métis spirit and green for the fertility of the Métis Nation. She did remember white represented the connection to the earth and the creator, but she had to be reminded yellow represented the prospects for future prosperity.

> There's probably more I could say (you know me).
> But one last thing … you know how I went on and on about David Thompson and the family connection?
> Well, I might have been off on that.
> Although I still think somehow there's a link …
> most likely with his wife, Charlotte Small.
> Food for thought.

Lost in thought, Harking barely noticed the whirring of her cell phone out on the kitchen table. Rushing out to grab it she read the message from Simi.

Where r u?

Suddenly realizing the morning was slipping by, Harking put the package aside and rushed upstairs to get ready for court. The general consensus in town was that Andrew Griffin had been working hard to get the charge against Tyson thrown out, but whatever happened, there was no way Harking was going to miss it.

CHAPTER 49

Sliding in next to Simi, Harking looked around the jammed courtroom and wondered how many of those present were there to see what happened with the charges against Tyson or if they were there for other matters.

Most people around town seemed to think that since Parks rarely satisfied the judge with the cases they brought before her, Andrew Griffin would win the day and have the charges dropped.

With no experience in these sorts of matters, Harking had no opinion one way or the other and relied on Simi to get her up to speed as proceedings began.

"I didn't think you were going to make it," Simi whispered. She gave Harking a stern look.

"Sorry. I got side-tracked," Harking tried to express her apology with her eyes.

"Well, I didn't think you'd want to miss him getting what he deserves," said Simi, nodding toward Tyson. He was sitting next to Thadius Grimes in the front row with his father directly behind them.

As Harking expected, Tyson only went partway to cleaning up his act for the court appearance, wearing a suit jacket on top of a t-shirt.

God. Talk about making a poor impression for the judge, she thought as she bored a hole into the back of Tyson's head.

As if on cue, Tyson turned around and caught Harking's glare, but as soon as their eyes met, he lowered his gaze and faced forward.

That's odd, she thought. *He seems to have lost his swagger now that he's in court. Wonder what's up?*

Turning to Simi, her friend gave her a reassuring look, but it did little to quell her apprehension. She knew from her latest chat with Shane there was a possibility Andrew Griffin might raise the issue of Match and her also being in the closed area, a complicating factor not lost on Harking.

Glancing at Match in the row across from her, she sensed from the look in his eyes he was also feeling apprehensive.

"Don't worry about it," Simi reassured her. "My father thinks Andrew Griffin won't challenge the charges."

"How does he know that?"

"He doesn't. But he thinks Tyson's father could have afforded a much better defence lawyer than Blabbius if he was going to fight this. Dad thinks he just wants it all to go away and not fester with more court appearances."

"Does that mean Tyson would plead guilty?"

"I think so, but you just never know. My dad says lots of people say one thing and do another when it comes to their day in court. Guess we'll see."

Feeling slightly more relaxed, Harking settled back in her seat, still wondering what she saw in Tyson's eyes.

Was he scared?

Perhaps.

But for something so relatively minor as being in a closed area in the park, the look seemed more serious.

But what else would he be concerned about?

Maybe his father?

Andrew Griffin had a reputation for being a no bullshit type of guy and Harking suspected he wouldn't like the attention being directed toward his family over the charge against his son.

But until the case was called, no one would know how things might shake out. If Tyson pleaded not guilty, Shane had said things could drag out for months, the court system being what it was. And even if he did plead guilty, it wouldn't be over right away since Shane indicated the park was going to ask for Tyson to do community service as part of his sentence.

Harking was mixed about that approach, realizing it would embarrass Tyson and possibly his father, and make living in town with the Griffins even more uncomfortable than it already was. But she also chuckled at the thought of Tyson having to suck it up and pay the price for ignoring the needs of the grizzlies and other wildlife using the trails on back of the lake. She'd love to see him doing ditch duty along the highways picking up the diapers and chip bags that drivers tossed with abandon out their windows as they passed through the park. Or something nice and visible in town like working the kids' booth on Parks Day.

I hope they make an example of you, she thought, watching Tyson as the judge entered the courtroom. *You deserve it.*

"All rise," the clerk solemnly declared as the judge took her seat.

Immediately the murmur of voices in the courtroom quieted as people returned to their seats before the judge called the first case.

"The first matter I'll hear today is Parks Canada and Tyson Griffin."

"His father must have pulled in some favours to get their case up first," Simi whispered. "This could be interesting."

Not knowing what to expect, Harking saw Shane Ross give her a surprised look as Thadius Grimes stood and faced the judge then turned and motioned for Tyson to do the same. Hesitating at first, Tyson was prodded by his father and finally stood up. "Tyson Emerson Griffin," the judge began, reading from the file in front of her. "You are charged with entering into a closed area in the national park, in contravention of a Superintendent's Order ..." The judge went on to recite the details of the charge word for word. "How do you plead?"

First turning to his father, who motioned for his son to face the judge, Tyson looked nervous. He shot a glance at Thadius

Grimes who looked back at Andrew Griffin and nodded before directing his response to the judge.

"My client would like to enter a plea of guilty, Your Honour," said Thadius, his voice barely audible to Harking and others in the courtroom.

When Tyson turned back to his father, the senior Griffin nodded, seeming to begrudgingly give his approval.

Without wasting a second, the judge turned to the federal prosecutor. "Can you please read the specifics to the court?"

As Shane Ross looked on, the prosecutor stood and read the court brief Shane had prepared in the event of a guilty plea, asking for the judge to consider a minimal fine considering Tyson's age, but also asking that he be sentenced to one hundred hours of community service, including among other tasks, educating trail users about the importance of respecting the park and refraining from using areas deemed critical for wildlife protection.

Harking and Simi could barely restrain themselves from laughing when the prosecutor finished, but held it together as Andrew Griffin turned and glared across the rows of people, directly at them.

"Oh my God," Simi whispered. "He looks pissed," she chuckled.

"Shhh," said Harking, gripping Simi's hand as the judge began to respond to the prosecutor's request.

"Do you have anything to say in response, Mr. Grimes?"

"Huh, would you excuse me for a moment while I confer with my client." Thadius Grimes seemed caught off guard and turned to Andrew Griffin, whispering something to Tyson's father who seemed flustered by Parks' request. Their exchange seemed awkward and prolonged until the judge interrupted them.

"Mr. Grimes, do you have anything to say in response?"

"Sorry, Your Honour. Yes, I do. Considering my client's young age and the fact that this is a first offence, we don't see the value of punishing him with community service. My client is happy to pay any fine you set, but extending the sentence to include community service seems a little harsh."

"Hmm," said the judge, as she listened to Thadius Grimes's argument while leafing through the file on her desk. "I'm not sure I agree, Mr. Grimes." She finally looked up at the pair. "Considering the recent incident involving one of the other young men in town, an incident I understand you were also involved in, Mr. Griffin, I'm inclined to agree with Parks on this matter."

"But, Your Honour ..." Thadius Grimes began to protest but was cut off.

"No buts, Mr. Grimes. This is a serious matter and I need to send a message. Therefore I'm going to agree to the request." She looked directly at Tyson, pausing briefly for emphasis before speaking again. "Mr. Griffin. You are fined one hundred dollars to be paid immediately to the court clerk. And you are sentenced to one hundred hours of community service, the details of which will be provided to you at a later date by Parks staff. Do you understand?"

"Yes, Your Honour," Tyson stammered, as his father sat fuming in the seat behind him.

"You're eighteen now," she added, looking down at the file on her desk. "And beyond the influence of your parents, although obviously that hasn't helped you up to this point." She looked at Andrew Griffin who squirmed in his seat. "Our courts see young people all the time who either shunned the good path their parents set out for them or didn't get the benefit of good parenting. I can't say which of these happened in your case, but I hope your parents can help steer you onto a better path from here on. Do you understand?"

"Yes, Your Honour."

"And will I see you in this courtroom again young man?" said the judge.

"No, Your Honour."

"Very good," said the judge. "You are excused."

Embarrassed and eager to make his escape, Andrew Griffin jumped up from his seat and went directly to the court clerk. Fumbling with his chequebook and pen as the crowd looked on, he quickly wrote a cheque, tore it from the book and handed it to the clerk. Waiting impatiently as the clerk completed the necessary paperwork, Andrew Griffin avoided looking at anyone else, then followed Tyson out of the courtroom, pushing him down the centre aisle past the crowd of onlookers. As he rushed his son by Harking and Simi toward the exit, Tyson's father had a look of contempt on his face.

Tyson, although initially looking bewildered, now glared at Harking as he passed by, mouthing an obscenity Harking easily deciphered.

Reacting without thinking, Harking raised a middle finger and stroked the base of her nose as Tyson passed by, quickly pulling it back as Shane shot her a dirty look and exited on the heels of Tyson and his father.

"Let's go," said Harking, keen to see what Shane was up to. Pulling Simi from her seat, Harking hustled her out of the courtroom but was brought up short when she saw Shane in the hallway in a heated discussion with Andrew Griffin.

Dragging Simi into a corner they watched the confrontation from a distance, only barely able to make out what either man was saying.

"Just don't give me ... reason to bring the police into this," they heard Shane warn Andrew Griffin. Standing toe to toe with the man, clenched fists by his side, Shane motioned to Tyson. "And ... touch one hair ... this boy's head, you'll have me to deal with."

Red-faced, Andrew Griffin muttered a profanity then turned and walked away. "C'mon Tyson," he yelled over his shoulder as he stormed out of the courthouse.

Hesitating, Tyson looked back at Shane as if he had something he wanted to say, but then seeming to have second thoughts, followed his father outside.

For a moment, Harking thought about catching up with Shane to find out what had transpired between he and Andrew Griffin but before she could he turned around, caught her and Simi looking at him, then disappeared through a side door.

CHAPTER 50

When Harking finally did catch up with Shane more than a week later, she was surprised how tightly he held his cards to his chest, unwilling to let Harking in on his plans for Tyson, other than to say he felt everyone deserved a second chance and he aimed to give Tyson just that.

For Harking, it was a reminder that compared to her own family life, everything she'd heard about Tyson's didn't sound so great. Simi had even hinted that her father, although never very open about his work with the RCMP, let it slip more than a few times that they had their eye on Andrew Griffin regarding his treatment of his ex-wife, as well as his son.

Richard Odili had usually clammed up when Simi pressed him for the details, but Simi felt certain there was some truth to the rumours floating around town. For those reasons, she told Harking she was also willing to cut Tyson some slack.

Harking, though, was less conciliatory but unable to nail down exactly what it was about Tyson that gave her reservations.

Part of it had to do with his overall attitude and disregard for others; but in that respect he was a fairly typical teenage male.

Part of it also had to do with her suspicions about why Marion left town; Harking was certain there was more to Phil Sykes's story about Marion's run in with Andrew Griffin and Tyson on the day she'd found Marion unconscious in her living room. And although she didn't think Marion had told her every-thing that happened, Marion had mentioned how Tyson had cut her off as she tried to make her way home and was sure he'd followed her. Harking felt certain that didn't help Marion's sense of security and influenced her decision to leave town.

To top it all off, Tyson had also led the boys to take risks that put Col in the hospital and jeopardized the lives of the mother grizzly and her cubs.

Even if, as Simi suggested, she was being overly paranoid about Tyson's role in Marion's decision to leave town, Harking just knew he was to blame for what happened with the bears. And she was determined to see he made amends for that.

The safety of the bears was paramount.

And Harking planned to keep an eagle eye on Tyson as he did his community service work.

There was no way he was going to get off easy.

She'd already heard from Megan Weaver that their first efforts to get Tyson to do outreach work around the importance of wildlife trails had been a bust, since anyone who knew him quickly blew him off when he approached them with the message.

As an alternative, Shane Ross had talked the railway into putting Tyson to work in the railyard, checking hopper cars to see which ones were leaking. The task was simple enough: walk along the string of railcars and note any piles of spilled grain sitting below each car's grain gates, the tapered chutes at the bottom of the railcars.

All Tyson had to do was record the car number and report it to the railyard supervisor. When the train pulled out of the yard, Tyson had to help a crew shovel the grain into bins and dispose of it. When that was done, he helped check the sidings close to town for other spills and clean them up as well.

For larger grain spills, the railway had access to a vacuum truck, but for smaller spills had to resort to manual labour, not Tyson's strong point.

According to Megan, riding herd on Tyson, staying on top of his every move to make sure he did what he was told, seemed to be more than the railway supervisor bargained for, and after only two days he wanted to turn the kid back over to Parks to complete his hundred hours of service.

But Megan said Shane promised the supervisor he'd oversee Tyson himself until his community service was complete, just to make sure he didn't worm his way out of it.

It didn't help that after a particularly bad week for grain spills, several black and grizzly bears had been seen on the tracks outside of town, focusing more unwanted attention on the railway, and by default, Tyson.

"I can't believe he's got any interest in doing the right thing for bears or any of the other wildlife in the park," Harking told Simi as they lounged on Harking's bed that evening, watching Netflix on her laptop.

"Maybe not," said Simi, tiring of Harking's rants. "But you can't blame him for the grain spills. That's a bigger issue that Tyson has nothing to do with."

"Still, he better do the work," Harking countered. "Or he'll be back in court. And considering what the judge said to him, she won't be pleased if he shows up again."

"Yeah, yeah," said Simi. "Just let it go, will you, and watch the show?"

■ ■ ■

The next morning Harking was up bright and early with plans to go for a ride and see if she could spot the bears outside of town. She'd heard a large male grizzly was seen on the tracks and someone had also mentioned seeing a sow and cubs as well. Harking hoped that wasn't the case since the mother grizzly seemed to be keeping her cubs away from town, but she wanted to find out for herself.

Harking was just going outside when she spotted Tyson headed her way. She knew he had to go by Marion's house every morning to report to Shane at the Parks office, after which Shane would drive him to the railyard.

But this was the first time she'd actually seen Tyson since the day in court.

223

As she watched him make his way down the road, Harking couldn't help but think he just didn't get the message. With a toque pulled down over his head and runners trailing their laces, the dirty t-shirt and ripped jeans sagging around his ass rounded out the picture of someone who Harking figured just didn't seem to give a shit.

Useless, she thought as Tyson picked up stones and drilled them at people's fences across the street.

He was almost at the intersection by Marion's house when he looked up and saw Harking. Hesitating, he turned and hurried across the road to the alley, stumbling and almost tripping on his laces as Harking kept him in her sights.

When he disappeared down the alley it was obvious Tyson was trying to avoid her.

Deciding to give him a little of his own medicine, Harking ran around the house and cut Tyson off, walking out the back gate and standing statue-like as he approached. Tyson hesitated at first but his swagger returned and he scowled at Harking as he tried to get past.

"Off to do your *community service?*" Harking chirped as she stepped out in front of him.

"What's it to you?" said Tyson, sounding indignant.

"You just better make sure you do a good job." Harking inspected Tyson from top to bottom. "Better than you do dressing yourself," she chuckled.

"Or else?" Tyson stepped closer.

"Or else I'll kick your skinny ..."

Harking stopped in mid-sentence, thinking there was something familiar about Tyson that she hadn't noticed before. Then she realized what it was. "Where'd you get that?" she challenged, motioning to the toque.

As if caught off guard by the comment, Tyson suddenly lost his swagger. "Huh, what this?" He pointed to his head.

"Yeah, that. That's my dad's."

Looking like someone caught red-handed, Tyson pulled the toque off his head. "I don't know how I ended up with it," he confessed under Harking's glare. "Somehow after the avalanche it ended up with my stuff. I didn't know who it belonged to so I just hung on to it."

"Well now you know."

"Sorry, I didn't realize it was your dad's." Sounding conciliatory he handed it to Harking. "If I'd known I would've given it back earlier."

Holding the toque in her hands, Harking was taken a little off guard by Tyson's response and was overcome by a sense of guilt about that day.

"You know it wasn't anyone's fault," said Tyson, as if reading Harking's thoughts. "Shit happens."

"Hmm." Unable to say anything more as the memories of that day stirred in her mind, Harking paused and regarded Tyson. He'd never once made any effort to suggest the avalanche was an accident, always leaving Harking to think she was to blame.

She wondered now if he was being disingenuous or not until he added, "There was *nothing* any of us could have done about it."

Filling the void of awkward silence, his words left Harking confused as she relived that day in her mind, the picture of what happened still not quite complete.

"I'm not sure," Harking said finally.

She was about to ask Tyson what other details he remembered about the avalanche when she saw Andrew Griffin charging down the alley toward them.

"Hey," he yelled as he came storming up. "What do you think you're doing?"

"Dad, no." Red-faced, Tyson intercepted his father's advance toward Harking.

"We were just talking."

"Well, you're supposed to be at work," Andrew growled. He grabbed Tyson by the shoulder then turned his attention back to

Harking. "And why does she have that?" he charged, pointing to the toque with his free hand

"It was her Dad's," Tyson explained, grimacing in his father's grip.

For a second, Andrew Griffin seemed lost for words.

"Her father's?" he finally blurted. "How come you had it?"

"I don't know. Somehow I ended up with it after the avalanche."

"It's not a big deal," Harking interjected.

"No?" Andrew Griffin's face contorted.

"No," said Harking, standing firm. "Besides it doesn't concern you."

"Why, you ..." Poised to explode, Andrew started to reply, but Harking quickly cut him off.

"If you want Tyson to get to work, why don't you let him go?"

Seeming to initially resent Harking's suggestion, Andrew Griffin wavered for a moment and turned back to Tyson instead. Releasing his grip he shoved Tyson away. "Get to work," he ordered. "And I'll see *you* at home later."

Tyson hesitated as if wanting to challenge his father, but Harking could sense his reluctance, his shoulders finally slumping as Andrew stared him into the ground. Finally turning, head slung low, Tyson walked away without once looking back.

Before he'd gone too far, Andrew turned back to Harking. "Now you listen to me, sister," he said, the fire in his voice reigniting.

"I'm not your sister," Harking interjected matter-of-factly, disgusted at Andrew's treatment of his son.

"Why you ..." Andrew Griffin raised a hand threateningly but instead of moving back, Harking stepped within striking distance.

Instinctively raising an arm to block Andrew her other hand was balled into a fist held waist-high, ready to respond if necessary.

"Don't even think about it," she countered, holding her form. "You think you can bully people to get your way, but I'm not scared of you." She paused for effect to let Andrew digest what she was saying then lowered her arm. "Yeah, I know, and everyone knows about you." She motioned to Tyson walking away down the alley. "And maybe he'd clean up his act if he had a better role model." She was about to walk away but stopped. "Like the judge said," she added coyly.

Harking smirked as Andrew's face blossomed into rage, but before he could erupt, she turned and walked back through the gate into Marion's yard, leaving him standing alone in the alley, fuming.

CHAPTER 51

After the encounter with Tyson and his father, Harking withdrew to the house, clinging to her father's toque as she curled up in Marion's favourite chair with a tea. Thrown off by Tyson's admission, she wracked her brain as she tried to piece together the details of everything that happened before the avalanche.

The backcountry trip into the park had been planned for a while and most of her classmates were excited, keen to get away from school and into what Dan Thompson often referred to as "nature's classroom".

Apart from Harking, the group included the usual cast of characters in her ever-competitive peer group, Match and Tyson among them, as well as a number of other students with backcountry skills and experience ranging from novice traveller to some like Simi who had more intermediate skills.

Harking had convinced her father to help with the trip and as the most experienced adult in the group, Dan Thompson was designated the lead while two teacher chaperones alternated with bringing up the rear, ensuring no student was left behind.

Determined to show her father she was a better traveler than even the boys, Harking followed his lead, keeping herself just behind her father but well ahead of Simi, Match, Tyson and the rest of the group.

Harking remembered the forecast was calling for snow, but nothing unusual. Still, she knew as well as any of them that mountain weather was notorious for being unpredictable.

Setting out from the parking lot, the going had been fairly easy as the trail wound its way through subalpine forests, gradually climbing toward treeline, avoiding steeper terrain and avalanche prone slopes. As the forest opened up, the snow-pack was deeper and a few of the lead students alternated with Harking's father, taking turns breaking trail until he decided to resume the lead.

As the weather worsened, heavy snow began to fall. When the wind picked up and temperature dropped, the up-until-then typical winter day in the mountains turned into a howling tempest.

Realizing they had to get to the cabin as quickly as possible, Harking caught up to her father. Yelling above the storm they quickly assessed options until Dan Thompson finally made the call. He'd break trail to the cabin to make it easier for the others, then come back to make sure everyone got there safely.

Crossing a couple of avalanche paths would be unavoidable so he planned to check them out first. Once he was sure the paths were safe he'd guide everyone across then continue to push on toward the cabin.

In hindsight, Harking wondered if he felt pressured to take chances he wouldn't have otherwise, suspecting he wanted to get it right for her, to have a win in her eyes, and maybe even more important, in the eyes of her peers.

She knew they thought he was a different cat, questioning how anyone could *throw away* (their words, not hers) a good paying job with the railway and hope to survive in Jasper without work. She also knew the gossip among her peers was precipitated by the trickle down effect of what their parents were saying, comments she was sure her father would have overheard, or suspected by their silence whenever he encountered one of them around town.

"There are no secrets," Marion would say.

When the others finally caught up to her, Harking told them her father's plan, stressing the importance of not surging ahead, the need to stay together as a group.

"But we should still take turns leading," Tyson had insisted.

"Yeah," Match agreed. "We'll make better time."

"No, I'll do it." Harking was adamant. "Stick with the plan so no one gets too far ahead or strays off the track. We've got to keep the group together."

Despite the boys' protests, but with the blessing of the other two teachers, Harking led the way with the boys right on her tail.

As conditions deteriorated, Harking struggled to keep her father in sight and often found it difficult to see the blur of figures behind her, waiting until they'd caught up before she would push on again.

At last she caught up to her father at the edge of the first avalanche path.

"Wait here," he yelled above the blizzard. "It's only a narrow chute but let me go first." By the time he was safely across the first of the others had caught up and he began herding them over to the other side.

"The next avalanche path is wider," he said to Harking, grimacing as the blowing snow cut into his face. "Stay well back until I give you the signal."

Once more he pushed on, breaking a rough trail that Harking tried to pack down as she followed, struggling at times to stay upright when one of her ski poles plunged into the deepening snowpack.

At one point, after stumbling to her knees, she was convinced someone else had pushed past, tripping her, but by the time she was back on her feet and hurrying ahead, she was convinced the only figure she could see in front of her was her father's.

Then she heard him shout a warning to stay back.

Wanting to approach as close as possible to the edge of avalanche path she continued for a short distance.

Then suddenly she heard a loud crack and her father shouting another warning.

I'm sure he was calling my name.
Or was he?
The next thing she knew she was being pulled downhill.

And when the madness stopped she was alone.

Searching frantically, she saw a partially buried body and assumed it was her father.

Quickly digging herself free, she struggled over to him and cleared the snow away from his head to ensure he had an open airway.

But when she turned his head, the face she saw was a blur.

Try as she might, Harking couldn't recall anything else.

That must have been when she collapsed.

But there was something about her father's toque that kept nagging at her.

What was it?

And why did Tyson have it?

Mentally exhausted, Harking curled up in Marion's chair and fell into a deep sleep. Awakening hours later to a dark house and realizing the day was shot, she went straight to bed.

CHAPTER 52

The next day Harking decided to get back on track, literally, planning to check out the latest bear sightings along the railway. If she found evidence of grain spills she would pick up where Marion left off and speak for the bears, taking her protests to Parks, and the railway managers if necessary, to make sure the grain was cleaned up.

Leaving the house, she pulled her bike out of the garage and headed out of town, taking the road for a short distance before turning off on the main trail paralleling the railway. She hadn't gone very far before she saw a small black bear literally lying between the tracks munching on a mound of spilled grain. Getting off her bike, she walked toward the bruin, waving her arms and yelling for it to move on, imitating Shane's approach on the day of the bear jam.

"Yo, bear. Go on. Get out of here," she called out as the distance between them shrank.

Casually, the small bear got to its feet and regarded Harking inquisitively before turning its attention back to the spilled grain. As Harking got closer, the bear finally relented, giving up its bounty and ambling off into the bush just as Harking stepped onto the tracks.

As far as she could see, small piles of spilled grain stretched off into the distance as if they had been placed there purposely, each one an attractant to bears and other wildlife drawn to the offer of free food.

As unbelievable as it seemed, Harking wondered if the stories she'd heard about railcars leaving the Prairies full and arriving on the coast empty were actually true.

Walking down the rail line, two-stepping at times to place her feet on the wooden ties and avoid the instability of the crushed stone used as ballast for the heavy steel tracks, Harking got a sense of the magnitude of the challenge in front of her.

It would take a work crew several days to clean up the mess. And there was no guarantee that the next train wouldn't repeat the process.

Now she understood why Marion had been pushing for the railway to not only bring in a vacuum truck and keep it in town, but to deal with the problem once and for all by repairing the leaking hopper cars, something she'd been advocating for over the past year or more.

Harking knew Shane and others at the park had also been saying the same thing, but for the railway it all came down to the bottom line. Repairing hopper cars cost money and there were a lot that needed fixing. For its part, the railway knew it had to do something and committed to making the repairs, but it would take years to fix all of the grain cars in its fleet.

Finally realizing the magnitude of the issue, Harking shook her head and sat down on the track, balancing her bum on the polished steel as she wracked her brain for options.

Marion was right. Fixing the hopper cars and solving the problem at its source is the only way to deal with this.

It might be inevitable that trains would kill some animals, but Harking knew that getting rid of spilled grain as an attractant would go a long way to saving many of them, not only in the park, but all along the rail line.

Harking was lost in thought when she sensed a tremor moving up through her body, causing her to sit up and take notice. Staring down the ribbon of steel to where it disappeared around a distant bend, Harking thought she could see a dark shape moving along the tracks toward her.

Jumping up, she immediately recognized the distinctive outline and movements of a large grizzly, its shoulders rolling

233

side to side as the large barrel-shaped body got closer and closer, seemingly oblivious to the locomotive just coming into Harking's view.

Without thinking, Harking began to run, screaming at the top of her lungs for the bear to get off the tracks as the locomotive raced toward them, its horn blaring, drowning out the noise of the kilometres-long string of railcars shuttling along behind.

Oblivious to everything else, including the noise of highway traffic paralleling the railway, Harking ran for all she was worth toward the bear, stumbling on the loose ballast as adrenaline propelled her toward her objective.

Only in the last moments, as the massive bear was dwarfed by the locomotive, did Harking see, out of the corner of her eye, the flashing emergency lights of the warden truck on the highway, its siren blaring.

Ignoring it, she ran headlong toward the bear until only a few hundred metres separated them, the blast of the locomotive's horn smothering her screams.

The train was almost on top of them when the bear suddenly stopped in its tracks, seemingly unconcerned about the crazed young woman running its way or the mass of metal hurtling up from behind.

Almost nonchalantly, it stepped off the tracks just as Harking herself was tackled out of the way of the locomotive, its brakes screeching as the engineer tried valiantly to avoid a collision.

"Jesus, Harking," Shane yelled above the roar of the train after their entangled bodies ground to a halt at the base of the railway embankment. Covered in dirt, blood seeping from several small nicks on his face and hands, he pulled himself to his feet. As the railway cars sped past, he looked at Harking lying in the bushes. "What the hell d'ya think you were doin'?" he yelled, fighting to be heard above the turmoil of the freight train.

Bruised and bloodied, Harking rolled on to her knees and slowly stood up.

"Trying to save the bear," she cried. "Just trying to save the bear."

"And trying to get yourself killed at the same time," Shane kicked the ground, furious. "You got a death wish or somethin'?"

As the last of the railway cars sped past, Megan Weaver ran across the tracks. Glaring at Shane she stepped between them and wrapped her arms around Harking, as if to shield her from the onslaught.

"Cause, if you do, don't do it in the park," Shane muttered, his voice finally losing its fire.

He turned to walk away but hesitated.

"Goddammit," he said, looking back at Harking through misty eyes. "We got enough dyin' on our hands. We don't need you to add to it."

CHAPTER 53

Lying in bed, her mind racing with the details of today's calamity, Harking finally succumbed to the dreams, rushing at her with the speed of a locomotive. But unlike the day's reality, the permutations and combinations of possibility brought a twist:

Biking along the old cutline, she sees the bear at the last moment; the fading rays of sunlight reflecting off the polished railway tracks giving definition to its distinctive shape, silhouetted against the mountains.

"Noooooo!!!" she screams, braking suddenly and jumping off her bike, the sound of the distant train lending urgency to the moment.

Throwing herself into the thicket she claws her way through, grasping alder and wolf willow as she pulls her body up the steep embankment and races across the open stretch of meadow toward the tracks.

"Go. Get out of here," she yells at the bear, her heart pounding, but the bear makes no movement away from the small mounds of grain spilled among the railway ties.

Her cries are lost to the shrill call of the monster barrelling down on them through a distant rockcut, the barely perceptible grade giving gravity an edge as the engineer tries to make up for lost time.

A few kilometres further and he will have to slow the train down for its approach to town and the massive railyard. But at this moment, the iron horse is headed for the barn and there is no stopping it.

Running for all she's worth, she's determined not to let this happen again.

The train is still not in view, lost behind a distant curve, but she knows only too well how quickly it can eat up the distance. Even when he sees the bear, the engineer will not be able to stop the train in time, despite his best efforts.

Screaming at the top her lungs, Harking is now close enough to make out the well defined hump at the base of the neck as the bear remains focused on the bounty of free food, slowly working its way from pile to pile.

Suddenly she realizes it's not the male grizzly but the mother.

And she's not alone.

There's at least one cub.

Suspecting there are more, Harking's convinced.

These are *her* bears.

Frantic now, she runs for all she's worth, screaming at the top her lungs.

But her efforts, amid the roar of the approaching diesel locomotive, seem to make little difference until finally the female bear looks up, first at her, then down the tracks toward the solitary, blazing light, fast approaching from around the turn.

Above the roar of the locomotive she screams for the bears, there are two cubs now, to get off the tracks.

But the sow seems unconcerned and the cubs follow her lead.

"Go. Get off the tracks," she screams once more, barely able to hear her own voice as the train's engineer blasts a warning.

But why isn't he slowing down?

Running hard, suddenly her foot catches on an upturned root and she cartwheels into the ground, tumbling and rolling, her bare legs burning, as she skids to an abrupt halt.

He has to see it.

Why isn't he stopping?

Lifting up on her elbows, she manages one final glimpse of the mother grizzly as it turns toward the train, the bear's final choice a bad one as the roar of the engines overtake them and barrels past, the rush of air and blur of railway cars pummelling her senses.

As the train speeds past, she can see the engineer leaning out of the window of the locomotive.

There is a frantic look on his face, as if pleading for a different outcome.

The sickening thud is louder than she would imagine for such a mismatched contest.

Burying her face in her arms, Harking's body shakes with the ground beneath her, as the train rumbles through the valley and around the distant bend at the base of the mountain.

Overcome with grief, her chest continues to surge long after the train has passed, until she finally looks up, her eyes rimmed with red, searching for the aftermath of the collision.

Then suddenly she is alone, standing, staring, overwhelmed by an ominous silence as the tracks clear.

Stepping across the bands of steel, shrouded by a veil of darkness, she expects to see the bears' lifeless corpses scattered in the fringes of alder and wolf willow.

But there is no sign of the mother grizzly

... or the cubs.

CHAPTER 54

Soaked in sweat, Harking pushed the bed sheets aside and stood up, then hobbled to the dresser. Exhausted from yet another tormented sleep and bruised and sore from yesterday's near miss, she checked herself out in the mirror, hanging her head as she reflected on what had happened.

So stupid, she thought.

She knew she was lucky to be alive.

Knew Shane had put his own life on the line to save her.

And yet she'd walked away without apologizing, leaving Megan and Shane standing by the side of the tracks looking at each other, while she retraced the steps to her bike and rode home, crying most of the way.

Standing in front of her mirror, she tugged at the few remaining strands of blue hair, grimacing as she massaged her bruised scalp.

What a mess.

Determined to change things up, Harking pulled a pair of scissors from the dresser drawer and headed to the bathroom, disappearing for a time until a voice called her out to the top of the stairs.

"I wondered if you were up there," said Simi, two-stepping her way to the top then stopping suddenly. "Wow."

"What do you think?" said Harking.

"Well, I like that you're going back to your natural colour," said Simi, running a hand through Harking's hair. "Blue didn't really suit you. Or orange, or whatever that was the other time." She paused and lightly slid her hand down the side of Harking's face. "Although they would go with the bruises. God, girl, what did you do to yourself?"

"What about the rest of it?" said Harking, brushing Simi's hand away, along with the question.

"Not so sure if I like the cut," said Simi. She smiled. "But hey, it won't take me long to clean it up."

"Yeah," said Harking stepping back toward her room and the dresser mirror. "That's probably not a bad idea."

"I heard some of what happened yesterday," said Simi, moving in behind Harking.

Harking muttered but said nothing as her eyes met Simi's mirrored reflection.

"It's a small town remember," said Simi. "There are no secrets." She took the brush from Harking's hand and ran it gently through Harking's hair then exchanged it for the scissors. "How are you?"

"Okay, I guess." Harking went on to explain the gory details of the previous day.

"Wow," Simi shook her head. "You're lucky Shane showed up in time."

"I know." Harking nodded.

Simi retrieved the brush and continued combing as she looked past Harking at their reflection. "By the way, have you talked to your mother and Col lately?"

"About what?"

"I don't know, the package from your dad, everything that's happened over the past few days. If nothing else, maybe you should reconnect and figure out where you're all at with each other."

"Hmm, yeah maybe. But I need to go see Shane first." Harking turned to look at Simi. "And Megan too. I kind of blew them off yesterday and I feel bad about it."

Before Simi could reply, a knock and the sound of the front door opening got their attention.

"Anybody home?"

Harking recognized Megan's voice immediately.

"We're up here," Harking called out. Together, she and Simi went to the top of the stairway. "Hi guys. I was planning to come see you today," Harking said as she and Simi headed downstairs. "I wanted to apologize for yesterday."

Harking immediately sensed a feeling of awkwardness.

"Hi, Simi," Megan began before turning to Harking. "You okay?" she said as Shane stood silently at her side, preoccupied with the brim of his Stetson as he pulled it through his fingers.

"Yeah." Harking tried to gauge Shane's silence and wondered what was up.

"You took a pretty good spill yesterday," Megan said as she motioned to Harking's cuts and bruises.

"More like a tackle," Shane mumbled, finally looking up to meet Harking's eyes.

"Oh well, I deserved it. How about you Shane?" She surveyed his bruised knuckles. "You okay?"

"Hell ya." Shane scuffed a boot across the floor. "That was nothin' compared to bein' thrown off Cassidy." Hints of a smile surfaced briefly then disappeared.

"Well, anyway, I'm sorry," said Harking. "What I did was stupid."

"Kinda," said Shane. "I know you care about the bears but running full tilt at a grizzly ... and a train for that matter, well, you're not going to win either one of those fights. But I might'a done the same thing in the moment," he added, spurred on by Megan's elbow to his ribs. His face contorted as he fought for the right words. "Kinda just delayed the inevitable, though."

"What do you mean?" said Harking, her concern rising.

"There was a grizzly killed on the tracks this morning," said Megan.

"The sow?" Harking asked, her voice rising. "One of the cubs?"

Megan shook her head. "A large male."

"It was feeding on an elk that got dinged by a train last night, "Shane remarked. "Then it got clipped itself."

241

"Its back was broken so we had to put it down," said Megan. "We hauled it away just before we came here."

Somewhat relieved that it wasn't the mother grizzly or one of her remaining cubs, Harking felt guilty about her reaction and hung her head. As much as she knew the large male might have eventually killed one of the cubs, losing another animal didn't help the park's grizzly bear population.

"I wish we had better news," said Megan. "No matter how you cut it, this sucks."

Shane nodded. "All the more reason to double down on the sow and cubs."

"But what can we do?" Harking pleaded.

"Give 'em space," said Shane.

"And keep enforcing the closures," Megan added.

"But the grain spills?" said Harking.

"Railway's bringin' in a vacuum truck this week," said Shane. "They'll clean up as much as they can."

"And the good news is the sow doesn't seem habituated to the grain," said Megan. "I think she's figured out the free meal isn't worth the risk."

"But what about the cubs?" Simi asked.

"Well, hopefully she's got them trained to avoid the railway. And if we see them near it, we'll haze them to reinforce the message."

"But at the end of the day, there's only so much we can do." Shane added. "It's gotta come from her."

CHAPTER 55

Upset by the news about the male grizzly, Harking said goodbye to Megan and Shane and decided she needed a change of scenery to take her mind off everything that had happened over the past few days.

"Where do you want to go?" Simi asked.

"I think I'll try to figure out some more of Dad's notes from the puzzle box."

"Mind if I come along?"

"No," Harking said, without hesitation.

"No, you don't mind or no you don't want me to come with you?"

"Sorry, no I don't mind," said Harking. She smiled. "Two heads are better than one. Maybe you'll be able to make sense of some of the notes I haven't been able to figure out."

Simi's eyes lit up.

"But I'm warning you." Harking's expression turning more serious. "It might be rough hiking."

"Oh well," Simi beamed. "Que sera sera."

A short while later, they were on their bikes headed out of town, stopping at the first overlook to get their bearings.

Harking had decided to start at the beginning, assuming there was some logic to the order of the waypoints, if that's what they were.

Standing at the overlook she pointed to the numbers in the margin of the page and asked Simi to read them out.

Plugging the numbers into the GPS, Harking pressed the GO TO button and watched the screen closely, the digital compass arrow suggesting she would need to travel southwest for a little over two kilometres. Looking at her map and roughly cal-culating the distance, she figured the waypoint was somewhere along the Athabasca River, and relatively easy to access.

Jumping on their bikes, Harking and Simi crossed the high-way and took the river trail, stopping occasionally to check the GPS and distance to the waypoint. As they got closer to the point, Harking took the lead and rode slowly along the trail, holding the GPS in one hand as she watched the distance reading go up and down, dropping to within a hundred metres then increasing again.

"What are you doing?" Simi asked when Harking stopped and got off the bike.

"Trying to find the shortest straight-line distance to the waypoint." Harking walked past Simi then stood still in the middle of the trail. "It's bouncing around a bit but according to the GPS this is pretty much it." She returned to her bike and pulled it into a clump of buffaloberry with Simi right behind.

"The bikes will be fine here," said Harking.

She stood with Simi and showed her the GPS screen. "See. When I press the GO TO button and follow the arrow, it's pointing us to that ridgeline." She motioned to an open ridge of scattered Douglas fir high above the river.

Simi nodded as Harking headed off, picking a route through the open forest of aspen bordering the trail.

"This way," Harking called out over her shoulder.

"I'm coming," Simi replied as she tried to keep up, finally catching Harking before she disappeared into a dense stand of lodgepole pine.

When Simi emerged on the other side, Harking was waiting for her.

"You okay?"

"Yeah," said Simi, gulping air. "But it's not a race."

"That's true, I guess." Turning, Harking started upslope with Simi tight on her heels. Gradually the forest of pine gave way to scattered Douglas fir, their furrowed trunks clinging to the rocky bands layering the hillside. Keeping one eye on the GPS, Harking led them higher and higher toward a band of cliffs that initially seemed impenetrable.

Stopping to catch her breath as Simi pulled up next to her, Harking surveyed the obstacle.

"Let's try that sheep path," she said, pointing to a barely discernable opening winding upward through the rocks.

"Sure," said Simi. She followed as Harking picked her way up the cliff band, finally squeezing through a tight section of shattered rock.

"Give me your hand," Harking said, just as Simi started to slide backwards on a patch of scree. Locking arms, she pulled gently but firmly as Simi grabbed the sharp edges of rock with her free hand and scrambled up next to her.

"Wow," said Simi, bending over to catch her breath as Harking dug out her water bottle and passed it to her. "That was quite the scramble." She took a long drink and passed the bottle back to Harking. "It's beautiful," she added, looking out over the valley.

"Hmmm." Harking took a sip of water then shoved the bottle into her pack. Looking at the GPS, she reoriented herself and pointed to an opening on the ridgeline.

"Just a few hundred metres more. That way."

Finally cresting the ridge top, they stood in the middle of an open patch of gravel and shattered rock. Beyond them the open forest gave way to a wall of rock arching ever skyward.

"I'm glad your father didn't tackle that," said Simi.

Harking laughed. "You and me both."

"But it is beautiful up here," Simi added, turning and pointing to the valley below.

The vantage point gave a sweeping view of the main river valley and several smaller valleys leading off from it, fingering into the subalpine. At this elevation it was also possible to get a feel for the subtleties of the topography, the forested slopes revealing pockets of benchland and smaller drainages that couldn't be seen from the valley bottom.

"It's stunning," Harking agreed. "I can't imagine a better view from anywhere else. Other than on top of the mountains," she added, pointing to the closest peak before turning her attention back to the surrounding panorama. "Wow."

She took a deep breath then returned to the task at hand, moving slowly across the ridge until the GPS reading indicated they were within a few metres of the waypoint. "Five metres," she said, as they both looked around the spot.

"What are we looking for exactly?" said Simi.

"That cairn," Harking replied, pointing to a small pile of flat stones, the mottled grey slate blending in with the surrounding scree. She made her way to the pile and pulled a rock from its face. Removing a second rock revealed a recessed cavity and a small waterproof container. "Bingo," she said, her eyes lighting up. Reaching in, she retrieved the clear plastic box. Sitting back, she handed it to Simi. "Go ahead, open it."

"But it's yours," said Simi as she sat next to Harking.

Harking shrugged and smiled. "It's fine. Go ahead."

Simi opened the lid and they both surveyed the contents: paper mostly, including a photocopy of a page Harking knew to be from one of David Thompson's journals. As she scanned it, she realized it included his survey notes for the broad expanse of valley below their location. There was also a folded photocopy of a hand-drawn map showing another part of the valley. A small piece of paper sitting at the bottom of the box was inscribed with a short message:

Good job Harking,
Now sit back, relax and look around you.
Remember this place.

Pondering the note, Harking wondered why it was made out specifically to her. How would her father know *she* would find it, and not someone else?

Sitting with her back to the cairn, Harking tried to figure out the map as Simi looked on. The location they were sitting at was circled and another location further up the valley was also marked. Other than that, there were no directions.

"So?" said Simi. "What do you think?"

"I'm not sure." Harking waved the map toward her friend. "There's not much to go on."

"So where to now?"

Harking thought for a moment then pointed back to the second location on the map. "The waypoint for the next cache might be hidden in Dad's journal. But we'll have to wait until we get back to Marion's to check it out."

"You want to try to get there today?" said Simi, raising her eyebrows.

"To the next waypoint? No way."

"Good." Simi sounded relieved. "I'm not sure I could do two in a row."

"No, let's wait until tomorrow," said Harking. "If you're up for it."

The next morning, they were up bright an early and headed farther down the valley. By noon they'd found the second cache containing another simple map pointing to a third. Since Simi seemed willing to give it a go, Harking decided to take advantage of her friend's help to find the next cache.

"It's back the other way," said Harking, pointing to the second map. "And actually, not so far from town."

Returning down the valley, they stopped in briefly at Marion's house to grab some snacks then headed out again. The third cache was the easiest to find, but unlike the others there was no new map.

"Thankfully," said Simi. Looking tired from the day's exploits she flipped through the pieces of paper from the third geocache.

"But I don't understand what any of these points mean," Harking said as she sat down and poured over the hand-drawn maps and the photocopied pages from David Thompson's journals.

"I don't think your father expected you to," said Simi, handing Harking a small piece of paper that they'd initially ignored.

It was another note from her father that repeated the earlier message, with the additional advice:

You'll need your mother to help with this last bit.

"Great," said Harking, flipping the paper over to see if there was any more to the note.

Simi smiled. "He's not going to let you off easy."

"What do you mean?"

"Your father made it so you have to speak with your Mom. It's obviously what he wanted."

Harking sighed. "Yeah, you're probably right," she said, resigned to the fact her mother might be the only one who could shed some light on the matter.

"And there are the other things in the package your father left behind," Simi added. "His instructions were pretty clear. The compasses were meant for all three of you."

"Whose side are you on anyway?" Harking asked, elbowing Simi.

"Yours, usually," Simi shrugged, "but today I'm on your dad's."

CHAPTER 56

Reluctantly, Harking decided Simi was right. It was time to reconnect with her mother. "Hey, Mom," Harking said when her mother picked up the phone. "Yeah, I'm okay. Um, can we meet in town tomorrow?"

When they met in the coffee shop the following day, Paige once again commented on how tired Harking looked. "The dreams again?"

"Yeah." Harking recounted the latest version with the train.

"Well no wonder," said Paige. "After what happened on the tracks."

"Yeah, I guess," said Harking. "Anyway, this is what I wanted to show you."

She spread out the maps on the small table and explained what she and Simi had been up to over the past few days.

Paige pondered the hand-drawn maps and reached for the photocopied pages from the Thompson journals and Dan's notebooks.

Slowly a smile surfaced on her face. "Okay, now it makes sense to me." She laid the maps out side-by-side and pointed to a location on the first one.

"You ended up on this ridge above the river, correct?"

"Yeah." Harking nodded.

Paige paused as if reflecting for a moment.

"But what about it?"

"What about it? Well, have you ever seen a better vantage point?"

"Not really, no," Harking conceded. "It was absolutely stunning."

Paige smiled.

"But still, what's so special about it?"

"It's where your father proposed to me," said Paige, biting her lip as her eyes filled up.

"Seriously? Up there?"

Paige laughed. "Yup. Way up there." She looked outside for a moment as if savouring the memory, then turned back to Harking. "It was actually pretty romantic." She pulled a tissue from her jacket pocket and wiped the corners of her eyes.

Harking waited patiently for Paige to regain her composure.

"And these other points?" Harking asked, her curiosity getting the better of her.

Paige pointed to the second location, hesitating again before she said anything as the flood of memories threatened to overwhelm the moment. "This was a bit of a scramble as well."

"Huhuh."

"But also beautiful."

"And?" Harking was impatient.

"It's where I told your father I was pregnant with you."

"You ... were pregnant with me?" Harking was incredulous. "And you climbed up there?"

"It wasn't that big of a deal," said Paige, straightening up in her chair. "And I wasn't about to let you slow us down." She sounded defensive, but smiled.

"The strong independent type," said Harking.

"You betcha," said Paige. "My mother would have freaked out if I told her, but I wasn't that far along. It wasn't that big a deal. You know, I hiked with Dan until just a few weeks shy of your delivery date. And I think things went more smoothly with the pregnancy because I did. Because I was in shape." She pointed at Harking. "And you don't seem to have suffered from it."

Harking raised her eyes momentarily and her mother pulled the third map on top of the others.

"This is a col on the ridge above town," said Paige.

"Where you told Dad you were pregnant again?" Harking guessed.

Paige nodded. "We decided your brother's name then and there," she added proudly, but then went silent.

"It never turned out quite like you planned," Harking said matter-of-factly.

"No." Paige's voice hardened. "Not at all." She shook her head. "It was a tougher pregnancy and I just couldn't keep going like I could with you. I don't know why. My mother's nagging didn't help—insisting I needed to slow down. She went on and on ad nauseum." Paige sighed. "To a certain extent, maybe she was right. I was physically and mentally drained. But everything turned out fine in the end. Col was a healthy baby and we never looked back."

"But it strained your relationship with Dad?"

"Absolutely," said Paige.

There was another moment of awkward silence before Harking gathered up the maps and journal pages. As they got up from the table, they stood looking at each other as if unsure what to do next.

"I'd like for you and Col to come over to Marion's place for dinner this evening."

"You mean *your* place." Paige smiled as she gently ran her hand through Harking's hair. "At least for now."

"Yeah, I guess." Harking sighed. "But even with Marion away, I can still sense her presence, kinda like she's watching me."

"Watching *over* you, more like it." Paige wrapped her arms around Harking and hugged her. She tried to step back before Harking could push her away, but Harking tightened her grip and whispered.

"I'm sorry things haven't been better between us."

"So am I," said Paige.

Harking relaxed her hold and looked up into her mother's eyes. "But *you* didn't do anything."

"Maybe not. But neither did you for that matter. We were both just trying to be ourselves."

"Strong independent types." Harking smiled. "Warriors even."

251

CHAPTER 57

The knock on the door that evening came sooner than Harking was expecting. When she answered it, expecting to see Paige and Col, she was surprised to see Tyson instead, standing there, a sheepish look on his face.

"What do *you* want?" Harking asked suspiciously, noting that Tyson had cleaned himself up, with his hair trimmed and combed and having ditched the saggy pants and tattered t-shirt.

"Take it easy." Tyson raised a hand. "I come in peace." He sounded cautious, offering a faint smile.

Harking held her ground, leaving Tyson standing outside, making him work for it.

Looking away then turning back to face her he said, "Thanks for standing up to my old man the other day. He's such an asshole sometimes."

"Whatever." Harking shrugged then stared Tyson down. "That's not what you came here for."

Tyson nodded silently in agreement.

"I remember how I ended up with your father's toque." He paused to look Harking squarely in the eyes.

"So *now* you remember?"

"Yeah."

"Well, go on." Harking's curiosity was getting the better of her.

"Okay, okay," Tyson started. "I know you said you don't remember a lot from that day, right?"

"Correct."

"But do you remember what the weather was like?"

"Yeah," said Harking, thinking back to the clear blue skies

252

and brilliant sunshine. "It was a beautiful bluebird day ... when we started. But so what?"

"But then the weather went for a shit," Tyson added.

"Yeah?" Harking recalled most of the first few hours on the trail.

"I'd left my hat at home, or I forgot it," Tyson admitted, leaving Harking still wondering where the story was going.

"When the weather crapped out," he continued, "your father saw me with nothing on my head and said he had a spare hat in his pack."

Tyson hesitated, seeming reluctant to go on

"He gave me the toque he was wearing and said he'd dig out the other one for himself." Again Tyson hesitated, looking up sheepishly at Harking, almost as if he was wondering when she might finally connect the dots.

As Tyson paused, seeming to search for the right words to say, Harking did recall seeing the toque.

But where?

"I'm sorry," Tyson said finally.

"For...what?"

As if a veil of fog suddenly lifted, Harking stared ahead in disbelief as she realized the toque was on, or next to, the partially covered body buried in the avalanche debris.

"For letting you think, it was your fault," Tyson added, his extended apology now lost on Harking as she was quickly drawn back to that day, recalling how despite the details having eluded her, the picture of what happened was now becoming clearer.

When the avalanche stopped she was in shock. Panicking and assuming she alone had been caught in the slide with her father, she had frantically looked around for him. She had no idea until later that Tyson and Match had also been caught up in the maelstrom.

When she saw the toque and the partially buried body she assumed it was her father and knew she had to get to him right away to clear the snow away from his head and open an airway.

But now, suddenly, in light of Tyson's admission, she realized the face that she saw when she turned it toward herself was not her father's.

"I'm also sorry about what happened to Col... and the bears...." Tyson started, but Harking raised a hand, stopping him before he could finish.

"I can't do this right now," she said. "I have to go."

Overcome by a rush of emotions, Harking eased the door shut, slumping against it, head bowed in disbelief. Suspecting Tyson had gotten past her that day and that *he*, not Harking, may have caused the avalanche, tendrils of anger flared up from the pit of her stomach as she closed her eyes, dwelling on the possibilities, including the sudden realization that while she'd assumed she'd found her father in the debris field, her distraction had meant no one had been able to get to him in time.

Dan Thompson was later discovered just beneath the surface of the snow, but in a situation where every second counted, it was irrelevant now.

Instead of digging her father out of the snowpack ...

... she had actually saved Tyson's life.

Stunned by the revelation, Harking leaned against the door for several minutes, leaving Tyson standing alone outside, head also bowed, practically touching the door. He waited for several minutes before he finally turned around and walked home.

Sensing he'd finally left, Harking retreated into the house, her movements zombie-like as she prepared for dinner and waited for Paige and Col to arrive.

"You okay?" Paige inquired when she met them at the door.

Harking deflected the comment with an excuse about being tired, the dreams still haunting her nights. She said nothing of Tyson's visit, still digesting its implications.

After dinner, still struggling to put Tyson's revelation to the side for the time being, she led Paige and Col into the living room.

"Are you sure you're okay?" Paige probed again, obviously concerned.

"Yeah," Harking lied. Straightening up, she breathed deeply through her nostrils and tried to focus. "I thought we could bring Col up to speed," she said as Col and Paige sat on the couch overlooking the maps and notes spread out on the coffee table.

"Good idea," said Paige.

"Bring me up to speed on what?" Col asked.

Harking started off slowly, explaining the clues their father had left behind and the geocaches she and Simi had visited while pointing out each item they'd found.

"I didn't know what they all meant but Mom was able to explain it."

"After a fashion," said Paige, turning to Col then flipping through the maps again. "These were some of the important points in our lives, literally. I'd completely forgotten about them until Harking showed me these maps."

Harking sat down opposite them and listened as her mother repeated most of what she'd told Harking that afternoon including where their father had proposed to her and where she'd told him about being pregnant with Harking. But unlike the earlier version, she added a little more detail.

"It was a major turning point for us," Paige explained. "Your father was ecstatic but we both wondered how it would change our lives. Not in a bad way. We were both over the moon in love. But we thought we'd lose our independence, our ability to take off when we wanted to. Your father more than me though. I was fine with slowing down, having a family and being a mom. It totally changed our life for the better."

"What about when you found out you were pregnant with me," Col asked bluntly. "Did I change your lives for the better? Sometimes I got the feeling I didn't."

"God, nothing could be further from the truth," said Paige, rubbing his back.

"For both of you," she added as she gently turned his head to face her.

Thumbing through the maps she pulled out the third one.

"This is where we hiked when I told your father we were pregnant with you, Col. It's one of our most favourite places in the park," she added as she scanned the map.

She hesitated and bit her lip, then pointed to a location that hadn't been marked. "This was another," she whispered, looking away from them both.

"But it was also the place I told your father we were probably through. I couldn't handle the fact that he was gone so much, working on the trains. I felt like a single parent. And when he was home, he was still gone; hiking, exploring, it never seemed to end. He said he needed it. Said it was his way to stay grounded and keep from going crazy. He thought it was unfair that I didn't get it. I could go any day I wanted and hike wherever I wanted, he said, as if I could just drop things and take off."

"But didn't he take us when he could?" said Harking.

"He did. He was great that way. But he usually just took one of you at a time so it's not like I got a break. We just seemed to be doing our own thing and never doing things together anymore. Before we knew it, we were like two people who'd lost touch with each other. It all came to a head when I told him I had a new job."

She stared at Harking, as if in disbelief.

"He hadn't even heard when I told him I'd been exploring opportunities outside of town. It seemed to come as a huge surprise and he kind of lost it. And I lost it. We said things we never meant to say but they stung. And once they come out, it's hard to put them back. It leaves you with a feeling like there's no going back on them. You can forgive perhaps, but there seems to be no forget."

Paige sighed.

"But that's all water under the bridge now. After everything that's happened, I only want to focus on the positive, to find the beauty in every day and think about the good times we shared. And honestly, you both represent the best of those times." She pulled Harking and Col into her arms briefly then sat back.

Freed, Harking disappeared down the hallway and returned with the puzzle box her father had left behind.

"What do you have there?" said Col.

"It looks like one of Dan's puzzle boxes," said Paige.

Harking nodded and handed the box to her brother then watched as he figured out how to open it.

"I don't get it," said Col, looking at Harking as their mother emptied the contents on the coffee table and spread them out.

Harking just shrugged as Paige pushed the compasses to the side and silently sorted through the envelopes, looking up and around before turning her eyes back to the papers in her hands.

"Any idea what it all means?" said Harking.

"Not really," said Paige, "but he left instructions." She waved a sheet of paper in the air then silently pored over the notes.

"I looked at those," said Harking. "But they don't seem to make a lot of sense."

"Well, there's only one way to find out," said Paige, finally looking up.

"I know," said Harking, "but it's a little late to do it today."

"Agreed," said Paige. "How about tomorrow?"

CHAPTER 58

Before the morning sun had crested the surrounding mountains, Harking, Paige and Col stood atop Old Fort Point, each with a copy of the journal page in their hands.

"This is it?" Col asked. "And why so early?"

"Because the instructions say to get here just before sunrise," said Paige, her head buried in the notes.

"So what do we do now?" Col asked

"I'm not sure," said Harking, looking over her mother's shoulder. "But let's follow Dad's directions and see where they take us."

"God knows what he wanted us to see," said Paige, shaking her head as she read the journal entry out loud and directed the scene. "Go over there, Col." She pointed off to the northeast. "It says to walk out at a bearing of northeast 68 degrees, for a distance of 20 paces."

Col followed the compass bearing and paced out twenty large steps.

"Harking, yours says southeast 30 degrees for roughly the same distance."

Harking followed her mother's directions, pacing the distance off as Col had done.

"And it says for me to basically walk downhill a few paces," said her mother, flipping over the page to continue reading the directions.

"What do we do now?" said Col.

"He's given us each a compass bearing to sight down," said Paige, as she read out the respective bearings to each of them. "Turn the compass dial to the bearing and sight down the compass." She laughed. "He's added a PS saying he's already set the declination but it might be off slightly by the time you get to use these compasses. He goes on to say don't worry about it."

Harking grinned. "Such a nerd."

Paige continued. "Then it says, 'From here you can see the most important things in your life.'"

"I don't get it," Col said after he sighted down the compass. Looking around he raised his hands in the air. "Edith Cavell, the mountain? Is that what I'm supposed to see?"

Paige shrugged. "I don't know."

"I don't get it either," said Harking. "I'm looking at Pyramid Mountain."

"And I'm looking up at Signal Mountain?" Paige said finally. "I don't get it either," she said under her breath. She flipped the page over then looked up and shrugged. "I don't know what it all means."

"From here you can see the most important things in your life," she repeated slowly. "The *most important* things in your life."

Slowly she looked around, a smile creasing her face.

"It's not the mountains," she said finally.

"It's not?" Col and Harking turned around, mouthing the words simultaneously.

"It's what's below the mountains."

"It's us," said Harking, excited with her discovery. "I'm looking right over you Mom, but it's you he wanted me to see."

"He wanted us to see *each other*?" said Col.

"Yes," said Paige, her eyes lighting up. "In a new light," she added, just as the sun broke above the surrounding mountains and drenched them in its glow.

"But he wrote this years ago," said Col. "How did he know we'd even need it?"

Paige smiled. "He didn't. Probably hoped we wouldn't. But you know your father. He was always prepared for the unexpected."

"Hedging his bets," said Harking. "Just in case."

"You father was all about building redundancy into his plans. If Plan A didn't work there was always a Plan B ... or C or D."

"And I remember him saying that sometimes Plan D is better than Plan A," said Harking.

"Exactly," said Paige.

"What did he want from this?" Col asked, as he and Harking walked back toward their mother. "For us to be together again?"

Before Paige could reply Harking looked at her and shook her head.

"I don't know if I can do that."

"I don't think he expected that," said Paige. "He was pretty pragmatic."

"So?" said Col.

"I just think he wanted us to remind ourselves, every now and then, that if we look around, we're pretty lucky ... pretty lucky to be living here among the mountains and pretty lucky to have each other," said Paige, her eyes glistening as she drew them into her arms. "I don't think it was anything more than that."

The three of them shared a quiet moment as the sun's warmth eased the chill in the morning air.

"You know the dream I told you about?" said Harking, stepping back to look into her mother's eyes.

"Huhuh, the one about the bear and the train?"

"Yeah," said Harking. "I had it again last night only this time it was a little different."

Paige listened but said nothing.

"The engineer on the train was initially ghostlike," said Harking. "I wasn't able to see his face." She hesitated. "Until last night."

"And?"

"Well, at first he was just a blur, a blank face. But suddenly he appeared leaning out the window of the locomotive, screaming at the bear to get off the tracks and screaming for me to stay back.

Screaming with all his heart. And as the train roared past ... I could see his face as plain as day." Harking paused and looked up at her mother. "It was Dad. And he looked devastated."

Paige sighed heavily and turned away.

"What is it?" said Harking.

"Oh," said Paige, turning back to face Harking. "I might as well get this over with."

"Get what over with?"

Paige sighed. "I haven't been entirely honest about why your father left the railway. And he kind of swore me to secrecy. It's not something he wanted known around town. And he definitely didn't want you to know."

"Know what?"

"The real reason he left the railway."

"I don't understand," said Harking. "I thought it was because they were looking for people to buy out. So they could downsize or whatever you call it."

Paige shook her head. "No."

"Then why'd he leave?"

"It was like in your dream," said Paige. "He was driving a train that had been delayed out east and was on a tight schedule to get to Jasper. He'd had other trips where he'd been unable to avoid wildlife on the tracks, and each time he came home from one of those, it was like a piece of his heart was torn out."

For a moment Paige seemed lost in thought.

"He hated himself for not being able to slow the train down," she said finally. "Or scare the animal off the tracks," she added.

"And when he'd report it, he felt it was often ignored. He wasn't even sure if the supervisors passed on the information to Parks and he definitely felt they never even considered any of his suggestions to avoid similar strikes in the future. On this particular evening he came home in tears. The train he'd been driving had been almost doubled in size in Edmonton because of a shortage of locomotives and the need to get all the cars to the coast. He said the train was more than three kilometres long."

"Wow," said Harking.

"Too long, he felt," said Paige.

"Anyway, as they were approaching Jasper, he saw a grizzly on the tracks. He figured it was eating spilled grain or maybe feeding on an animal that had been killed earlier, cleaning up the remains. Either way, it wouldn't move. Normally he might have been able to slow the train down, but this train had too much momentum behind it and at the speed he was going, he just knew there was no way to stop in time."

Paige's voice sounded defiant as she continued.

"Dan laid on the train's horn, but the bear was indifferent. He said the bear almost seemed to be challenging the train. But it was a fight it couldn't win."

Paige paused. Seeming distracted she scratched her head as if re-evaluating the story. "God, he cried like a baby that night as I held him in my arms in bed. But the more I think of it ... I would have done exactly what he did."

"Which was?"

"Well, the next morning he walked into the railway superintendent's office and told him he felt there were things the railway could do differently to reduce the number of animals being killed, things he'd raised before but which had been largely ignored. He told him he'd always worried that someday he'd be the one driving a train that killed a grizzly. When it happened, it was the last straw."

"God, he must have felt so bad," said Harking.

Paige nodded. "He was devastated." She put a hand to her mouth and looked away. "I probably didn't help by telling him he had to go get his job back, that we couldn't afford to live here on one income."

She turned and faced Harking again.

"He said he'd never go back, that he'd find other work. But that was the beginning of the end for us. From then on it seemed like all we did was fight. Money was tight, we had two kids to raise, and this isn't a cheap place to live. He'd take odd jobs, but it was never as much as the railway paid. And the more time he spent out in the park when he wasn't working, the more he wanted to be out there, to the point where he gave up looking for work. It just wasn't sustainable financially. We couldn't make ends meet. We were going deeper and deeper into debt."

Paige's voice sounded desperate.

"When we split up and you and Dan decided to stay here in town, I honestly didn't know how that could work. But you were both so headstrong and adamant; I finally convinced myself I had to take Col and leave. It took some time but I was able to get on top of things financially and whenever I had extra, I sent it to your father."

"I didn't know that," said Harking.

"I know," said Paige. "There's a lot we didn't share with you, even though you were probably old enough and responsible enough to handle it. When he was killed in the avalanche, I knew there was no way you'd come live with me. I thought I was going to lose you both."

Paige put a hand on Harking's shoulder and looked her in the eyes.

"So I asked Marion if she would consider taking you in."

"*You* asked Marion?"

"Yes."

"I thought she came to me on her own."

"Oh, she probably would have," said Paige. "If I'd waited. But I went to her first. I said I'd pay your board, but she was offended by my offer and told me in no uncertain terms you were welcome to stay with her as long as you wanted. But she didn't want any money. She said having someone else in the house would ease the loneliness she felt since Malcolm died, especially someone younger like yourself. And with Susan having moved away, it made even more sense." Paige smiled. "She'd always been fond of you."

"God," said Harking. "I feel terrible. All this time I thought ..."

"I was the bad cop," said Paige.

"Kind of," said Harking. "Oh God, I'm so sorry, Mom." As tears rolled down her face Harking fell into her mother's arms. "How can you ever forgive me?"

"Hmph," Paige sighed. "How can I not?" Reaching out she pulled Col into their embrace. "We're family. And I love you both so much."

CHAPTER 59

Another day, another unexpected knock on the door.

When Harking answered it this time she was surprised to see Megan Weaver, looking surprisingly *normal* out of her park warden uniform, wearing a pair of biking shorts and long-sleeve riding shirt.

"Hey," she said, hesitating for a second. Other than their one interaction that day on the railway tracks and another time after court, she didn't really know Megan that well.

"Hey," Harking replied.

"I was just heading out for a bike ride but Shane called and said he'd spotted the mother grizzly and cubs outside of town. He thought you'd be keen to see them." "Yeah," Harking's eyes lit up. "I'd love to."

There had been no sightings of them for a week or more so she was excited about the news.

"Well, get whatever you need and come with me." Megan motioned toward her car sitting by the curb.

"Sure." Harking grabbed a hoodie and closed the front door behind her.

"Sorry, it's a bit of a mess," Megan said as Harking slid into the passenger seat. "It looks like I've been living in here." She laughed. "We've been crazy busy at work and I haven't had a chance to clean it out."

"No worries," said Harking. "I'm not exactly the tidiest myself."

They smiled at each other as Megan started the car and headed out of town.

"So," said Megan. "How've you been?"

"Good."

265

"That's good." There was an awkward silence as Megan drove through town and turned onto the highway. "Shane said the bears were down the Snaring Road, feeding on buffaloberry."

"Cool," said Harking. "Hopefully they stay away from the train tracks."

"Ten-four." Megan seemed to catch herself, skewing her face as she watched Harking's response. "Sorry, couldn't help it. The Ten Codes are etched in my brain."

"No worries," said Harking. "I get it."

"Anyway," Megan continued, "I agree with you and hope the bears don't get sucked in to the grain spills, even though they're like a free meal."

"Not really free," said Harking, playing Devil's advocate.

"No, that's true. Sadly, they do come at a cost, especially if a bear gets habituated to them."

"Exactly." Harking was resolute.

"So ... what are your plans for the summer?" Megan inquired, changing the subject. "You're finished school, right?"

"So finished," Harking sighed. "I'm working at the bike shop for the summer then we'll see. I don't really know beyond that. Mom's planning to travel so while Marion is away I'll stick around and look after her house. And my little brother, I guess." She raised her eyes at this last point.

"How's he doing, by the way?"

"Pretty good. Might have to ride herd on him a bit to pry him away from virtual reality, so I can show him actual reality, but that's pretty par for the course with kids these days."

"Riding herd," Megan chuckled as they turned off the highway and headed down the Snaring Road. "I thought you weren't into cowboy talk? Sorry," she added quickly after catching Harking's stare, "Shane let that one out of the bag."

"Fair enough. Yeah, I kind of like putting Shane on the spot with his cowboy shtick, but I know he comes by it naturally." Harking paused. "So what else did he tell you about me?"

Megan seemed to think about her response. "He said you'd make a good park warden. He thinks you have the right stuff."

"The right stuff? What exactly is that?"

"Mainly that you care about the right things, the bears for example."

"Hmph."

"And that you have balls." Megan looked over at Harking and grinned. "Guy talk, but you know what he means."

"I guess."

"It's not every teenager that would take on the world. We need more young people to give a shit about nature." Megan shot a serious look at Harking then motioned further down the road. "There's Shane," she said as his park warden truck came into view, parked along the road next to a clearing. "Let's see what's up."

As Megan pulled in alongside Harking rolled down her window.

"Howdy, ladies," Shane said, unapologetically. "Glad you could make it Harking." He motioned toward the clearing. "The bears are still there, taking their sweet time, feeding on buffaloberry. Pull ahead a bit and you'll be able to see them."

"Sounds good," said Megan, leaning across Harking to speak.

"I'll jump in the backseat if you don't mind," Shane added. "We can watch them together."

"Ten four," said Megan. She pulled the car ahead, angling it slightly along the side of the road.

"See them there," Shane said as he slid into the back seat and pointed across the clearing.

"Yeah," said Harking, as Megan nodded in agreement.

"They seem pretty focused," Megan noted as they watched the bears slowly make their way through each bush. "The mother's not paying any attention to us at all."

"But she knows exactly where we are," Shane offered. "She's a good mom. Exactly what we need."

Just as Shane spoke the mother grizzly stopped for a moment and sniffed the air then resumed feeding.

"Take these if you want to get a real good look," said Shane, handing a pair of binoculars to Harking.

"Thanks." As Harking lifted the glasses to her eyes and focused on the bears she was impressed by the clarity of the view. "Wow." Concentrating on the mother grizzly she sensed that although she was feeding, the female bear was also keeping one eye on the two cubs, literally following in her footsteps. Harking smiled as they seemed to be systematically working each bush, the mother bear selectively targeting the higher berries as the cubs took advantage of the lower hanging fruit.

"Cool," she said under her breath as she watched the mother grizzly pull single berries off the branches.

"Do you want to take a look?" Harking offered the binoculars to Megan.

As Megan glassed the bears Harking continued to watch the cubs as they mimicked their mother, the feeding interrupted from time to time by short bursts of cavorting as they pushed each other out of the way, trying to get the upper hand on a particularly full branch.

"So they've been staying away from the railway?" Harking asked, turning around to speak to Shane.

"Near as I can tell." Shane remained focused on the bears then turned his attention to Harking. "My take on it is they've been staying out this way because there's a better berry crop here, or at least it seems to be ripening up sooner. I expect they'll gradually work they way around the valley."

"Avoiding town?" said Harking.

Shane nodded. "So far so good. Hopefully we can track what's happening and keep folks out of areas that have a good berry crop."

"That's easier said than done," Megan said matter-of-factly, handing the binoculars back to Harking.

"True," said Shane. "But all we can do is try. Hopefully

the bears will show us what's working and what's not. The fewer reports we get from folks, the more that tells me the bears are successfully avoiding us.

"I know we talk about bear management," he continued, "but hell, we don't manage wildlife or ecosystems. The best we can do is manage our own activities so we minimize our impacts *on them*." He motioned toward the bears. "Really we're in the business of *people* management."

Shane's voice took a more serious tone.

"If we get it right, the bears'll do just fine."

Harking hadn't thought of it quite like that and was impressed with Shane's take on how things worked.

"Well, I should be getting back to work," Shane added. "You two stay as long as you want. And you can hang onto the glasses. I'll get them back from you later, Megan." With that he got out of the car and walked back to his truck. Slowly, so as not to disturb the bears, he turned the truck around and disappeared down the road.

Harking and Megan continued to watch in silence until the three bruins finally disappeared into the forest at the edge of the clearing.

"Pretty cool, eh?" Megan smiled.

"Yeah."

"One of the benefits of working for Parks," Megan suggested.

"I guess."

"Give it some thought," said Megan. "Parks always has openings for seasonal park wardens, but the competition is pretty stiff. In the meantime, summer jobs give you a foot in the door. Even volunteering on some of the wildlife projects isn't a bad way to go. The more experience you have the better your chances of getting in."

Harking took a deep breath and sighed.

"I'm not sure. Not sure what I want to do. Not sure if Parks is who I want to work for."

"Fair enough," said Megan. "Just food for thought. But don't knock something before you try it."

CHAPTER 60

"So you're sure you don't want to come?" said Paige, as she stood with her kids at the train station.

Harking shook her head. "No, this is something you need to do on your own. You've been looking forward to a train trip across Canada for a while. Besides, with Marion deciding to stay with her daughter for longer, someone has to look after her place."

"And you Col?" Paige asked. "You'll be all right here?"

Col smiled and looked at Harking. "I don't know. I guess we'll see."

Harking nudged him in the shoulder with her fist. "Depends if he's learned how to listen to his elders."

"Yeah, right," said Col. "You're barely two years older."

"Older though," said Harking. "And don't forget it."

"Okay, you two," said their mother. "And you wonder why I worry."

"Don't worry," said Harking. "We'll be fine." She nodded to Col. "I'll keep him in line and get him outside as much as possible."

"Yeah, right," Col mumbled.

"And away from the video games," Harking added. "I think I'm going to cancel cable and pack away the video games."

"What?" Col protested.

"That's right," said Harking.

"Mom!" Col looked at his mother for support.

Paige frowned. "She's just pulling your leg, Col."

"Am not," Harking countered, digging a knuckle into Col's side before turning back to Paige. "Anyway, that's not for you to worry about. Go. Enjoy yourself. Maybe you'll find another soulmate."

Paige raised her eyes. "You think that's what I'm looking for?"

"I don't know. Maybe. Sometimes we don't know what we're looking for until we find it."

"Is that why you plan to do some volunteer work for Parks?" Paige asked.

"Kinda," said Harking. "Megan sort of talked me into to it, but hey, how'd you know about it?"

"Doesn't matter," said Paige, waving off the question. "But I know you'll do great. You're made for it."

"Think so?"

"Know so." Paige smiled and hugged them both. "Take care of yourselves," she said before turning to Col. "And listen to your sister."

"He will," Harking interjected. She pinched Col's arm until he cried out and jerked his arm away.

"You two," said Paige, shaking her head. "I've got to go," she added as she looked at her watch. She hugged them both then walked toward her train, looking over her shoulder just as Shane Ross rushed out of the train station, nearly running into her.

As Harking and Col looked on wide-eyed, Shane and Paige engaged in a short but animated discussion before hugging and parting company.

Catching their stares Shane waved then bolted off in the opposite direction.

"What's that all about?" Col asked after Shane had left.

"No clue," said Harking with a smile. Wrapping an arm around Col, she pulled him along the line of cars until they found their mother, sitting by the window, peering off into space.

When she noticed them, she quickly wiped her eyes with a tissue and smiled just as the train began to move from the station.

"Call us when you get there!" Harking mimed holding a hand to her ear.

"I will," Paige mouthed, their voices now muted by the creaks and groans of steel wheels rolling on the track.

"C'mon," said Harking, as she pulled Col along, trying to keep up to the train as it picked up speed. Sensing his resistance, she finally stopped and waved to her mother one last time then watched as the train slid out of the railyard and headed east.

"Fine," she said, turning back to Col. "Let's head home. I've got some chores lined up for you."

"Yeah, right."

"Yeah, right!" Turning away, Harking headed for the exit without looking back.

"What kinda chores?" Col shouted. When she didn't respond, he ran to catch up. "Hey, wait a minute," he called out just as Harking disappeared around the corner of the train station.

CHAPTER 61

Keeping one eye trained skyward, Harking picked her way through the patch of buffaloberry, the clusters of crimson fruit weighing down each thin branch, competing with the fleeting glimpses of scarlet moving through the canopy of lodgepole pine as a trio of ravens followed her progress, seeming to humour her efforts.

Damn ravens, she thought, as she tried to concentrate on the telltale flashes of red leading her further and further away from the main trail. *Shut up for once.*

Following a barely discernable path uphill through the detritus of forest litter, Harking pushed her way through the branches, crouching and waddling duck-like to avoid becoming ensnared in the bramble of thick bushes. Stumbling on a hidden root, she launched herself into a massive spider web before bolting upright, sputtering and wind-milling her arms as she plowed through the maze into a small clearing.

Swearing and spitting, she ran her hands across her face and forehead, combing her fingers through her hair to pull out the knots of matted needles, twigs and cobweb.

"Arghhh," she cursed as she wiped her hands down the legs of her pants to get rid of the last remnants of the sticky mess. Jumping up and down, she shook like a dog in a last ditch attempt to regain her composure.

Looking around as if expecting someone to be watching her antics, Harking quickly scanned the empty treetops then collapsed in a heap on the moss-covered ground. Pulling her pack around and settling it between her outstretched legs, she unzipped the front pocket and pulled out her water bottle. Raising it to her lips she took a final gulp then held the bottle up to the sky, swirling it to locate any remaining thirst-quenching drops.

Finding none, Harking tossed the bottle down, let out a sigh and wiped a hand across her lips. Reaching into her pack, she pulled out a tattered copy of *A Field Guide to Western Birds* and lay back on the cool moss. Thumbing past the sections on owls and kingfishers to a colour drawing of a Pileated wood-pecker, she scanned the description on the opposite page and read aloud.

"Common but wary ... solid black distinguishes it from other large birds ... except crows and ravens ... *damned ravens* ... and some hawks. Conspicuously red-crested in all plumages."

That was it, for sure, she thought, discounting the next closest option, the near-extinct Ivory-billed woodpecker from the deep southern States, as an unlikely possibility.

Scanning the other drawings, Harking was absorbed by the variety of similar species, noting the fine details separating one *Piciforme* from the other and reminding herself of the other possible options defined by the range maps, the Common Flicker, one species of Sapsucker and a few other smaller woodpeckers.

But still it wasn't the bird she was looking for, the rare Lewis' Woodpecker. Unlike other woodpeckers it didn't really cling to the trunks of trees so much as perch, but it was its iridescent green back and salmon-red underbelly that really dis-tinguished it from all other North American birds. A tourist had reported seeing one but Harking wanted to be the first in Jasper to confirm the sighting and add it to her life list.

Lost in her musings, Harking was oblivious to the nearby drumming until a small woodchip hit her squarely on the fore-head. Startled, she dropped the guidebook and peered into the canopy as a large black bird worked its way around the trunk of a dead lodgepole pine, stopping frequently to peck away at the scaling bark and punky wooden core.

Slowly pulling a pair of binoculars from her pack, Harking lay still and watched the bird, a large Pileated Woodpecker, its brilliant red head cresting into a sharp spike.

As the woodpecker worked its way around the tree, a freefall of bark and large rectangular wood chips accumulated at the base, a telltale sign that Harking's father had pointed out on a search for its smaller cousin a couple of years ago.

No matter how many times she thought about him and the advice he'd given her about always being aware of her surroundings, the irony of his words still caught in her throat as she recalled the avalanche. And although he was gone, she now realized that in so many ways he lived on in her and Col, and would continue to influence them both, like their mother would. There was little doubt in Harking's mind that just as Marion insisted, Harking was as much her mother's daughter as her father's.

The rekindled relationship with Paige would no doubt also give Harking a better appreciation for everything that had happened in their past and help guide her future. With Marion away, Harking figured she'd appreciate her mother's advice more now than ever before, but only time would tell.

With one phase of her life over, Harking knew it would soon be time to focus on the next one. The family of grizzly bears might continue to consume her free time, but they couldn't continue to be her obsession. As Shane had said, there was only so much people could do. Ultimately, the bears would have to figure out how to find their own way.

And so would Harking.

EPILOGUE

Months later

Leaving the lakeshore far behind, the grizzly led her cubs away from the river valley, their interest shifting away from the last clusters of buffaloberry to bearberry and Hedysarum roots as they headed to higher ground, the sounds of the highway and railway quickly fading into the distance.

In a few days she would find what she was looking for and begin digging their den into a gravel slope high above the valley bottom, eventually sequestering her family inside to wait out the long winter months.

Buried deep beneath the drifts of snow their bodies would slowly succumb to the isolation, nourished solely by their efforts over these past several months of continuous feeding. With more than enough fat put on by late fall, springtime would find them lean but healthy, ready to repeat the cycle.

A few years earlier, the mother grizzly had emerged from a similar den along with *her* mother and sibling, both newborn cubs eager to escape the confines of winter and explore the new world opening up before their eyes.

Lean and hungry, her mother had led them downslope to spring's first offerings, a moose carcass buried in the snow at the bottom of an avalanche chute, gradually revealed as the warming sun sent the snowmelt into an adjacent creek, churning its way toward the river, where shoots of fresh grass and horsetails would draw the family of bears further and further away from their den site.

Surviving their first three years, the cubs were eventually driven off by their mother's new suitor, a large male that would stop at nothing to have them gone.

Escaping him, the cubs eventually separated.

While her brother was drawn even further from their birthplace, the female rarely ventured into new territory, always returning to the river valley where she, too, eventually encountered a young male with a singular focus.

Emerging from her den the following spring with three cubs at her side, her survival instincts led her to repeat much of what she'd learned from her mother, and what she'd discovered herself.

Survival was a function of chance; that summer's bounty would be enough to get them through until the next year, as long as the hazards associated with other bears *and people* could be avoided.

Survival was also a function of choices made.

While the wrong ones had deadly consequences, making the right choices increased the chance that in time, and with a little luck, her cubs would also repeat the cycle, setting the stage for the next generations, a future with bears and other wildlife coexisting on an ever changing landscape in an ever changing world.

ACKNOWLEDGEMENTS

Harking is my first book outside of the *Dyed In The Green* series, and my first work of young adult fiction. It was inspired by our work in Jasper National Park to document the effects of human use on wildlife movement in an area around the town of Jasper referred to as The Three Valley Confluence.

That work, initially intended to assess the movement of wary large carnivores including cougar, wolves and bears ultimately became as much a study of human use as a study of wildlife use, with our initial findings suggesting that not only were people using well-established wildlife trails for hiking, biking and horseback riding, they were taking over these trails, likely displacing wildlife to less secure and more energy demanding travel corridors or possibly forcing animals into situations where they faced an increased probability of encountering people, with an increased likelihood of conflict.

As we collected remote camera data and the picture of human and wildlife use began to come into focus, we communicated our findings to human users, hoping people would voluntarily shift their use back to the park's official trails. That wasn't always the case however, and more aggressive management was proposed including area closures and enforcement.

Today, some of the areas we identified as critical wildlife movement corridors around the town of Jasper and Jasper Park Lodge are closed to human use, and monitoring suggests people are complying with those closures, which is a good thing.

But as the numbers of visitors to our parks increase and human use continues to expand into what were typically referred to as the shoulder seasons of spring and fall, long term monitoring will be required to determine if wildlife, especially large carnivores including grizzly bears, wolves and cougar, continue to use these areas and the park's high-quality montane habitat.

Coincidentally as I write this, we are in the throes of a global pandemic that has resulted in a virtual shutdown of human use not only in our parks and protected areas, but everywhere. In the absence of a huge influx of people in places like Jasper National Park during the spring of 2020, wildlife responded by showing up in greater numbers and in areas not normally used in recent years. Although other factors including weather may have influenced wildlife behaviour this year more so than in the past, species such as grizzly bears may be showing us that their preferred habitats overlap with human use areas even more than we suspected.

This phenomenon, if we want to call it that, is occurring throughout the world, highlighting the need to better understand wildlife use as well as our own impacts on that use, if we are to coexist with other species.

My greatest hope from writing this story is to help communicate the need to develop a better appreciation for the needs of wildlife, not only in our parks and protected areas, but everywhere, so that we can better adjust our own use to accommodate other species we share this planet with.

Having the opportunity to view and appreciate wildlife and wild places is a privilege that is becoming increasingly rare throughout much of the developing and developed world. While our parks and protected areas are intended to maintain and enhance these types of opportunities, the increasing demands and levels of human use we inflict on these special places compromise our ability to sustain wild places and the wildlife that rely on them for their survival.

Changing our expectations and our own behaviours is critical if we are to coexist with wildlife into the future.

■ ■ ■

Along with the lessons learned from our work in Jasper National Park, this book has also benefitted from the input of numerous people, once again including my primary editor Kate Scallion, cover artist Dan Stiles and layout designer Iryna Spica.

Despite pursuing a law degree, Kate found time to review and edit early drafts of this story and once again provided valuable advice and suggestions to improve the manuscript.

For his part, Dan continues to *get it* the first time around. Ever since working on the cover for my first book, *Dyed In The Green*, Dan has nailed the cover concept for each of my books, encapsulating the story in a powerful cover image that attracts both first-time and seasoned readers alike.

Iryna also deserves special thanks for taking the time to listen to and translate my ideas for how I would like the final book to look and feel into a layout that is both pleasing to the eye and easy to read.

I am especially grateful for the efforts of these three key players.

I am also grateful to Jody Carrow for helping me with Harking's story. Having grown up in Jasper and being familiar with the park and the community, as well as having a solid background in writing and editing, Jody's manuscript review and suggestions as well as final edits immensely improved the final story.

I am also indebted to several advance readers, especially Janet Mercer, Gwen Pemberton, Eli Whittington, Taite Marcoux, Angela Spooner and Bella Leopkey. Their feedback on the draft manuscript helped refine Harking's story and shape its outcome.

As always, my family is a big part of any writing venture, providing invaluable support, advice and suggestions as well as keeping me grounded in reality. I wouldn't be able to do any of this without them.

Ultimately though, writing *Harking* was my task, and any errors or omissions may be attributed solely to me.

If you'd like to provide feedback, please check out the links to my websites on the next page. I'm always happy to hear from readers. And if you enjoyed *Harking* please stay tuned. She may return. (Full disclosure – I am considering completing *The Harking Trilogy* including *Book Two – First, Nature* and *Book Three – Second Nature*.)

Apart from *Harking*, you might also be interested in checking out my *Dyed In The Green* series, the first fiction series about Canada's national parks. Once again, if you do and if you enjoy those stories, please help spread the word.

Word of mouth advertising is the best kind.

There are many ways to increase awareness and build appreciation and support for our parks and protected areas. My primary objective is to use story to attract readers who might not otherwise be drawn to learn about our national parks, including the opportunities they present and the challenges they face. I hope my stories raise awareness about these challenges and promote changes in attitudes and behaviours that support coexistence with the other species we share this planet with, not only within our parks and protected areas, but everywhere.

EGM, July 2020

ABOUT THE AUTHOR

A former Canadian national park warden, George Mercer is the award-winning author of the *Dyed In The Green* fiction series about Canada's national parks. Prior to turning his attention to writing George worked in six national parks across Canada, including eight years as a Park Warden and Wildlife Specialist in Jasper National Park, Alberta.

During his time in Jasper, George introduced the use of remote cameras to assess wildlife and human use of trails in the park and was also the first to use GPS collars in the park for woodland caribou and wolf research and monitoring. These projects led George and his co-workers into every part of the Three Valley Confluence area of Jasper as well as more remote backcountry locations. The insights and knowledge gained from that work provided the foundation for Harking's story.

George continues to be passionate about parks and protected areas and this passion forms the backdrop for much of his other fiction and non-fiction writing, which can be followed at www.georgemercer.com and www.writenature.com.